FASTEN YOUR SEAT BELTS!

History and Heroism
in the
Pan Am Cabin

FASTEN YOUR SEAT BELTS!

History and Heroism in the Pan Am Cabin

Valerie Lester

Paladwr Press

This book is written in memory of
Petra Browne and Fran Wood,
and is dedicated to Pan American's flight
attendants, wherever they may be.

Published 1995 by Paladwr Press,
1906 Wilson Lane, Apt. 101, McLean, Virginia
22102-1957

Manufactured in the United States

Maps by R.E.G. Davies

Edited by R.E.G. Davies and John Wegg

Typesetting/Layout and Jacket Design by Spot Color

ISBN 0-9626483-8-8

First Edition
Second printing 1997

Contents

vi

Maps

by R.E.G. Davies

Cartoons

by Jerry Daly

Foreword

by Jeffrey Kriendler

Had Valerie Lester listened to me, not a single page of this book would ever have been written.

Not that I thought that the story of Pan Am's flight attendant corps would make dull reading; nor did I doubt that she could put her engaging outline to paper. On the contrary; throughout my 24 years with Pan Am, I was always one of the strongest advocates for flight attendants and had faith in Val's literary skills and determination to get the job done.

When she first approached me, soon after Pan Am's shattering collapse, I was overcome by sadness and truly felt that her mission would be doomed to failure. "Who would publish your work?" I asked her. More to the point, "Who would buy it?" I scoffed.

Well, in true Pan Am flight attendant fashion, Val was not to be discouraged. She had the will and persistency to get the job done, like so many of her flight attendant colleagues who had that Pan Am 'can do' spirit.

The men and women who proudly served Pan Am as flight attendants were the company's public persona and contributed richly to its stellar reputation around the world. Almost everyone who worked for Pan Am felt that one of the company's greatest strengths was its cultural diversity, which was a reflection of Pan Am's incredible expanse across the globe. This was perhaps best exemplified within the ranks of flight attendants whose profession required psychological and technical skills to serve the travelling public.

I join Valerie in saluting the many contributions which Pan Am flight attendants made to bring the company to greatness. I commend and congratulate you, Val, for the time and effort you have exerted to tell the Pan Am story through the eyes and words of the greatest group of professionals ever to serve the public aloft.

Acknowledgements

In addition to all those I interviewed as subjects for this book, there are many others (not all of them flight attendants) who have helped me with their knowledge, insight, and kindness, in response to my probing telephone calls and letters. My warmest thanks go to Ralph Abrams, Millie Adams, Jeanne Bayer, Sebastine Amédume-Beaumier, Yasmin Bhalloo, Joanne Buerklin, Diana Cable, Fred Cate, Verne Chaney, Mary Higgins Clark, Chuck Cobb, Ulla Davis, Maria Engel, (the late) Robert Ford, Robert Gandt, Mary Goshgarian, Jane Gottschall, Christopher Gregory, Pat Hogan, Opal Hess, Joe Kapel, Sally Kaplan, Nicole Kapochena, Harry La Porte, Jimmy Leahy, Virginia McKillop, Ada Pena, Philip Parrott, Dale Reedy, Paul Roitsch, Eiichiro Sekigawa, Barbara Cliff Stoodley, Lilian Walby, and Marcia Young.

To Gerri Wilkins and the members of the Annapolis chapter of World Wings International, I offer warmest thanks for three years of steady encouragement and good parties.

Jeff Kriendler cheered me when my spirits flagged, and supplied me with wise counsel, facts, names, numbers, and a great view in Miami; William Brown and Gladys Ramos introduced me to the Pan Am Archives at the University of Miami, and Karen Hudson helped me dig; Lucinda Jameson housed me when I visited Seattle; Barbara Sharfstein gave a luncheon at Twin Peaks so that I could meet some San Francisco giants; Yoko Ishikawa entertained me regally with the World Wings chapter in Tokyo; Pat and Paul Kaplan were my refuge in New York; Marge and Carl Gray read and listened in Maine; John Pratt flew me to Portland (Maine) in his Mooney to pick up Dorothy Kelly and bring her to Islesboro; Joan and Peter Hockaday provided practical ideas in Maine and a fabulous party in San Francisco; Pam and Tom Taylor offered steady advice and encouragement in Washington, D.C.; also in Washington, Jane Lester provided a *pied à terre* and rock-like faith in the enterprise; my children, Toby in Jerusalem and Alison in Tokyo, read eagerly and offered long distance counsel.

R.E.G. Davies, Curator of Air Transport at the Smithsonian's National Air and Space Museum, has been enthusiastic about this book ever since I sent him the two sample chapters on Dorothy Kelly and Pamela Taylor. I cannot conceive of learning more from an editor, nor having as much fun. With his encyclopædic knowledge of aviation, he has saved me from some giant clangers, and my prose has become leaner thanks to his careful pruning. Imagine my experience the day I handed in the final draft: it was a cold but bright November morning, half an hour before working hours at the museum. Ron and I sat on a bench in the huge central hall, with the sunlight sifting between the wings and spars of the historic aircraft suspended from the ceiling. Over our heads, to the left, was *Voyager*, the skinny marvel that flew non-stop around the world; above us, on our right, was the *Spirit of St. Louis* and the Wright brothers' 1903 *Flyer*. The privilege of being in that environment at that particular moment is something I shall never forget.

Hang on; there are still two special people. Grace Walker has been my mentor during this long journey, ever ready to listen and to offer good advice. I especially thank her for interviewing Katherine Araki for me in Hawaii. Without Grace's wisdom, support, good judgment, and humor in the tough moments, this book would have been a sorry thing. And thanks to Jim; kindest critic, best friend.

Author's Preface

Then the doors closed and the engines started and the beast turned and faced the wind. The spray, the great spray of their future was thick now and they were hidden from view. See the windows strange and low! Imagine the huge angles that mark its height, that speak for its breadth! Now it races! Now it thunders! Now it lifts! Now it roars! Into the kingdom of air! Into the kingdom of air!

Tim Binding, *In the Kingdom of Air*

The day before I was born, my mother watched, cheering, as my father made his first solo landing in a private airplane at a small airfield in Cheshire, England. If *in utero* experience influences a baby, I was certainly affected that day. I have always been interested in flying.

Shortly after my birth, we sailed to Barbados where we lived until my fourth birthday. The first clear memory I have is of a Pan American Sikorsky S-42 flying boat in which we flew when my father was transferred to Jamaica. There was no direct flight to Kingston, and we made several hops— Barbados to Trinidad to Venezuela to Colombia—before what was then a long haul north over the Caribbean. A boat with wings was enormously attractive to a child who had learned how to swim at the same time as she took her first steps. To be under water in something that flew, to swim in an airplane—for that is what it seemed like to me as the water streamed past the windows and we sped through the waves—was, so to speak, elemental.

Five years later, my mother christened a Pan American Convair 240 on its inaugural flight to Kingston. She stood high up on a platform, and I watched from below as she leaned forward, holding a huge silver chalice, and poured water from the rivers of Jamaica over the nose of the aircraft. When she pronounced the words: "I christen you *Clipper Jamaica,*" the whole airport jumped and clapped. Later on that day, I was invited to join her and my father on board a special flight around Kingston Harbour, but as I climbed the steps to the airplane, I became panic-stricken and refused to enter the cabin. I could not imagine how a person breathed in the sky. My mother tried

Mrs. H.R.E. Browne (Petra) christening Clipper Jamaica, *14 July 1948.*

everything in her power to persuade me to step aboard, but I dug in my heels, and the aircraft took off without me. I spent the next half-hour alone at the airport, climbing up and down the aircraft steps, as my parents circled above, breathing effortlessly in the brand-new Convair-Liner's pressurized cabin. They lost no time in telling me how silly I was when they returned to earth, how wonderful the flight had been, and how easy it was to breathe on board. After that, I never turned down another opportunity to take a 'plane ride.

When my father was transferred to West Africa and I was sent to boarding school in England, I used to fly unaccompanied to Nigeria for my school holidays, always dependent upon the kindness of flight attendants. My favorite was the one who lent me her hat and apron and invited me to help with the meal service. When I was 11 years old, I decided to become a stewardess.

✈ ✈ ✈ ✈ ✈

In 1962, at the age of 22 and bilingual in English and French, I was hired by Pan American in London, at a time when the airline was expanding rapidly and hiring slews of young women who spoke a second language. My particular group was sent to San Francisco for training, and I met my room-mate, Frances Stickley (Wood), as we flew over the Pole to the other side of the world to begin our careers. Following training, we were both based in New York, where I flew for the standard two years before marrying a passenger. After raising two children, I took a B.A. and then an M.A., since when I have alternated between teaching and writing.

Fran, however, continued to fly and then moved into higher and higher echelons of flight service management, always keeping the company's interests first in her heart. No challenge seemed too great for her, and when it came time for a flight service representative to fly to Tenerife in the aftermath of the world's worst airline disaster, Fran was the first to volunteer. Five years later, in a truly ironic and ignominious twist of fate for one who was so heroic, she was struck and killed by a pick-up truck while crossing a street in Miami. The driver had been blinded by the sun.

On 4 December 1991, the unthinkable occurred. Pan Am died. In the far corners of the world, the shock waves reverberated as denial set in and people

Fran Wood in 1964.

chanted over and over: "It cannot be." "How could this have happened?" "Pan Am could never die." Slowly, denial changed to low wails of sorrow as reality struck home. The last Clippers had set out on their final journeys, the crews dispersed, the mechanics washed their hands, the ticket counters closed down, and the whole mighty engine of the world's most influential airline ground to a halt. The Pan Am family was left with little but memories, and each ex-employee suffered the loss in his or her own particular way. Several of them resorted to taking their lives.

    In my case, the death of Pan Am was followed a week later by the death of my mother, and this, combined with the loss of my heroic roommate and my early memories of flying, started the germination of the idea for this book. I needed to generate something positive from all this annihilation. For a while, I considered writing about heroism in the cabin in general, ambitiously taking on all the airlines of the world, but I rapidly became discouraged by the enormity of that task (not to mention the hubris), and found myself increasingly drawn to recording the history and heroism of Pan Am's flight attendants in particular. There, at least, I had something of a head start. I began to talk to friends about my idea, and received nothing but unqualified encouragement. I hurried off to the Library of Congress and did a search of literature about flight attendants and histories of Pan American. I found that 'flight attendant' (a genderless title which came into being at the time of the 1964 Civil Rights Act) was the preferred designation in the card catalog, preferred to stewardess, steward, purser, air hostess, or cabin crew. I discovered that there are precious few books by or about flight attendants, although the notorious *Coffee, Tea, or Me?* is in its twentieth printing.

    I started reading the various histories of Pan Am, always on the alert for any mention of cabin crew. It had struck me that, in the eyes of passengers, flight attendants had the power to make or break a trip. They were the public face of the company, dealing directly with the consumer in an almost ambassadorial role, and for that reason alone were of supreme importance, quite apart from the fact that in an emergency they would be called on to save lives. I fully expected to find plenty of material about cabin crew in the histories, but as I sifted through minutiae about engines, contracts, deals with the government, regulations, and negotiations, my hopes for documentation began to wither. I searched more and more frantically for any mention at all of hostess, purser, stewardess, steward, or flight attendant. It was almost as though flight service had been expunged from the record. In the few instances in which flight attendants are mentioned, the light that is shed is meagre and depressing, and they are never mentioned by name. Let me show you what I mean:

There is no mention at all of flight attendants in Matthew Josephson's early history of Pan American, *Empire of the Air.*

In P. St. John Turner's *A Pictorial History of Pan American,* the sole mention of a flight service term occurs in a description of the problems encountered with the advent of the 747:

> Unfortunately, call button requests for hostess service tended to be transferred into an action switching on the reading light—perhaps someone else's—and in some cases lights would flash on and off at dramatic points in the film soundtrack. (p. 154)

In Marylin Bender and Selig Altschul's 605-page history, *The Chosen Instrument: Juan Trippe, Pan Am, The Rise and Fall of an American Entrepreneur,* I found:

> On behalf of the C.I.A., which was encouraging tribal chiefs in the Indonesian archipelago to revolt against Sukarno's regime, [Sam] Pryor facilitated equipping the cabin of a Pan Am plane chartered to Sukarno with bugging devices. Not to be outdone by the Russians, who provided a blond interpreter on an Aeroflot plane so bewitching that Sukarno took her back to Indonesia, Sam engaged a couple of prostitutes from the red-light district of Hamburg to pose as Pan Am stewardesses. "I was afraid to expose our Pan Am girls to him," he said. "Our girls are nice girls. Why, my friends ask me to get their daughters jobs as Pan Am stewardesses." (p. 480)

In *An American Saga: Juan Trippe and his Pan Am Empire* by Robert Daley, a 529-page book, stewards are mentioned on the first trans-Atlantic passenger flight:

> As soon as the flying boat was out over the Atlantic the steward passed through handing out a passenger list....At last the steward announced dinner.....The stewards began to make up berths,.... [Betty Trippe's] mind was filled with observations...Shouldn't the berths be made up before leaving to make it easier for the stewards? Because at eight thousand feet, the making up of a berth was strenuous work, and the stewards felt it.....

> Breakfast was served en route to Marseille; at an altitude of ten thousand feet eggs and coffee took twelve minutes to boil. The stewards worked hard, then and always. They not only served all meals to the thirty-four people aboard—in addition to the twenty-

two passengers there was a crew of twelve—but they also handled all baggage, made up berths, took charge of passports and
landing papers in each country.

Stewardesses fare less well in that book. The only mention of them I could
discover occurs during the description of Juan Trippe's retirement announcement:
...he looked out over rows of stockholders, about eight hundred
people in all. Pan Am stewardesses in powder-blue uniforms
moved up and down the aisles handing out company literature.
He rapped for order, and in a low, droning voice began to read a
45-minute stockholders' report. (p. 441)

While I mourned the fact that I would be unable to lean on the above
histories for valuable information pertaining to flight attendants, I recognized
immediately that it was even more important than I had thought to document
the cabin crew's contribution to the company and to reveal their heroism. It
was time to swing into action, but once again I almost swooned at the enormity of the task. I had no idea where to begin. My two years as a stewardess
early in the 1960s hardly equipped me to tell a 64-year tale. The advantage I
had was a passion for the subject and a love of the oral tradition. (At the
university where I work, I make my first-year students read *The Iliad* aloud in
the course of a single day. It takes about 18 hours.) I wanted to *hear* flight
attendants telling their own stories. I decided to track down those who, for
reasons of heroism or historical significance, were important to rounding out
the Pan Am story. I would interview them and then incorporate their stories in
my book, using as much of their personal testimonies as I could.

To find them, I started my own networking. I joined World Wings International, an association of ex-Pan Am flight attendants. I travelled all over the
country and went overseas to interview willing victims. Everywhere I was
received with open arms and encouraged to keep going. On my journeys, I
would ask complete strangers "What do you know about Pan Am?" and the
response would usually involve the intervention of a flight attendant. I kept
listening and amassing material. I gave a lecture, 'Heroism in the Pan Am
Cabin,' at George Washington University. But the more material I collected,
the more frightened I became that I might omit the greatest story or the most
heroic deed. I still wake up in the night with a certain apprehension.

However, the other side of fear is hope. My hope is that *Fasten Your
Seat Belts!* will encourage the unearthing of more cabin history. Remember,
this book is idiosyncratic. It is determined by the people I have met, the stories
I have listened to, and is based on choices that I alone have made, the most

important of which was to write about Pan Am's historic and heroic flight attendants. (The names of those whose stories I focus on appear in bold face in the text.)

Recently, a writer, the husband of one of the subjects in this book, asked, "Where's the chapter on layovers, Val? You'd sell a lot more books if you included sex." He's right, of course. I do not deny that there was sex—lots of lovely sex. Nonetheless, I responded rather snappishly that it was high time someone presented another, overdue, view of flight attendants. By the same token, he could have asked why I chose not to write about smuggling, pimping, spying, thieving, and drug and alcohol addiction. Those topics also sell books, and Pan Am flight attendants were exceptionally exposed to temptation and international intrigue; the wonder is that so many of them were able to resist the lures.

If I have omitted tales of your favorite Pan Am cabin pioneers and heroes, or if you wish to retrieve the cabin histories of other airlines, quickly set about recording them. These histories are too precious to be allowed to evaporate, like Pan Am itself, into thin air.

Valerie Browne in 1963.

The First Stewards

*The purser seated the passengers and handed each a packet that
contained a wad of cotton and another of chewing gum. The cotton was for plugging up your ears in the hopes of muffling some
of the otherwise unmuffled roar of those engines against the un-
lined metal hull of the boat. The gum, if chewed vigorously, would
pop your ears and equalize the pressure when the plane changed
altitude. It also gave the nervous, and we had quite a few, something to chew on. The purser's second act of passenger service
came later, when he handed out the lunch boxes. If his sounds like
a lazy job, it wasn't. After takeoff, he had to make out and verify
all the ship's papers before the next landing. There was a blizzard
of papers, with half a dozen copies of each. At that time our little
aircraft when it entered port, was treated like a twenty-thousand-
ton liner.*

William M. Masland, *Through the Back Doors
of the World in a Ship That Had Wings*

No flight attendant was on board to accompany pilot Cy Caldwell
and seven sacks of mail from Key West to Havana on the single-
engined Fairchild FC-2, *La Niña,* on 19 October 1927, the day of
Pan American's first flight. Juan Trippe, a young entrepreneur, and for 41
subsequent years the presiding genius of Pan American, had borrowed the
seaplane from West Indian Aerial Express in order to fulfil the statutory
requirements to qualify for the country's first overseas air mail contract. Nine
days later, on 28 October, by which time the airport at Key West had been
completed and Trippe had received delivery of a Fokker F.VIIa, the Key West
to Havana route was officially inaugurated. No flight attendant was on board
that day either to accompany Huey Wells, Ed Musick, and 772 pounds of
mail. On 16 January 1928, Pan American inaugurated its passenger service
for a fare of $50 one way. There was still no flight attendant, but the need for
one was becoming readily apparent.

Stewards had already been hard at work in Europe for several years.
Germany claims to have provided the first cabin service, on 17 March 1912,
with Heinrich Kubis as their first air steward. He tended to passengers aboard

1

the Deutsche Luftschiffarts A.G. (DELAG) dirigible, the *Schwaben,* during 1912–14, and then became the chief steward on the *Hindenberg.*

As early as 1922, British stewards were serving food on Daimler Airway (later Imperial Airways). With the advent of Armstrong Whitworth Argosy aircraft in 1926, Imperial experimented with luncheon, promptly at 12 noon, on board its Silver Wing service from Croydon to Paris, having recruited stewards from existing rail and ship services to serve the meal. The experiment was successful; Imperial Airways advertised its de luxe luncheon flight to the general public in 1927.

During the 1920s, the French company, Air Union (later Air France) experimented on its Blériot aircraft with meal service and attendants provided by the Wagon-Lits Company. It was called the Avion Restaurant, but it was not successful. However, in 1929, they tried again on board the Lioré et Olivier 21s, this time hiring six British stewards for their primarily English and American clientèle. The stewards' recruiter, Jack Bamford, writes: "The requirements were that they must have previously have been waiters, that they spoke good French, and that their weight should be no more than that of a jockey. Try finding six like this in the West End! Especially when besides all this they had to be personable, smart and healthy! However, with perseverance, by advertising and by considerable enquiry, I at last assembled a team. One came from the Savoy, one from Claridge's and one from Scotts."

Early in 1928, Deutsche Luft Hansa hired its first airplane (as opposed to dirigible) steward, Albert Hofe, and later that same year Pan American

Unknown steward (perhaps Amaury Sanchez) working aboard a Pan American Fokker F-10.

hired its first steward, **Amaury Sanchez**. He was a 19-year-old native of Puerto Rico and was working in a New York fraternity club when Pan American's general traffic manager approached him about a new job. Admiring Sanchez's competence and easy manner with the club members, the manager invited him to work as a steward out of Pan American's brand new base in Miami. He offered him $100 a month and the rare opportunity to fly.

"I was scared as hell on my first flight," Amaury explained to the *Miami Herald*. "It took two hours to get from Miami to Havana. I had a little portable chair in the back of the airplane, and my only instructions were to keep people happy and not too scared. I was young and crazy in those days."

Young and crazy though he may have been, Amaury Sanchez was obviously gifted for his job because Pan American soon began hiring stewards for all its passenger flights, and introduced refreshments on board in 1929. Pan Am would continue to hire stewards rather than stewardesses until the beginning of 1944, in spite of the fact that women had been aloft since 15 May 1930, when Ellen Church of Boeing Air Transport (later United Air Lines) became the world's first airline stewardess.

Passengers were thrilled with the novelty of flying, and during 1928 more than 1,100 people boarded Pan American aircraft for flights between Florida and Cuba, while the fleet grew to seven and the number of employees rose to 118.

By 1930, the company employed ten stewards. **Charles (Bebe) Rebozo**, one of the original ten, says that he joined Pan American (at age 17) because being a steward was an excellent job in those days. His training consisted of one flight to Havana on a ten-passenger tri-motor Fokker, the aircraft on which he worked exclusively during his one-year career as a steward, after which he became a navigator. He left Pan American for more lucrative pastimes, which included flying a small airplane over Miami and if he saw land he fancied, he bought it. This laid the foundation for his career as a property mogul. Sixty-four years after his career as a steward, Bebe Rebozo has only fond memories of Pan American: he recalls that all his flights were exciting, the pilots were aces, and Pan Am, with its total of 300 employees, was a wonderful company to work for.

The airline soon began reaching out to more distant Caribbean islands and to Central and South America, building bases at each stop along the route, hacking airstrips out of thick jungle, dropping supplies from the aircraft, and fending off hostile Indians. It was impossible to build landing strips in some locations, either because of inaccessibility or because of volcanic terrain, and that problem was solved by bringing in an aircraft 'that carried its own airport on its bottom,' the amphibious Sikorsky S-38.

Using the Caribbean and Latin America as its training ground, Pan American pilots accumulated wisdom and experience about long-range, over-water flying, and the stewards took on more and more responsibilities: for passenger comfort and safety, for the paperwork that accompanies international flying, and in some cases even for calculating weight and balance of the aircraft. By 1931, travel by air had become so popular that Pan American acquired its first four-engined aircraft, the Sikorsky S-40 flying boat. The first into service was christened *American Clipper,* and the prefix or suffix 'Clipper' was used for all Pan American aircraft that followed. The S-40 had a range of 800 miles and could carry 40 passengers, catered to by two stewards.

Juan Trippe then began to dream about an airline that could cross the major oceans. He spent months travelling to and from Europe by ship, arranging meetings with the air ministries of Britain, France, Germany, and Holland. He also negotiated with Washington, Bermuda, and Canada. And he gazed regularly at the globe, peering down at those little specks in the Pacific: Midway, Wake, and Guam, the stepping stones to Asia. In June 1931, he wrote to the six major aircraft manufacturers requesting designs for "a high-speed multimotored flying boat having a cruising range of 2,500 miles." Four of them laughed at his request, but Sikorsky and the Glenn Martin Company were willing to consider it.

Meanwhile, the famous aviator, Charles Lindbergh, now closely associated with Pan Am, suggested to Trippe an attempt to fly from New York to China—via Alaska. Robert Daley in *An American Saga* continues: "Trippe was enthusiastic, and promised every support. Lindbergh would be accompanied by his wife Anne, aged twenty-five, who had been taught Morse code by Leuteritz [Pan American's radio genius and chief communications engineer] and who would operate the standard Pan American sending-and-receiving radio telegraph during the flight. Obviously, this flight, which would carry the young couple over unknown areas of the globe, was hazardous, and Anne was just a slip of a girl, but when the danger to her was pointed out to Lindbergh, he merely smiled and said, 'But she's crew.'"

No flight attendant climbed aboard the Lockheed Sirius on 27 July 1931, when Charles Lindbergh and Anne Morrow Lindbergh set off from College Point, Long Island, on their long journey halfway around the world. In the days that preceded their departure, however, they provisioned and loaded their aircraft in much the way that an early steward would, making sure there was plenty of fresh water, food that would not spoil, and first aid equipment. In *North to the Orient,* Anne Morrow Lindbergh describes their preparations: "Our craft, the *Sirius,* with its six-hundred-horsepower Cyclone engine, was equipped with gasoline tanks which would carry us for two thousand miles, and with pontoons that would enable us to land in Hudson Bay, on the many inland lakes throughout Canada, along the coast of Alaska and Siberia, and among the Japanese islands...aside from the general equipment indispensable for our everyday flying, we must carry a large amount of emergency supplies: an adequate repair kit and repair materials; a rubber boat, a sail and oars; an extra crash-proof, waterproof radio set; parachutes; general camping equipment and food supplies; firearms and ammunition; a full medicine kit....And we must not exceed our limited weight budget. Every object to be taken had to be weighed, mentally as well as physically. The weight in pounds must balance the value in usefulness."

By the middle of 1934, Trippe's six years of haggling, planning, negotiating, and making agreements for landing concessions in Europe, Canada, and the Azores had not been translated into action. In addition, although the Lindberghs' summer transit from New York to Nanking had been successful, winter flying problems in Alaska had proved insurmountable. Also, because U.S. diplomatic recognition of the Soviet Union was only then becoming a reality, landing rights in eastern Siberia could not be taken for granted. Defeated for the moment in crossing the Atlantic and in reaching China via the Arctic, Trippe began once again to focus on those tiny pinpoints in the Pacific: Wake, Midway, and Guam. If he had installations for water-based aircraft on those islands, he would be able to reach Asia over water; furthermore, all the staging points as far as Manila would be U.S. territory, thus avoiding international traffic rights problems. Sikorsky and Glenn Martin had worked miracles, and he was just about to receive delivery of three Martin 130 and three Sikorsky S-42 flying boats. On 3 October 1934, Juan Trippe announced to the Secretary of the Navy that Pan American was ready to fly the Pacific. His announcement was a little ahead of realism. He still had the problems of stretching the payload-range of the flying boats and of building and equipping bases across the Pacific. The story of Pan American's establishment of seaplane bases across the Pacific is absolutely fascinating, and is dealt with at length in *An American Saga, The Chosen Instrument,* and *Pan Am: An Airline and its Aircraft.*

According to William M. Masland in *Through the Back Doors of the World in a Ship that Had Wings,* stewards were already at work in the Pacific well before passengers made their first crossings. He relates that André Priester, Pan American's chief engineer, the ever practical Dutchman, discovered that flight crews who pioneered the routes from island to island across the Pacific "subsisted on a diet of baked beans and peanut butter. Advised of this curious diet, he ordered a steward to join the crew to see to it that the flight crew ate a more balanced meal."

To trace the route by which flight attendants working for Pan American found themselves in the air is always interesting. Let us go back to Miami for a moment and listen to **Jerry Galindo**, who joined Pan American in 1934 and who worked on the flying boats in the Latin American Division. His story is full of a boy's passion for flying in the earliest days of Pan American.

"When I was a kid, I lived in Key West, and my grandmother and my aunt managed an apartment building close to the ocean on the main street, Duval Street. We were on the furthest point in Key West, half a block from the South Beach, and from there you go direct to Havana. In 1927, when I was about 14, Pan Am started flying out of Key West, and the first pilots came there and rented apartments. One of them was Shorty Clark and another one was Ekstrom, and they were way old-timers, way back. I used to wash their cars. They'd give me two dollars and I'd spend a half a day washing the orange clay off the cars because they'd come in from Georgia or wherever. Then I started making little model airplanes.

"Those pilots always put the wing down when they passed over the apartment; they were at maybe 500 feet, headed for Cuba. To me that was the most wonderful thing I had ever seen. I got the bug there and then. Some of the pilots' wives were a little nervous. They would run down to the bootlegger to buy booze after their husbands left. And I would say 'How could she do that to him? He's a hero. Look what he's doing up there.'

"A couple of times they took me up flying. The first time they took me up, they wanted to check-ride an old tri-motor Fokker, and they gave me a ride for about 30 minutes, and I went ape. It was something unbelievable in those days. Every time they'd come in, I'd be right there to say hi to them."

Jerry had fallen in love with flying and with Pan American, and he was determined to find work with the airline. He knew that he could not be hired as a pilot because he did not have a license, but he had heard that Pan American was hiring young men to be stewards. He continues:

"When I was 20 years old, I took the Florida East Coast train from Key West to Miami to see Juan Trippe about a job. He had dated my mother, who was divorced then; a couple of times he took her to dinner or something. Anyway, he was sick, and Mario Martinez, the general manager, was in the office. He said 'We'll hire you, Jerry, but we can't hire you right now because you're only 20 years old.' I got my aunt who was a judge to give me a birth certificate, but he saw through it because he was an old Key Wester himself. I still have the affidavit saying I was 21 years old.

"I wanted that job, and I sat in Mr. Quickley's office—he was the operations manager in Coconut Grove—for days and days until he hired me. He finally said 'Do you want this job?' and I said 'Yes, SIR!'

Jerry Galindo at work on a Boeing 307 Stratoliner.

"Right away, I started work on the flying boats. Pan American had acquired the S-42s by then. When we landed the boats at Dinner Key, for instance on Sundays and holidays, there would be thousands of people who had come to watch the 'planes arrive. The place would be packed. When you'd go through Customs and want to get home, you had to push your way through the traffic because of all the people who would come out there to watch those 'planes on a nice day."

Coming home to Dinner Key was the easy part; life on the line was full of adventure and hazard. By this time, Pan Am had acquired the pioneering New York, Rio and Buenos Aires Line (NYRBA), and Jerry describes what it was like flying down to Buenos Aires:

"We flew the S-42s only in the daytime hours. In the beginning, we landed at night, using flares on the Amazon and other rivers where we landed, but the Indians would come out through the dark in canoes to investigate the lights. That's why we flew only in the daytime. On the way south, we over-nighted in San Juan, Trinidad, Belém, Recife, Rio, and Buenos Aires.

"Two of us worked on the flying boats. Pan American hired a lot of maitre d's to be stewards. Italian, German, French. They would visit the kitchens on the ground to see how the food was prepared and to make sure that the cooks washed their hands when they came out of the bathroom. It wasn't very sanitary some places. Sometimes a passenger would open up an egg and there'd be a biddy in there.

"I remember in 1939—I was a purser by then—in the flying boats, the women—I wasn't a bad-looking guy—the women catered to me a lot more than they did other guys. These women would say 'Why is it that you can go up and down and you don't get sick?' Well, I was serving lunch to this one lady and I came out with this one, and I swear to God it happened. I got personal with her and I said 'Now listen, the reason I don't get air sick is I take a tape and tape it straight up and down across my navel like a cross.' She says 'You do?' And I said 'And that's the reason I don't get air sick. I put tape, Band Aid, across the navel.' Honey, maybe a month or two later, I'd have this one and that one come to me and whisper, 'Hey, I got the tape!'"

Jerry likes to recall the good times, but there was another side to working in the flying boats for cabin crew in those days. Horace Brock in *Flying the Oceans* reminds us: "In the Antilla [Cuba] accident, as in virtually every one, the purser was the hero. The entrance hatch in the S-43 and S-42 was in the top of the cabin to keep the sides closed and watertight. Access to the entrance hatch was by a gangway run over to the top of the hull from the shore or dock, and the passengers then went down a short companionway inside the cabin to their seats. In a crash it was the purser and steward, if there were two cabin attendants, who would carry or push the passengers up the companionway and out into the water. In these landing crashes there might be no time for inflating rubber boats or formal evacuation procedures. No purser ever left the cabin till he had gotten all of his passengers out of it, and some died in the attempt. The stewards and pursers were all, at this time in LAD [the Latin American Division], Cuban-speaking [sic] men, and we held them in esteem as crew members."

Even though Jerry thoroughly enjoyed working with the passengers, he never overcame his desire to fly the aircraft. He started taking flying lessons, saved his money, and bought a small airplane.

"While I was working as a purser, I started flying my own 'plane. At that time, I often took the controls on the Pan American 'planes to Rio. Those guys let me fly! You see, Pan American pilots didn't like the Army pilots they hired during the War. And if an Army pilot made a couple of mistakes, I'd hear the bell 'Dingdingdingding.' I knew what it was. It meant the Army co-pilot had goofed and the captain would embarrass him by making me sit up there. It was embarrassing for me too, because I wanted to be nice and friendly to the Army co-pilots. I didn't want those guys to hate me. Not all of the Pan American pilots let me fly, but there was this one guy I'm thinking of specifically. I flew with him to Rio for a long time, and that's the way I logged my hours. In 1943 I got my commercial license.

"Now, in 1942, I left the Rio run—they put me almost in charge of the Africa/Orient division, and that was Miami-based and was the Army Air Force department of Pan American [the military had taken over much of Pan American's equipment and personnel for use during the Second World War]. I couldn't get used to being on the ground, so I had a buddy of mine take over and let me fly as a purser, then he'd take over in the office, and then I'd come back and I'd take over. Miami to China, you know. We'd fly from Miami to China. We'd go down to Natal, Natal to Ascension, Ascension to Accra, Accra to Khartoum, Khartoum to Aden, Arabia, Aden to Karachi. This was Pan American under a military guise."

Because of the War, it became harder and harder for Pan American to hire young men as stewards, and on 21 November 1943, the company formally hired their first training group of women. "When we first got stewardesses, Pan American had me go on observation flights to check out the passengers' reactions to having them on the line. When I saw how the folks never took their eyes off the girls, and never once looked at me, I told the company 'They're in. They're in.'

"Let me tell you how I got friendly with the chief pilot. We had a DC-3 flight out of Miami, and I'm standing in the back of the plane trying to check this and that and I hear somebody saying 'Hey, you,' and he snaps his fingers, 'Hey, you,' he kept hollering, he never knew me from Adam, and he kept snapping his fingers. I ignored him completely. Well, first thing you know he comes back and says 'Hey. You deaf?' And I say 'Yeah.' He says 'We want a lot of coffee and a lot of sugar, and a lot of cream. A lot.' I shook my head and didn't answer. After we took off, I took the whole damn thing of coffee, one of those two quart containers, a quart of cream and a whole box of sugar, and I put it on a tray and in the center of the tray I put a condom. I put the whole shebang in his lap. He looked down and he said 'What's this for?' And he pointed to the condom. I said 'Sir, you can put it over your head and they can call you Captain Prick!' So we became the best of friends, and when I was in Rio, where he was chief pilot, I was always invited to his apartment."

Jerry Galindo is unusual in the history of flight attendants because he made the move from cabin to cockpit, although not the Pan Am cockpit. (In recent years, Kathy Brown, who worked as a stewardess for Pan American and then United, has now become a pilot for United.)

"After I got my pilot's license, Pan American wanted me to come as a pilot for them, but old man Priester, the Dutchman in New York, wouldn't let me. So in 1944, when I was 30 years old and it was still during the draft, I called up Jacksonville, the main office of National Airlines, and talked to the chief pilot, who then interviewed me on 2 January 1945, and hired me. When they heard that National had hired me as a pilot, Pan American was so nice to me. They worked out my paperwork to transfer me immediately over to National so that I would eliminate the draft. I went from ten years as a purser with Pan American straight to being a National pilot.

"From then on, I was very lucky. I was a co-pilot for only nine months before I was made captain. When I would fly from Miami to Havana, I would pass the chief pilot from Pan American, and in Havana I'd be waiting for him when he came in. Our planes were much faster than theirs. I'd go up high and then I'd dive it down and cruise right by him like he was standing still. The co-pilots would envy me. They'd say 'I've been here 22 years,' 'I've been here 15 years,' or 'I've been here nine years, and I'm still the god-damned co-pilot and you are with National only nine months and you're a captain.' I was the envy. They would talk about me.

"Pan American people would call me 'The Legend.' It wasn't that I was so great or nothing. It was the idea that I was the only one that moved out of the ranks. I was the only one. A lot of the pursers didn't think I could ever make pilot. Most of them are dead now. For some reason or other all the old stewards have passed away."

Even though he had made the switch from purser to pilot, Jerry was unable to forget his days in the cabin. If the crew was overworked, he would leave the cockpit and lend a hand. He did this on many occasions and only once got caught. He likes to tell the story of that occasion.

"This is the one I got written up for. I was flying a 'plane from New Orleans across the Gulf to Miami. Before we took off, I knew that the stewardess was feeling very bad. She was sitting in a chair and I said 'What's the matter?' And she says 'I don't know. I feel terrible.' I said 'Get on the airplane and we'll see what happens. I can help you.' She says 'No, no, thank you. I'll do it.' Anyway, when I got on the airplane the kid was knocked out, so I got out of the seat after the climb, took off my hat and my jacket, and went in the back and started preparing the trays. The two of us, the girl and myself, we served 80 passengers or whatever the hell it was. We only had an hour and 40 minutes to serve all these people between New Orleans and Miami. So we had to work like a son of a gun. Just before we arrive, I go back to the cockpit and land the airplane, and that's the end of that. So now, two or three days later, I get a 'phone call to come and see the chief pilot, and he says 'You're the only one we can think of that would do this.' I said 'What are you talking about?' He said 'We got two letters here from passengers which said they are very happy to know that National Airlines now has pursers. They wondered why we never had pursers before. The only guy we can figure that would leave the cockpit and go back and serve the goddamn passengers is a guy named

Galindo. Is that you?' They aired my ass out. I said 'Gee, I guess so. I was only a couple of minutes.' He said 'Bullshit. They said you served the whole way through and you were wonderful.' But they really ate my ass out over that one."

Jerry Galindo worked as a flight attendant for ten years for Pan American and was a captain for National Airlines for 19 years. Like many stewards before and after him, he had a business on the side and for 27 years ran two men's stores at Miami airport, selling airline uniforms among other items of clothing.

"So now I'm 80 years old. They gave me a big party, balloons, T-shirts with 'Go Fuck Yourself' and so on. I still get around, I'm still the same, I haven't changed, my vocabulary hasn't changed. My favorite expression when any girl comes up to me: 'Oh, let me tell you this one.'"

War Stories

On the eve of history's first global conflict, in a world that was depending more and more on the airplane, Pan Am alone had the equipment, the crews and the experience to transport men and materials across oceans and continents literally to any place on the earth.

The First Fifty Years of Pan Am

As Pan American grew, so did its complement of cabin crew. In 1934 alone, stewards provided service to the more than 100,000 passengers who flew to Central and South America, the Caribbean and Alaska. As the company racked up one first after another, the stewards of the 1930s and early 1940s were presented with challenges both in the air and on the ground that their modern counterparts would find inconceivable.

In 1935, Juan Trippe's dream of an airline that could cross the Pacific came true with an air mail service, and in 1936 passenger service across the Pacific was inaugurated. Flight Steward L.R. (Bob) Merrill was on board the *Hawaii Clipper,* a Martin 130 flying boat on the historic six-day flight from San Francisco to Manila. (The passengers included two women whose occupation was listed as 'World Traveller.') And at last, on 20 May 1939, the *Yankee Clipper* accomplished the first commercial flight carrying passengers between the United States and Europe. Albert Tuinman, who had been a chef at '21' before working for Pan Am, and René Mezzanin were the cabin crew for that historic flight. (Sometimes the temptations presented by international flying proved irresistible. Shortly after the War began, Mezzanin was caught smuggling in Europe and served a term in jail).

Pan American had already staged one of its publicity blitzes for the press, offering journalists the opportunity to cross the Atlantic before the first fare-paying passengers. Alice Rogers Hager, a well-known aviation writer in the 1930s and 1940s, was one of those invited to cross the Atlantic on 17 June 1939. In her book, *Wings Over the Americas,* she describes the scene on board the Boeing 314:

"Our 'flying pressroom' was the scene of violent activity. No calls for Copyboy echoed through the cabins, but every few minutes one of the stewards would be waylaid and asked in wheedling tones if he couldn't rush some more 'takes' up to the radio men. By the time it was dark outside and seven o'clock had rolled around, they were looking despairingly at their watches and asking us repeatedly if we weren't hungry. But over the noise of the clicking keys no one paid any attention. At last Captain Winston came down, wearing his most engaging smile, and before we knew it typewriters had been stowed temporarily; the ladies had gotten mysterious word that the captain would appreciate it if they would dress for dinner, and the stewards were fairly running to get the tables set.

"In the tiny but elegant chrome and leather ladies' lounge five of us were a tight fit, but we managed to shuck ourselves out of traveling gear and into evening finery. What with our going-away orchids and such, we really did justice to that first night's flight, establishing a custom that it was hoped would stick, since it would set the standard of the service as a luxury line of the air. The men on board, not having been warned, hadn't a black tie among them, but they cheered our performance and compromised with clean faces and freshly brushed hair.

"Each of the tables in the smoking compartment amidships, which automatically became the dining salon during meals, bore its centerpiece of flowers, and with the compliments of the captain, who came down to join us at his own table, champagne was served. So we toasted him and his crew and the trip that was sending us across the ocean as recorders of history in the making. After dinner it was back to the typewriters again, and I shall never forget the sight of Inez Robb, in an elegant frock by Schiaparelli, pounding away for dear life against that nine-o'clock deadline."

On board the return trip, when the pressure for deadlines was off, Alice Hager wrote in her journal:

"This morning, at ten minutes after two, the steward shook my curtains and said, 'Captain's compliments, Madame. Venus is about to rise.'

"Two of us did roll out of the warm comfort of our berths at that summons, threw on a few clothes, and went with Captain Winston up to the flight deck and back to stand on the little ladder into the star hatch. The conical glass 'blister' on the topmost point of the midwing surface is the vantage from which star positions are 'shot' by the navigator...

"Had it been anywhere but where it was, the scene would have been faintly romantic but not out of the ordinary. In mid-ocean, isolated from the water below by that deep layer upon layer of cloud, it was fantastic.

"To right and left stretched the tremendous wing surfaces of the plane, with the engine nacelles lifting proud heads above the leading edge. Directly behind us, the great three-finned tail reared itself, sturdily reassuring, familiar human handiwork. Beyond was the infinite—the procession of the planets wheeling upon their courses and guiding ours. To the right stood Mars, Jupiter, Saturn, large and faintly golden. To the left, just above that billowing argent cloud floor, Venus walked in rosy beauty. If one had never worshipped before, then was a time when divinity was too much present not to bow the heart in reverence."

But I digress....

Hunter-Gatherers At Botwood

Before the U.S. officially entered the Second World War, Pan American was already involved in missions across the Atlantic. Some of the accounts of the stewards' ingenuity during these missions are recounted in Philip J. Parrott's *The History of Inflight Food Service*, and one of the prime examples of stewards' amazing resourcefulness occurs in a story that **Jerry Cameron** recounted to Phil and me. But first, let us take a look at Jerry's career up to that point.

He was hired by Pan American in 1940 as a port steward, and his job entailed loading and unloading the galley equipment and commissary

A training session with Jerry Cameron.

supplies, and washing and stacking tableware when the Clipper arrived at North Beach marine terminal (which later became LaGuardia Field). The facilities at North Beach were primitive, and Jerry had a tiny cubbyhole in which to work. He hosed the dishes down and then washed them in a bucketful of hot water, which he heated over an electric hot plate. Then he would prepare the galley for the next departure.

Jerry worked as a port steward for three months, at a salary of $100 per month, watching the cabin crew coming and going, thinking that a job in the air would be a gift from God. He had plenty of time between the Clippers' arrivals and departures, and the company required that he attend flight steward training classes so that he would understand the job perfectly and be able to complement the service crews in the air with his service on the ground. On every occasion he could, he demonstrated his interest in becoming a flight steward. Three months after he started work as port steward, Jerry was hired as the eleventh flight steward in New York, his salary was increased to $125 per month, and he embarked on his 38 years of flight service with Pan American.

A few months after Jerry started flying, he was assigned to one of the special trans-Atlantic missions. "We had eight or ten intelligence chaps as passengers on board, and we landed at Botwood, at the far northeastern tip of Newfoundland, to top off the tanks. After topping off, we started our take-off run and blew an engine. So, there we were, stuck at Botwood, and you couldn't find a more primitive or worse place to break down, but you don't choose those things.

"There was a fellow who always came out from a Royal Canadian Air Force base by boat to the 'plane. He brought fuel and helped with maintenance. He saw us return that day, and took me and the skipper ashore to look the situation over. We found an abandoned R.C.A.F. Quonset hut with part of it fixed as living quarters, with some pretty good equipment consisting of a long table, ten folding chairs, a big wicker davenport, broken down but still comfortable, a large camp stove, a big heater, and ten bunks. We decided to set up housekeeping there. We learned later that this facility was used for fishing parties.

"Eddie Lockwood was the steward with me on the flight, and we made several trips with the boat getting all the supplies we had aboard to feed and house everyone from the 'plane and into the Quonset hut. We only had food for two more meals, so I asked the skipper to include that information in his wire to New York for repair parts. He said we had to give New York credit for some sense and they would know what commissary supplies we needed, so he kept his message to maintenance requirements. Let me tell you what they sent, along with the parts he requested: six gallons of ice cream, 20 quarts of milk, and a case of bourbon. There was, of course, no refrigeration in the Quonset hut.

"Eddie and I went fishing, but all we caught were some small bass, but we needed some real food. On our take-off run we had seen some little fishing villages along the shore, so we figured we might find some food to buy. I had a cash fund of $500 for buying supplies on the trip, so I gave him $100. We decided to buy as much as we could on the first go, because if we had to come back they'd probably jack the prices up, or else tell us to go scratch, because Americans weren't too popular there until we really got into the War. I took one side of the lake, and Eddie took the other.

"It was several hours before we returned to camp. We picked up everything we could, including a spring lamb. This was August or September because the leaves were beginning to show some color, and by that time the lamb weighed 20-25 pounds. Between us we had four chickens, a bushel sack of potatoes, some turnips, and 17 or 18 eggs in a bag, but a couple of them were broken by the time I got back. I had borrowed a wheelbarrow to cart my supplies back.

"Now came the bit about killing the lamb. Being a farm boy and raised around all sorts of animals, we had to slaughter pigs, sheep, calves, and chickens. That was all part of growing up. But I had been caring for this little lamb and had become fond him, so I hoped someone else would volunteer. Well, nobody was about to do so. Fortunately the skipper had a .38 pistol, so I took the little lamb out behind the Quonset, shot him in the back of the head. Felt pretty badly about it, but I did it, and then I skinned and cleaned him up. The chickens were no problem—just wring their necks. We made soup from the chicken carcasses, along with potato and turnip and cabbage. It thickened up pretty good with the continuous boiling of the potatoes in it. We were short on seasoning; all we had from the supplies on board was salt and pepper and the hot sauce we used for shrimp cocktails.

"We received an awful lot of compliments from the passengers and crew. They were all very nice—played a lot of poker and told stories, and, of course, we had the case of bourbon."

The Cannonball Run

"The Botwood flight was just cutting my teeth," Jerry Cameron continues. "After the War really got going in Europe we couldn't fly to Southampton or Foynes any longer, although we still flew regularly scheduled trips to Lisbon. Before the U.S. joined the Allies, much of the rest of our work was in three flying boats, NC18603, 18604, and 18605, the *Yankee, Atlantic,* and *Dixie*

Clippers, working on the Cannonball Run, the 11,500-mile express route that Pan American operated from Miami to Karachi or Rangoon. Part of that work involved special missions carrying arms and ammunition to the American Volunteer Group (A.V.G.)—to General Joe Stilwell and to Claire Chennault. The A.V.G. was based in Kunming, China. Supplies were sent to Chabua on the Indian border, and the A.V.G. flew them over the Hump to Kunming."

The Hump was the notorious route to China over the Himalayas, legendary for the dangers it presented. Many of the pilots were American mercenaries from the disbanded Flying Tigers working for China National Aviation Corporation, a Pan American-associated company. Crews would often have to fly up to 20,000 feet without oxygen to cross the mountains; the weather was vicious, and Japanese fighter 'planes were an ever-present threat. One Pan Am-owned aircraft returned from a trip over the Hump sporting more than 3,000 bullet holes. After the U.S. entered the War, the A.V.G. was joined by Army Air Force flyers.

"On one occasion, we took the flight from New York to Miami, where we loaded up with machine guns and other munitions needed for fighting the Japanese in China. No passengers, just a cockpit crew of 15 and two stewards. We travelled together all the way from New York to Rangoon. I had a brand new steward with me, Ed Hable, so new that he didn't even have a uniform. He did what he was told, but wasn't the energetic type.

"We left home base several days before Pearl Harbor. As we were flying somewhere over West Africa, I remember the captain coming downstairs from the cockpit, Captain R.O.D. Sullivan, the best pilot there ever was, and saying to me: 'Do you have good eyesight? We have to decipher this message by flashlight.' Why he picked me instead of one of the other 15 crew members, I don't know. Anyway, we deciphered the message together and it said: 'We are at war. Refer to plan A.' That meant operating without any communication and in total radio silence.

"We had to make short hops along the way because we were so heavily loaded—San Juan, Trinidad, Belém, Natal, Dakar, Lagos, Léopold-ville. Once we got to Lagos, we followed a route that was provisioned by Imperial Airways, and scrounging food from them wasn't too difficult. We would go ashore in little bunda boats. By the way, the Congo River runs pretty swiftly, and sometimes whole pieces of land would break away from the river bank, forming small islands, which would sail down the river towards the Clipper. Someone from the cockpit crew stayed on the boat all the time, ready to run up the engines and move out of the way. If one of those floating islands got stuck under the seawing, it would tear the airplane away from its mooring.

"The day after we set down at Léopoldville, Bob Ford and his crew came in from San Francisco. We sat on the water with them. That was the first time I met the stewards, Barney Sawicki and Verne Edwards. [More about their amazing, inadvertent round-the-world flight in the next section.] We flew from Léopoldville to Port Bell on Lake Victoria, and then set off for Khartoum. On our way we found ourselves in a tremendous dust storm. We were in that storm for hours. Do not forget; we couldn't use the radio, and navigation was done by dead reckoning alone. We couldn't fly too high because climbing expended too much fuel and we couldn't fly too low because the sand would clog the carburetor screens. We were in flight for about seven hours on dead reckoning, knowing that there were some high peaks with lower passes that were charted through. That is when I found out that Captain Sullivan was somebody special. All at once the airplane tipped up on a wing. Everything came loose. Some ammunition flew out of the restrainers. What a mess. Later I climbed up to the cockpit and said 'What the hell happened there?' The first officer was still stunned, shaking all over. Sullivan said nothing. I asked him to assign someone to help us clear up the mess.

"A little later, the first officer came downstairs and again I asked him what happened. He said 'I don't know. That man must have radar like those underwater creatures. We couldn't see anything, but all at once he wrenched the wheel.' In those days, most of the flying was done by hand. They did have a half-baked automatic pilot they called George, but it was not accurate and they had to keep adjusting it. R.O.D. Sullivan was probably one of the strongest men for his weight that you could imagine, and when the mountain came right up under us, he yanked that great big airplane with all his might, and tipped the wing over the side of the mountain peak. With superhuman strength, he did with that giant, heavily loaded Clipper what you do with a little fighter plane. Only when we had safely set down on the Nile at Khartoum did we recognize how close we had come to disaster.

"When I asked Captain Sullivan how he knew the mountain was there if he couldn't see it, he said 'I felt it.'"

"From Khartoum we flew to Aden, and you can't imagine how hot it was. The only way to keep cool on the ground was by pulling a sheet over yourself and having somebody throw a bucket of water at you. We scrounged some more food there before flying on to Karachi, which was a good place to get supplies, being a major base out East for Imperial Airways. We spent three days there because we needed a lot of maintenance by then. There was one engine in particular that had to keep going, Number Three, because it powered the galley. If they lost Number Three, they would get cold food only. They paid a lot of attention to Number Three.

"We flew on to Calcutta. That was a real hole. Imperial Airways had already withdrawn, and the whole operation was run by the British Admiralty. They grounded our airplane, along with the cargo, waiting for further orders. They let us sit on there on the Ganges River and bake our tails but good.

"Our captain was an ex-Navy commander and was not about to give up his ship to anyone, with or without orders from above. He refused to hand over our airplane and its load to His Majesty's Navy. So we sat there for three days, waiting for orders from President Roosevelt. Imagine how hot it was in that airplane and how it stank on that river. There were dead cows floating down, and we used grappling hooks to push them away from the seawing so that they wouldn't tear us from our mooring. Let me tell you, don't punch a hole in a bloated dead cow, like one of our fellows did....

"It was my job to find food, and the British weren't about to offer any because we wouldn't hand over our aircraft. Food became a serious problem, but by hook and by crook, we went scrounging. Ed Hable and I went straight to the Great Eastern Hotel in Calcutta to buy some food. They refused to give us anything because we did not have a requisition.

"I had plenty of money because Pan American always gave the chief steward an emergency fund. I found one of those little fellows on the street who changed dollars into rupees, got a big wad of rupees, and then I found a

"We ran like hell ... and we cleaned those suckling pigs up pretty good"

taxi driver and offered him enough rupees to make him interested in doing exactly what I asked him to.

"We drove round to a ramp at the back of the Great Eastern, where I left the steward to keep watch. Then I went down the ramp into an underground kitchen in the hotel. It was about 9 p.m. and the evening meal service had been completed. The place was deserted. On top of the stove, just out of the oven, cooling, I found a bunch of roast suckling pigs, fixed for the next day's menu. I had some two-gallon, glass-lined thermoses and stuffed four suckling pigs into them, along with some vegetables of a kind I didn't recognize.

"I was just about ready to leave when someone came into the kitchen. We ran like hell, got in the taxicab and took off, with a couple of Indians chasing us. When we got back to the airplane, the crew gorged themselves. They would have eaten anything at all, and we cleaned those suckling pigs up pretty good.

"Word finally came from President Roosevelt that our captain was to proceed on his mission without interference. The British finally agreed to give us some food—cold meat and bread—and fuel, which we had to load from 48-gallon drums, using wobble pumps. Everybody took turns at that crank, and we're talking three hours of pumping fuel. I wasn't very clean when I went to work after that. Smelled pretty bad.

"Finally we left for Rangoon, and had some problems landing there because the water was uncharted for aircraft. But we were certainly expected because there was somebody waiting for us, and we all unloaded the ammunition.

"On our return journey, we were able to overfly many of the stops because we had no cargo to slow us down. We rested when we could. We had piles of bags that we lashed down and used for resting on. If you weren't on watch, you lay down wherever you found a place. We did all our sleeping on board. That ship could fly 20-25 hours at a stretch when you had the winds behind you."

During the War, a river of arms, supplies, and personnel flowed from the United States to Africa and Asia in Pan American aircraft with Pan American crews. Even when the War was over, the company still continued to assist the military. Jerry concludes: "We still had a couple of contracts to bring the killed and the wounded back from Europe. Pan American asked me to get up a crew of 35 stewards to work this contract. I hired them, trained them, uniformed them, and had them working on the line from February to August of 1944. In 1945 we were back to flying commercially."

The Long Way Home After Pearl Harbor

The ultimate foraging challenge came to **Barney Sawicki** and **Verne Edwards**, San Franciso-based stewards who found themselves on the way from Nouméa to Auckland as members of the crew of the *Pacific Clipper* on 7 December 1941, Pearl Harbor Day. Barney and Verne are no longer alive to recount the story of the Clipper's amazing 25-day odyssey as it returned to the U.S. the long way round, but Barney confided to a friend several years ago that provisioning the *Pacific Clipper* during those 25 days was the most difficult task of his life. Even though it was difficult, he and Verne were eminently successful because Captain Robert Ford describes them as "very hard workers who did an excellent job of providing for us."

A colleague of Barney's describes him as "a short stocky fellow with a big head on him and real strong hands; he was a masseur on the side." Another says "He was the crudest son of a gun I ever met, noisy and brash, and his English was quite fractured. Built like a buck. He had that brush cut, and his hair stuck right up." By way of contrast, Verne Edwards was a quiet, reserved type. He and his wife were both concert pianists, students of Joseph Levine. How I wish we could peer into the cabin of the *Pacific Clipper* to watch the interpersonal dynamics between those two stewards, a truly odd couple, on their extraordinary journey around the world. I have had no indication, however, that their courage and skill were anything but stellar.

As you read the adventure story that follows, try to sense the spectre of war in the Pacific and imagine Flight Steward Barney Sawicki and Assistant Flight Steward Verne C. Edwards on board the *Pacific Clipper* as they face the same dangers as the nine-man cockpit crew. Then try to visualize them as they go ashore at each stop in little launches or row boats, and set out in search of the local markets. Think of them as they resort to sign language to broker their deals. Think of them desperately trying to find sources of reliable water. Try

Barney Sawicki

Verne Edwards.

to imagine the blistering heat in the galley as they prepare meals, and the lengths to which they must go to prevent the food from spoiling as the cabin itself becomes an oven in the equatorial sun. Think of the flies, the mosquitoes, the snakes, the fear of the unknown each time they leave the Clipper, and the heat, the heat, the heat, as the Clipper makes the first circumnavigation of the earth by an airplane following an equatorial route, actually crossing the Equator six times. Imagine them as they prepare the bunks for yet another night on board and then shake out the sheets and blankets the following morning. Think of them as they keep the cabin looking as fresh, tidy, and cool as possible. Remember them in their white jackets, remaining calm, and ask yourself if the *Pacific Clipper* could have reached New York without them.

Two hours out of Auckland, just starting the northeast-bound course to the States, Captain Ford received the Condition A radio flash, which warned him that his route back via Honolulu was blocked and advised him to proceed to Auckland in radio silence and await further instructions. The crew waited there for seven anxious days, knowing that their Boeing A-314 was invaluable to the U.S. at war but would be an easy target for the Japanese if they tried to return via the Pacific. The Clipper was quickly given a coat of camouflage paint.

Finally word arrived from headquarters: "Return home the long way round." Exactly how this would be accomplished was left to the crew. They were on their own for what was to be the first round-the-world flight by a commercial airliner. They had to pioneer the route and set down in harbors that no flying boat had ever approached. There would be no weather forecasts, no mechanical support along the way, and they would have to scrounge for fuel and food wherever they could find it, in places where they had never set foot.

Before the *Pacific Clipper* could set off, a further set of instructions arrived. The crew was to return to Nouméa in French New Caledonia to pick up stranded Pan American personnel and fly them to safety to Australia before setting off on the journey home. Captain Ford put together a flight plan, and after Barney and Verne gathered together the final provisions, the Clipper flew through the night to Nouméa. At dawn the stewards welcomed 22 Pan Am men, women, and children and treated them to first-class service on the flight to Gladstone, the first aerial crossing ever between New Caledonia and Australia.

Barney and Verne found enough fresh water and provisions for the 11-hour journey to Darwin. Captain Ford took off with the fuel tanks one third empty, because no 100-octane fuel was available in Gladstone. On that direct route, there was no body of water on which the Clipper could land in Australia's hot, dry, summer December, but they arrived without incident, and as soon as they set down in Darwin's harbor, Barney and Verne went ashore for provisions for the next leg of the the journey. They found a city that was mad with fear—fear of air raids, fear of invasion. Women and children were to be evacuated the next day. The pubs were full, occasionally disgorging their patrons to continue their fighting and vomiting in the streets. A violent tropical storm lit up the city and its harbor with slashes of lightning, and thunder terrorized an already terrified populace. It was under these conditions that Barney and Verne hunted and gathered. At dawn, the *Pacific Clipper* took off again for Surabaya in the Dutch East Indies, making its way in radio silence across the Timor Sea. As they approached Surabaya, they were suddenly joined by four British fighter 'planes, whose pilots, confused by the camouflage and angered by several recent air raids, were trigger-happy and ready to blast the strange bird out of the sky. Fortunately, their radio operator on the ground asked them to scrutinize the Boeing for identifying marks. One of the pilots climbed and then dived over the Clipper, glimpsing the Stars and Stripes on the top side of one of the wings. Escorted by the fighters into Surabaya, the Boeing made a safe landing in the harbor, a harbor that was strewn with mines.

No 100-octane aviation fuel was available in Java, so the crew topped up the tanks with automobile fuel for the 21-hour flight across the Indian Ocean to Trincomalee on the east coast of Ceylon (Sri Lanka). There were no charts for the flight, so the Clipper flew low, beneath the cloud layer, always on the alert for lights or land. The most astonishing sight they saw was that of a surfaced Japanese submarine, whose crew was out on deck taking the air. Captain Ford quickly thrust the Clipper up into the clouds before the enemy could fire the deck gun. The next challenge for him was to set the airplane down in Trincomalee harbor, where no giant 314 had ever landed before. Following that 21-hour flight, the crew rested for a day, during which the challenge for Barney and Verne was to find water and food in completely strange surroundings, in burning tropical heat.

On Christmas Eve, 34 minutes after taking off from Trincomalee for Karachi, oil started gushing from Number Three engine, and the Clipper turned back. Once on land, the flight engineers went to work. For two days they labored, borrowing material and making the necessary tools and parts on board a British warship. It is interesting to speculate as to what kind of Christmas dinner Barney and Verne served on board the *Pacific Clipper.* Canned ham or Trincomalese curry? Plum pudding or exotic tropical fruits? One thing we can be certain of is that the meal was presented with style, using Pan American's fine china, flatware, and glass.

On 26 December, heavily loaded with aviation fuel, the Clipper lumbered across the harbor and rose slowly, skimming over the encircling palm trees that circled the harbor. On and on it flew, over the vast Indian countryside, finally arriving in Karachi in the late afternoon, where the crew immediately headed off for long soaks in the Carleton Hotel bath tubs. The next day, Barney and Verne provisioned the aircraft for the following leg: Karachi to Bahrain.

In Bahrain, the crew refueled once again with automobile gasoline, which made the engines pop and spit in a frightening manner. But they kept going, sputtering across the Arabian Peninsula and the Red Sea and into the Sudan, where Captain Ford set the Clipper down at Khartoum, near the confluence of the Blue and the White Niles.

On takeoff from Khartoum, the Number One engine lost part of an exhaust stack, which made a noisy engine even noisier and presented a serious fire threat. However, knowing that spare parts for Boeing 314s were unavailable in Khartoum, even for ready money, Captain Ford grimly set off southwest across the Sudanese desert. Hours later the landscape began to change from desert to rolling countryside to jungle. Finally the crew sighted the Congo River, a dark brown, muddy ribbon. As they set down on the river at Léopoldville, they became aware of how fast it flowed. Tying the Clipper up to a mooring was no easy task; stepping out into the fierce equatorial heat and humidity was stunning.

It was New Year's Day 1942, when two Clippers sat on the Congo at Léopoldville. It was the day that Barney Sawicki and Verne Edwards flying west met Jerry Cameron flying east. Jerry recounts: "They were a sorry-looking lot when they got in. Barney looked pretty raunchy, but then he always looked raunchy and sweaty. He and Verne were still in their stewards' uniforms. They had encountered many more provisioning problems than we did because they set down in outposts where the Clipper had never been, whereas we had a planned itinerary."

Although provisioning in Léopoldville presented no severe problems apart from that of moving around in the dire heat, and although there was plenty of aviation fuel available, the take-off from Léopoldville proved to be the most terrifying of the entire 25-day trip. The thirsty Clipper had taken on 5,100 gallons of gasoline, enough for the long haul across the Atlantic. In the dense, tropical air, the heavily laden bird—the fuel weighed 33,660 pounds—refused to lift off the water. On and on she roared downstream, finally letting go of the water just a few feet before a series of cataracts. Still the Clipper refused to gain altitude as Captain Ford guided it down the gorges of the Congo; the ailerons had locked because the heat had caused the metal to expand. Finally, the nose lifted and he was able to throttle back after *three* minutes of running the engines at take-off power.

Anne Morrow Lindbergh in *Listen! the Wind* describes a similar take-off from another African river, the Gambia, in words which do more justice to the experience than mine can. This is what must have been rushing through the stewards' minds as they hurtled down the Congo:

Here we go. Hold on. The roar, the spray over the wings. Look at your watch. Won't be more than two minutes. Then you'll know. You can stand two minutes...We are spanking along. We are up on the step—faster, faster—oh, much faster than before. Sparks from the exhaust. We're going to get off! But how long it takes. Spank, spank—we're off? Not yet—spank—almost. Splutter, choke—the engine? My God—it's coming then—death. He's going on just the same. We're off—no more spanks. Splutter—splutter. What is wrong? Will he turn? Will we land?...Yes—we're off—we're rising. But why start off with an engine like that?

But it smooths out now, like a long sigh, like a person breathing easily, freely.... We turn from the lights of the city; we pivot on a dark wing; we roar over the earth....We were dependent on you just now, River, prisoners fawning on you for favors, for wind and light. But now, we are free.

Exactly 23 hours and 35 minutes later, the *Pacific Clipper* was back in the New World, setting down at the harbor at Natal, after a journey of 3,583 miles, the longest nonstop flight in the history of Pan American. All the crew members went ashore during the four hours it took to refuel and to repair the Number One engine. When they clambered back on board, their maps and petty cash were missing, and as they took off, the damaged engine blew its exhaust stack immediately, and thundered menacingly for the nearly 14 hours to Trinidad.

In Port of Spain, the crew of the *Pacific Clipper* finally bathed and slept, 40 hours after their perilous takeoff from the Congo River.

A 16-hour journey to New York lay ahead, and when Barney and Verne woke from what was probably the soundest sleep of their lives, they provisioned the Clipper for the final leg of their round-the-world odyssey. Easy. The provisioning network was well in place, and in English-speaking Trinidad there was no need to resort to sign language as they did their marketing. They took off in the early afternoon.

It was freezing cold in New York on 6 January 1942. At 5:54 a.m., the officer on duty at LaGuardia marine terminal was startled out of what he thought must be a dream. He could not believe his ears as he picked up the transmission: "*Pacific Clipper*, inbound from Auckland, New Zealand,

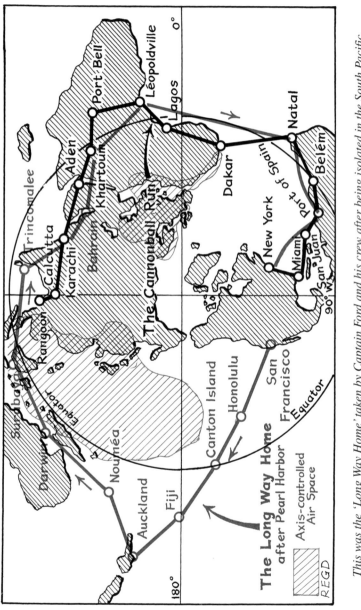

This was the 'Long Way Home' taken by Captain Ford and his crew after being isolated in the South Pacific, following the Japanese attack on Pearl Harbor in December 1941. Pan American's wartime 'Cannonball Run', a vital supply line to the China Theater of wartime operations, is shown in black.

Captain Ford reporting. Due arrive Pan American marine terminal LaGuardia seven minutes." He thought someone was pulling a fast one. He was wrong. Seven minutes later the Boeing floated down out of the sky onto the icy water at LaGuardia. Because the crew had nothing but tropical clothing with them, Barney and Verne handed out blankets. Then the 11-man crew, wrapped like cocoons, climbed out of the *Pacific Clipper* into the bone-chilling air of New York, after a 25-day, 31,500-mile journey.

Barney Sawicki and Verne Edwards had, unintentionally, become the first stewards to fly around the world.

Pan Am and the Naval Air Transport Service

Shortly after the bombing of Pearl Harbor, the Naval Air Transport Service (N.A.T.S.) took over Pan American's Pacific operation lock, stock, barrel, and experience. They needed that experience just as much as they needed the equipment because they were incapable of air navigation over the ocean. Pan American was able to provide them with professional navigators, radio operators, and crews, all with considerable flying experience.

In 1942, at the age of 19, **Ted Johnson** was studying at the University of California with every intention of becoming a physician; at the same time, he was well aware of Uncle Sam's increasing need for young men to serve in World War II. As luck would have it, an encounter on the street with a fellow Freemason steered him in the direction of Pan American and entry into a career which provided him with a priceless education, countless opportunities to use his medical intuition, and a significant way to contribute to his country's war efforts in three wars in the Pacific. In fall 1942, he was interviewed by Harry La Porte, who was to hire so many stellar flight attendants in his time. Ted started work for Pan American and N.A.T.S. on 1 January 1943. He describes his training:

"An ex-chief from the Navy gave the cabin crew extensive training on the ground, including emergency equipment training, seamanship, knots, semaphores, signalling. Then we were put into the galleys and trained under chefs for three months before we made our first flight.

"My first trip was on a Boeing 314 Clipper test flight, and we were on board to see if we got airsick or not. We flew round and round for a couple of hours while they were testing the airplane and training the pilot. If you didn't throw up, you were in. I had no problems. Then we went into class again for three months' further training. When I was hired, there were only 50 stewards;

Sam Taormina (with injured arm) and friends.

at the end of all that training, there were 125, and I went from being very junior to very senior in no time at all. I became a senior steward on my second flight."

Sam Taormina, who became a Pan Am steward in 1942, adds: "We had to learn how to survive on islands, what to eat, what not to eat. We carried a small survival bag with a pouch to convert salt water into fresh and instructions how to split coconuts with a piece of wood, if you had nothing but coconuts to eat. We thought that it was just part of a game and never wondered what we were getting ourselves into. If you think about it, we were sitting ducks. We had no weapons to defend the plane, and the enemy could shoot us out of the sky any time they chose. The captain was allowed to carry a pistol, but that was the only weapon on board. I don't know if that was to take care of himself or the crew."

The stewards wore Pan American uniforms on the Clippers between San Francisco and Honolulu, but from there on into the war zones on board the Consolidated and Martin PBMs, they wore 'Pinks'. These uniforms resembled the N.A.T.S. officers' uniforms and were made of soft, light brown material. They bore Naval Air Transport epaulettes and an insignia on the collar with S for Steward on it. A round patch on the arm was inscribed with Pan American above and N.A.T.S. below.

"People don't seem to believe what we did in those days," Sam says. "When we came back from a trip, we never had long stretches of time off. After a couple of days, we went back to Treasure Island to work in the kitchen. We had to wash all the plates that came off the airplanes to have them ready for the next 'plane going out. We would work for eight or ten hours, and we'd come back the next day and do it all over again, until they said 'You're going out on a trip.' There were no bids or lines; they just said 'Time to go,' and off we went." (Later on, cabin crew would bid for 'lines,' which consisted of a month's pattern of flying. Some lines were considered much more desirable than others, and this is where seniority played an important part.)

"The passenger deck was designed to simulate the comfort of a modern home and was divided into nice sections with deeply upholstered seats," continues Sam. "Some of the compartments could be converted into berths for up to 36 passengers. There were comfortable dressing rooms for men and women, where they had plenty of space to change for dinner or into their night clothes." Between San Francisco and Honolulu, the stewards used steam tables and pressure cookers to provide hot meals on the 314s for as many as 74 people on board, serving 12 people at a time, four at a table, in the lounge area. Outside mealtimes, the lounge became the social center of the Clipper where people would gather to play cards and converse. The tablecloths and napkins were of fine Irish linen; the settings were bone china; the silverware shone and the glassware sparkled. In accordance with maritime tradition, the captain would always be seated with the most important and most interesting passengers. Several times during the War, Sam found himself seating Admiral Chester Nimitz with the Clipper's captain.

Sam adds, "We were not allowed to bring garbage into Treasure Island, so when we came close to the Farallon Islands, we knew it was time to toss the garbage out the back door. We had large paper bags—we called them turkey bags—and lots of masking tape. If there was fog over the islands, though, that garbage might come pretty close to hitting San Francisco."

Out of Honolulu on the PB2Y-3, whose capacity was between 26 and 30 passengers, the sole steward cooked on two electric burners, and would serve four passengers at a time on a card table in the rear of the aircraft, encouraging each group not to linger, but to move back into the cabin so that he could serve the next four.

"Before a flight, we actually had to go out and buy the provisions and bring them on board. I often made stew from scratch. I'd peel the potatoes and the onions right out of the grocery bag, brown the meat, and add the vegetables. One time I even made dumplings," says Ted Johnson.

"When we were beyond Honolulu," continues Sam Taormina, "we had to buy our food at different stations for the following hop. We couldn't keep much fresh food on board because there was no proper refrigeration, merely a block of ice out of San Francisco and another out of Honolulu; beyond that there was no ice at all. We'd start out at Treasure Island with enough food to get us to Honolulu, an 18-22 hour flight, and then we'd buy food at other stops in the Pacific and southeast Asia, except for Wake, Canton Island, Midway, and Guam, where Pan American had its own commissaries. There they would stock us up with cans. Flying out of those islands, we'd serve canned beef stew, canned ham, or canned chicken à la king. If we served the meal on toast, we would advertise it as 'on the shingle.' The passengers leaving Wake, Canton Island, Guam, and Midway would be delighted to get anything we served because there was practically no food at all on those islands. When they stepped on board the airplane, those canned meals looked like first-class to them.

"Once in a while, we'd have a really good cook. There was one famous Italian steward, Pancho Aliati. He used to be the maitre d' at Ciro's in Hollywood, and he joined Pan American because he didn't want to go to war. Since he had been recommended by his Hollywood cronies, he assumed he would be made supervisor of the station. Instead, he found himself out on the line like the rest of us. He carried some fancy condiments in a little case, and he did things that none of us could do. The crews loved him because he cooked first-class. When they flew with me, they got chicken à la king; when they went with Pancho, they were served pheasant!"

High Drama at Funafuti

On the South Pacific route out of Honolulu and into the war zone, the Pan Am/ N.A.T.S. crews flew to Canton Island, Funafuti Atoll, Fiji, Espiritu Santo in the New Hebrides, Guadalcanal, and Brisbane, Australia. The flying boats operated during daytime only, but when war activities began heating up, the Navy wanted speedier service. As a result of this requirement, when each aircraft arrived, day or night, it was immediately refurbished, refuelled, and supplied with a new crew. The passengers, high-ranking officers, would continue on to their destination. A total blackout was ordered, which necessarily ruled out landing lights in the harbors; on moonless nights, the pilots would be left to rely on radio instructions from the 'crash boat' about where there might be other traffic.

Depending on how you think about islands, Funafuti can be regarded as a small island or an enormous atoll, surrounded by vast expanses of Pacific Ocean. It was the scene of many wartime disasters and adventures. **Ted Johnson** describes arriving on the infamous atoll with a full load of 'gold braid,' just as the Navy was amassing ships in the harbor for the invasion of Tarawa:

"We landed in Funafuti to gas up on our way to Guadalcanal; the waves were 30 feet high and a typhoon was advancing on us. We were stuck in the harbor, so we wallowed around and around, and the ground personnel were unable to gas us. Night was coming on, and we had to get the passengers off because, by that time, they were all terribly seasick. We finally tied the airplane up to a buoy and took the passengers off in small boats. This was a neat trick because the boats were bobbing up and down and we were bobbing up and down, but we didn't lose any passengers in the water.

"The captain told Operations that the only way we could save the ship was by sitting in it all night with the engines turning, and facing it into the wind. He knew that the buoy could not last out the storm. He went out there with two pilots and one engineer and sat all night in up to 100 m.p.h. winds. It was the best move he ever made. Next morning ten Consolidated PBYs were washed up on the beach, along with all the lighter boats in the harbor. Only one flying boat was unscathed. Ours.

"They gassed us up, and we put the passengers back on, even though the sea was really rough, with deep troughs. It turned out that there was water in the fuel, and we flailed around for about three hours, trying to get rid of that water. The more time passed, the more urgent it became for all that brass to go north, but instead, they were turning green, throwing up a storm, and becoming weaker and weaker. Finally, I went to the skipper and said 'Captain, we just have to get these passengers off otherwise they are going to be dead before we are airborne.' He called out a small boat and all the passengers disembarked, but we continued to go round and round until we finally got all the water out of the fuel. By that time, we had used up so much fuel that we had to overnight, tied up to the stern of a tender.

"We were all assigned duty watches, and they gave me the last watch. I said to one of the pilots 'What in hell good is it if the wind stops and we start drifting into that ship? I can't start the engines.' He said 'No one else can do it that fast either, Ted. You just yell like hell, and we'll come up and try.' We all slept on board, and it worked out fine, although I found my watch quite scary. I went on duty about 3 a.m. and saw the sun come up. I woke the crew at 6 a.m., and then we discovered that we had lots of water in the bilge. We had an enormous bazooka pump on board, about 12 feet long, and we had to take up the floorboards just aft of the cockpit to get down into the bilge, and somebody had to get up to the top of the pump. I, being the smallest, climbed up, stood on somebody's shoulders, hung onto the frame of the airplane with one arm, and pumped like hell with the other. The pump was about four inches in diameter, and it drew up huge amounts of water on each pull. I had to change arms several times, but kept going as long as I could. Suddenly someone yelled 'Hey, you did a damn good job. There isn't much left.' We had pumped enough out to allow us to take off.

"We took off without the passengers because we had no way to take care of them and the inside of the cabin was a wreck. I had no supplies, nothing. All that was left was a piece of ham and some stale bread."

Sam Taormina ran afoul of Funafuti, too, and vividly recalls:

"It happened during the time when I was stationed for six months on Canton Island. The steward on the Australia flight came in to Canton with a bad cold, so I took his place. Already on board were Admiral Cecil, the planning strategist for the invasion of the Philippines, along with his strategy board of four captains. Admiral Cecil had just left President Roosevelt in Honolulu and was on his way to General MacArthur's headquarters, carrying the invasion papers in a small valise.

"En route to Sydney, we stopped in Funafuti to refuel. In those days, to check the magnetos on the engines, the airplane would circle on the water first left and then right, revving the engines. When the cockpit was satisfied that the engines were all working, they would radio the crash boat in the area and say 'We're ready to go,' and the boat would respond 'O.K., you're cleared to go.' Then the captain would try to make sure that there was nothing in front of the aircraft, which wasn't easy because there were no lights and the water was just as black as the sky.

"We took off again in the wee hours of the morning. All I remember is the unusual, sudden, steep left bank of the aircraft. I don't remember the impact. I must have been knocked out at that point."

The PB2Y-3 flying boat had hit a ship anchored out in the lagoon, and the impact tore off the left wing. All the passengers, including Admiral Cecil, in the bow of the airplane, were killed on impact. Three crew members, the navigator, the engineer, and Sam Taormina, were the only survivors, all of them flung from the aircraft at the point where it split in two. (This is one case in which seat belts would certainly not have saved lives.) Although he has absolutely no memory of what happened next, Sam must have swum some distance until he found something to hang on to. It was the anchor chain to another boat.

The crash boat then had the miserable job of picking up any floating bodies, and Sam was tossed aboard with the dead. The first thing he remembers is a voice say "Look out! This one's alive." The next thing he remembers is being in the Quonset hut hospital on a gurney. Looking up, he saw a bag of yellow plasma hanging overhead and asked "What's that?" An orderly responded "That's blood." Sam looked again and said "You're kidding me. Blood is red and that's yellow." The orderly responded with a smile: "You're going to be all right. Go back to sleep."

Sam, who suffered considerable damage to his right arm, was the least seriously wounded of the three crew members, and he was able to leave Funafuti in less than a month. However, once he reached Honolulu, he found that flights to San Francisco were full, and there was no room for him on the Clipper. When he was offered a place on a Navy PB2Y-3 plane to Alameda, he jumped at the opportunity because he needed to return home as quickly as possible for a skin graft; his right arm had been covered in grease to prevent the skin from healing and scarring until the grafting took place.

In layout, the PB2Y-3 was mostly a cargo plane, and Sam quickly realized that it was standing room only all the way home, a flight of 19 hours. In Pan Am/N.A.T.S. uniform, with his right arm in a sling, he held onto a strap with his left hand. Straphanging next to him was a war correspondent, returning from action in the Pacific.

"What happened to you?" the correspondent asked.

When Sam explained that he had been in a crash at Funafuti, the correspondent questioned him further:

"Were you with Admiral Cecil?"

"Yes," replied Sam.

"How come you're standing up? How come you don't have a seat?"

"There are no seats left," Sam replied. "I'm standing up, just like you are."

"Just a moment," said the correspondent, calling an orderly. (Stewards aboard the Navy planes were referred to as orderlies.) "Go and tell the captain that you have a man down here, standing up, a man who was in the airplane crash at Funafuti with Admiral Cecil, a man who needs a seat, a man who should not have to stand after what he's been through."

The orderly disappeared. A few minutes later, an officer was deprived of his seat, and Sam sat down at last. A little later, he was shown to a bunk, where he stretched out and slept all the way to Alameda.

The military moves in mysterious ways. Early in 1994, Sam Taormina received an honorable discharge from the Air Corps, three medals, and a gold Air Corps pin; more than 50 years had elapsed since he had flown with the Naval Air Transport Service/Pan American in the Pacific.

To Casablanca with F.D.R.

Philip Casprini was born in New York City. He joined Pan American in 1941, but before then he had studied at City College and worked in the dining room of the élite St. Regis Hotel, where he was entertained by glamorous floorshows each night even as he was earning good money as a waiter. An admirer of Charles Lindbergh, Phil became interested in his political organization 'America First,' which was concerned with keeping America out of World War II. Phil discussed it with his colleagues at the St. Regis until the maître d' took him aside and asked him not to propagandize. At the same time, a friend of Phil's, a former St. Regis waiter, encouraged him to join Pan Am. The company decided to hire him, so long as his draft board agreed. Pan Am provided him with a letter declaring that he was needed as a crew member; to Phil's surprise, the draft board accepted Pan Am's request, and he embarked on his flying career.

On 12 January 1943, after two years of flying, Phil found himself on a trip that was far out of the ordinary. "We had no idea who would be on board. I was simply told we were going to Miami, and that Pan Am had assigned two Clippers to the trip," says Phil Casprini.

The crew members flew to Miami and spent the night in a hotel. On the morning of the 12th, cockpit and cabin crews assembled and were told to prepare for a flight to Port of Spain, Trinidad. Phil recalls: "We still had no idea what was going on. They didn't explain anything to us."

At Port of Spain, the mystery was finally revealed. President Roosevelt was on his way to Casablanca to meet Winston Churchill and Charles de Gaulle to negotiate the terms of surrender for the Axis. (The Axis was the 1939 alliance of Germany and Italy, which later included Japan and other countries.) Al Tuinman, Pan American's chief steward, and Eddie Garcia

Phil Casprini

were chosen as cabin crew for the *Dixie Clipper*, serving President Roosevelt, Harry Hopkins, his assistant, and seven other passengers, including two admirals. Phil Casprini and Gus Garreau would work on the escort Clipper, whose passengers included another admiral, members of the press, and several communications experts. This would be the first flight an American president had ever taken overseas and Pan American's first White House press charter.

From Port of Spain, the two Clippers made the long flight over the Atlantic to Bathurst on the westernmost bulge of Africa. When the aircraft set down at the mouth of the Gambia River, a warship was waiting. For security reasons, its name was never revealed to the crew. Phil watched in awe as the President was lifted by a crane from the Clipper, gently swung across the water and over the warship, where he was lowered slowly onto the deck to the cheers of the watching seamen. Phil comments: "He was perfectly safe, perfectly comfortable. It wasn't as though he was hanging from a helicopter."

Phil continues: "From Bathurst, F.D.R. was flown to Casablanca. The conference lasted several days, and time was hanging heavy on our hands. We had nothing to do, and I can remember sitting on the seawing one day, gazing at the water, thinking how good it would feel to take a swim. A couple of Marines were assigned to protect the President and the Clippers, and I was chatting to one of them. I said to him, 'The water looks so inviting, but I've heard there are too many sharks round here.' He brandished his automatic weapon and said, 'Go right ahead! Don't worry about sharks. Take a dip, and if I see a shark, I'll take care of you.' 'Forget it!' I replied."

President Roosevelt cuts the birthday cake presented to him by Al Tuinman on board the Dixie Clipper.

Phil recalls that the atmosphere on board the escort Clipper on the return flight was very relaxed and vacation-like; the atmosphere aboard the *Dixie Clipper* was heady, and to cap it off, Al and Eddie presented the President with a birthday cake, champagne, and caviar to celebrate his 61st birthday. The President was then inducted into the Short Snorters Club. (Short snorters were a fad during World War II. They were dollar bills signed by travellers across the ocean, and the object of the exercise was to acquire famous signatures. A short snorter signed by Roosevelt was eminently desirable.)

On arrival in Port of Spain, the President, his party, and the Pan Am crews dined together at the army base. "He shook hands, talked to all of us, and signed short snorters. He was very impressive," recalls Phil, "but he was already pretty deaf. If you spoke to him, he didn't know what you were saying."

The following morning, the President boarded an Army aircraft for the journey back to Washington, and the Pan American crews returned to New York in the two Clippers. "When I got back home," says Phil, "I went out to a bar for a drink and showed my short snorter around. That was the end of it. I never saw it again."

✈ ✈ ✈ ✈ ✈

Disastrous Loop at Lisbon

After the wonderful experience of the Casablanca trip, **Phil Casprini** felt he had the world's greatest job and wanted to fly forever. Little did he know what lay in store for him on 22 February 1943, little more than a month later.

"On this trip, we took a regular scheduled flight from New York to Bermuda, and many of the passengers got off there. For the continuation of the flight to the Azores and Lisbon, we had 38 people on board, including the crew. The other steward, Craig Robinson, was a very nice kid. He was an artist, and he had taken the job with Pan Am because he felt it would give him the opportunity to see places he would like to paint. We were looking forward to being in Lisbon because it was very exciting in those days."

Several State Department officials and members of the press were on board the *Yankee Clipper*. The first Clipper to cross the Atlantic, it had made 240 crossings by this time. Most of the other passengers were entertainers at the start of a tour to Army camps in Europe and North Africa, including the singers Jane Froman, Yvette, and Tamara; Gypsy Markoff, an accordionist; Grace Drysdale, a puppeteer; and the dancing duo, Lorraine and Rognan. The colorful entertainers were a change from the usual passengers flying across the Atlantic in wartime—military and government personnel—and the atmosphere was both relaxed and sparkling, an atmosphere that would be destroyed in one tragic instant.

"We flew from Bermuda to the Azores, and then from the Azores we headed to Lisbon," Phil continues. "It was nightfall and somehow or other we made a bad landing there. Instead of landing as you would with the hull of the 'plane, the left wing dipped into the water. We were going about 90 m.p.h., the usual touchdown speed, and the 'plane flipped. The next thing I knew, I was under water, coming up to the surface. I found myself outside the 'plane, and it was like a nightmare. As I surfaced, I saw the tail of the airplane sticking out of the water. The forward part of the 'plane had submerged, but it was so big that the tail and a good part of the fuselage was sticking out of the water, way up in the air. I thought, 'Gee, that's funny. I'm *in* the airplane. How could it be that I see the airplane out there?' It's funny that I could rationalize like that even though I had been seriously injured.

"I had been flung through a rent in the fuselage into the water about ten yards from the aircraft. [Phil did not have time to fasten his seat belt.] I had two fractured vertebrae, a fractured left hip, a broken left arm, and four crushed ribs. Yet you survive all these injuries. I don't remember pain at the time, but it was difficult to breathe because of my ribs. When the ribs get caved in, you can't breathe very well. I could hear some muffled voices and was vaguely aware of people crawling on the fuselage, but no one close by. Lots of objects were floating around from the airplane, and I found myself holding on with my good hand to a mail sack. They float. I held onto it until the motor launches came from the shore. By that time it was pitch dark, and they had big powerful lights, and they found me and picked me up. They laid me down on the floor of the launch. At that time I started to get cold because I was in shock." It is interesting to note that Phil did not notice the cold until this point. The water of the Tagus River in February must be ice cold.

"Then they put me in an ambulance. Hey, listen to this! The driver must have been a maniac, racing through the streets. He'd forgotten to close the back door, and I could see the streets flashing by, and I thought 'My God, this is it.' But he finally got me safely to San José hospital. It was a wild ride."

On arrival at the hospital, Phil was visited by a Catholic priest, who, recognizing the severity of his injuries, administered extreme unction. In a desperate attempt to save Phil's life, the doctors resorted to a blood transfusion. Phil continues: "They didn't have the things we have today; they just took some Portuguese man, laid him down alongside me, opened his veins and mine and let his blood come in. The funny thing is that I could feel this warm blood coming in like it was new life. Maybe this guy had been drinking a lot of Portuguese wine, and I was feeling great. But after I had received the blood and was coming back to the few senses that I had left, I started to feel the pain. If someone even came up to the bed and touched it, oh, my God, the pain. If you move a broken hip, a broken spine...

"They made me lie in bed for two and a half months, and performed an operation on my hip to make the bones knit. When it was time for me to get up, they gave me a leather corset that would hold me together. The hip did not knit, and when I returned to the States, I went to Presbyterian Medical Center for another operation. It's held up. Perfect. I can't do all the things, but I can still walk. That's the important thing. I was on crutches for about six months."

Phil recovered, but others were not so lucky. Craig H. Robinson, the steward/artist perished. In fact, of the 38 people on board, only 14 survived, including the captain, five of the ten-man cockpit crew, and all the entertainers except Roy Rognan and Tamara. Jane Froman was gravely injured; her life was saved by John Curtis Burn, a co-pilot, himself badly injured, who held her above water and comforted her until they were rescued. Five years and 25 operations after the crash, the two were married.

Once he had recovered enough to start working again, Phil had a tough decision to make. Should he return to flying or not?

"Would you believe it, I went back to flying again! My first flight back was one of those trips where we would go to Lisbon, down to Africa, over to South America, and then up north again."

But Lisbon was Phil's nemesis. The Clipper landed safely, but after it took off again for Africa, the captain was unable to level off. "We went round in a circle but he couldn't level off because the ailerons had locked. We kept going around and around, and finally I received word from the cockpit to tell the passengers that we might have to make an emergency landing and that they should strap themselves in again and take their shoes off. It was the same river where we had ditched!

"So, here we are going round and round for about 45 minutes. Finally, the captain sent a pilot into the hold to check the cables operating the ailerons. Apparently, one of the pilots, going down to release the airplane from the buoys, must have hit the aileron control, probably with his hat, and locked it. As soon as they discovered that, they unlocked it and were able to make a perfect landing. But by that time, they had dumped all the fuel, and we had to get out and refuel before setting off again.

"After that, I said 'I've had it,' and Pan American gave me a job in the reservations department."

Lisbon still did not leave Phil Casprini alone. He continues: "Subsequently, I was called to testify in court. Jane Froman and Gypsy Markoff were suing because they thought the captain was responsible. I was given a deposition by the company lawyers and I told them everything I could. I was presented as a witness for the company. But I'm a total loss when it comes to legal matters; when I was on the stand, the prosecuting lawyer cross-examined me and got me to admit that somehow or other, the captain could have been at fault. The Pan Am lawyers were disappointed because they expected me to stand up for Sullivan.

"This is what I believe happened at Lisbon. The ship was supposed to approach that landing straight. You don't approach a landing at a right angle and then make a steep turn, trying to get in line. There were landing lights on the river and it was dusk. The pilot has to go maybe two miles in a straight line coming in for the landing. Sullivan didn't do that. He was a kind of cowboy. He came in at a right angle, and made a steep turn. I was looking out the galley window at the time, I wasn't strapped in, and I saw the wing. It was almost vertical. Holy Smokes! I never saw a 'plane as steep. We weren't going fast enough to level off. He tried to level off for the landing, but the 'plane never did get leveled off. So we ditched."

When the War ended in 1945, Pan American needed to cut back on its personnel in the Pacific. Remember Ted Johnson, back on Funafuti? He picks up the story at the end of the conflict: "There was nothing for the Pacific flight service to do at first. Pan American had ordered DC-4s, but they hadn't yet arrived, and the flying boats were in terrible shape by then. All the spars were cracked, and they were barely holding together. Maintenance had drilled holes where the cracks were to prevent further cracking, but the 'planes were all write-offs.

"They let off a lot of stewards. They went up the list, according to seniority. Finally Harry La Porte came to me and was just breaking the news in the office when Bob Kamera, the supervisor, overheard the conversation and said 'No, no, Harry. You've got the wrong person. We want Ted.' Another ten minutes and I would have been out the door. Close call.'"

Once the DC-4 went into service and the public began to fly for business and pleasure again, the employment situation improved, and Pan American's Pacific Division started hiring. (At this point women were added on the Pacific routes.) Although unpressurized, the DC-4 was a much faster airplane than the flying boats, and could make the trip to Honolulu from San Francisco in as little as ten hours, carrying 40–50 passengers. The one-way fare was reduced from $278 to $195. In the tail section of the aircraft, there was a small, efficient galley, with electric ovens. Ted adds, "The food was prepared and put aboard chilled, and we had a good icebox, so we could give a proper meal service. And the service steadily improved as we acquired Stratocruisers, Constellations, DC-7s, and finally the jets."

Women On Board

I want to do it because I want to do it. Women must try to do things as men have tried. When they fail, their failure must be but a challenge to others.

Amelia Earhart

Not until 1944 did Pan American finally hire stewardesses. T.W.A. had hired women in 1935 and American Airlines in 1933. In 1934, Swissair's Nelly Diener became the first European stewardess. But as early as 1930 Boeing Air Transport (B.A.T., later United) had hired Ellen Church, a nurse, to become the world's first airline stewardess.

Before she made that significant step, Ellen had taken flying lessons with dreams of becoming a commercial airline pilot. When she showed up in B.A.T.'s office to try to convince them to hire a woman pilot, Steve Stimpson, the San Francisco district manager, dissuaded her. In the conversation that ensued, the idea of having 'sky girls' on board the company's Boeing 80 tri-motors was born. Stimpson had been trying to persuade B.A.T. to hire cabin attendants for some time, and had recently hired three 'couriers,' all male. However, the notion of having women aboard appealed to him, particularly if they were nurses.

When she left the B.A.T. office, Ellen Church had the task of finding other suitable candidates. She searched for them in hospitals in Chicago and San Francisco, using all her powers of persuasion to attract the right women. Find them she did, and together she and Steve Stimpson trained them—and herself—in preparation for a three-month trial period on B.A.T.'s Chicago–San Francisco route.

At 8 a.m. on 15 May 1930, Ellen Church took off from Oakland Airport, bound for Chicago, and a new career for women was born.

Pan Am's First Training Group

"Passengers who have travelled extensively via domestic airlines frequently ask why Pan American Airways has stewards rather than stewardesses. The

*Pan American's first stewardesses: Elsbeth Erhart, Lois Smith, Gloria Smith,
Dorothy Mills, Doris Stimson, Louise Taylor, and Dorothy Larsen.*

answer of course, is that the Clippers make long flights over great distances
through isolated territory, and the job has always been considered a little too
strenuous for a young woman."

This was the company line. It is tempting, however, to look a little
further than that bit of publicity. It might be equally true to say that the
company hung on to its men-only rule because it enhanced its quasi-military
appearance; the fact was that, during World War II, it was moving in tight
formation with the U.S. military. The presence of stewards rather than stewardesses was also thought to reassure those travellers suffering from the
jitters. Curiously, Boeing Air Transport hired women in 1930 precisely
because it felt that the presence of women would do much to reassure *their*
passengers who had the jitters.

The military nature of things, however, became the undoing of the men-
only rule; by late in 1943 Pan Am could not find enough suitable men to be
stewards because so many had been drafted for the war effort. On 21
November 1943, after a lengthy hiring process, letters were mailed to eight
young women inviting them to become Pan American's first stewardesses. All
eight entered training; seven completed it.

In April 1944 the company literature trumpeted: "The first air stewardesses to fly the international routes of Pan American World Airways are now
members of the flight crews of the PAA Clippers operating out of Miami.
Trim and attractive in their powder-blue uniforms and pert flight caps, seven

pretty girls have broken the long-standing unwritten tradition of Pan American's 17-year history of all-male flight crews and now fly regularly on the Clippers to Nassau, to Havana, and to Mérida, Mexico. First of their sex to 'win their wings' and become members of Pan American's highly trained flight crews, the girls were selected on the basis of ability, aptitude, and appearance .....Pan American's 'ideal stewardess' is blue eyed, with brown hair, poised and self-possessed, slender, 5 feet 3 inches tall; weighs 115 lb, is 23 years old, actively engaged in some participant sport, an expert swimmer, a high school graduate with business training—and attractive....So successfully has the first stewardess class met all tests that company officials have placed the stamp of approval on the plan and have permitted the enrollment of additional classes." Immediately upon shedding the all-male, quasi-military rule, the company perceived that 'attractive' was indeed the way to attract customers.

The first seven 'girls' to be assigned to duty aboard the Clippers were: Elsbeth Erhart, Dorothy Larsen, Dorothy Mills, Gloria Gene Smith, Lois Smith, Doris Stimson, and Louise Taylor. They were certainly attractive but they did not fit the profile as easily as the company publicity would have you believe. With these seven, Pan Am had hired the first in its long line of powerfully idiosyncratic women.

Lois Smith (Kelley) was a recent widow, her husband of two weeks having been killed in the War. (She was one of two widows in the first training group.) Before she applied to Pan Am, she had been working as a legal secretary to earn her keep, but her ambition was to become a photographer. When she saw the advertisement announcing that Pan Am was recruiting its first female cabin crew in Miami, she went along with the intention of photographing what she knew would be an historic event and to find out if she could land a job in Pan Am's darkroom. When the recruiters saw Lois, they immediately recognized that not only was she beautiful, she was spunky. They invited her to apply to be a stewardess. Lois insisted that flying would make her sick and that her interest in the airline was purely through the lens of a camera. The recruiters were insistent; the recruiters were persuasive; the recruiters claimed that she was exactly the type of person they were looking for. Lois capitulated, and filled out an application, which was thrown into the hopper along with 2,000 others. Eventually, the field was narrowed to 1,000, then to 100, then to 50, and then to eight, and sure enough, Lois Kelley was one of the eight to be chosen. The company directors were personally doing the hiring. "Some asked for one girl, some for another," says Lois, who learned after the interview that she had been chosen by Harold Gray, the chief pilot. She claims that she could see no consistent reason why particular women were chosen and others were not. There were no standard guidelines. For example, the first seven ranged in height from 4' 11" to 5'9", a differential which stands out in their class photo when compared with the narrower height range in photos from later years.

Training for the first group of stewardesses began early in 1944, and was conducted by the chief stewards, including Jerry Galindo (see page 6). The trainees were consulted about their uniforms and chose the color—sky blue—and a skirt with kick pleats for ease of movement. They were provided with uniforms and company jewelry but had to furnish their own shoes. They were told to think of themselves as hostesses in their own living rooms with the passengers as their invited guests. This differs markedly from the recommendation put out by Imperial Airways (later B.O.A.C., still later British Airways) that their stewardesses "be willing to undertake the duties of their task which should be described to them as similar to those of a domestic servant." Even so, Pan Am's first women were offered aprons. Their response was "No, thanks. Take your aprons...." Lois adds, "If we were hostesses in our living rooms, of course we would not have worn aprons. Aprons were for kitchens, not living rooms."

Once their training was complete, the first women worked on Sikorsky S-40 flying boats between Miami, Nassau, and Havana. They were up at 4 a.m. and home at 11 p.m., working three or four round trips in a day. Lois says that it was extremely challenging for women to work on the flying boats: "I didn't really like them. When you took off, the water rose up over the windows and you felt as though you were in a submarine. I always had the feeling we weren't going to make it, that we'd drown. In order to bring nourishment to the flight deck, we had to scale a ten-foot ladder, which was hard enough to do without carrying cups of coffee. I was terrified one time when I was climbing up that ladder during a tropical storm and I noticed the propellers engulfed in rainbow-colored fireworks. I thought the aircraft was on fire, but when I told the pilots, they laughed their heads off. It was St. Elmo's fire." (These lights appear on masts of ships and on wing tips, propellers, and noses of aircraft in storms, often accompanied by a fizzing sound.)

"Another problem we had was with condensation. The metal ceiling sweated dreadfully. It was often so intense that the cabin crew had to hand out umbrellas, one for every two passengers—we never had enough—so that they didn't get soaked to the skin. Everything was wet, and it made it very difficult to serve food. And I remember one flight on which we carried 70 people in a 'plane that was designed for 40." Lois eventually complained to the manage-

"Condensation ... was often so intense that the cabin crew
had to hand out umbrellas."

ment about the difficulties of working on flying boats, and shortly after that
the women worked only on DC-2s and DC-3s. "I was pretty vocal; the other
girls were terrified. I was their spokesperson."

Food service was also difficult in those days, and not only difficult but
often disgusting. "There were lots of British people flying in the Caribbean
and the menu catered to them; it was *always* lamb, gravy, and peas," Lois says.
"These items came on board in heavy thermos jars, 2 feet high, 10 inches in
diameter. The lamb was green because it had been in the thermos so long. The
food was sometimes elusive because at every stop the stewards would sell parts
of our commissary—the consommé, the dessert, everything but the meat and
potatoes. By the time we got ready to serve several stops later, they'd sold
everything. We couldn't report them; we were afraid of them."

The first group of women was received warmly by the passengers,
perhaps a little too warmly. "Sometimes we had to fight them off with the six-
inch hatpin that was part of our uniform," adds Lois. In spite of that initial
response, she felt that Pan Am stewardesses were the most respected of all the
airlines' women; this was probably because they were still regarded by the
public as an arm of the military. To continue profiting from that impression,
Pan American insisted that, when the crew was ready to board, the captain

should blow a whistle and the crew would march out to the aircraft, with the lone stewardess last in line.

After working for several months in Miami, Lois was transferred to Pan Am's newly opened base in Brownsville, Texas. From there she worked south as far as the Canal Zone. "At each stop we had to walk up and down the aisle, spraying the aircraft with insecticide, and you absolutely could not breathe. You had to kill all those foreign bugs. Huh! When I think of all the harm that did to *people*... and there was always some creep on board, a spy from the office, to make sure you sprayed enough. When we landed, Agriculture would come out with the big spray guns and crawl into the belly to attack all the luggage.

"We laid over in Guatamala; loved Guatamala, loved the marimba music that floated up from the hotel courtyard. When we flew into the Canal Zone, we had to place frosted plastic over the windows half an hour before landing so that the passengers couldn't see the Canal and the secret installations there. It made them furious.

"And all the servicemen in the Canal Zone! I'd have a date for breakfast, for lunch, for dinner. My mother thought I'd die of dating.

"Our uniform was 100% wool and sometimes it would be 117 degrees down there, but nothing stopped us. There we'd be, drowning in perspiration, but still marching out in a neat little line, carrying the all-important briefcase."

"Sometimes we had to fight them off with the six-inch hatpin that was part of our uniform."

Shortly after the first women had completed their training, **Louise Taylor (Leonard)**, another of the seven, gave an address to new recruits about the work of a Pan Am stewardess during wartime. She told them: "Of course a casual bystander at the airport, watching one of us step briskly up the steps as the last member of an otherwise all-male flight crew to board the ship, might suspect that we have merely enlisted on a series of aerial teaparties shuttling to and from tropical wonderlands. As a matter of fact we're doing a man's job, side by side with men in wartime....We are responsible not only for the comfort and health of passengers during a trip but for the checking and orderly delivery of passenger, cargo, and 'plane documents from port of exit to port of entry. Papers vital to the national security are in our charge, as well as passenger valuables and precious cargoes. Travelling on merchant seamen's passports, we combine the functions of the purser and steward on an ocean liner. We supervise the loading of mail and cargo before the take-off. We handle coded radio messages relating to reservations; we must decipher such things as air-way bills and government bills of lading, manifests, consular invoices, certificates of origin and priority ratings; and we are familiar with all the requirements of our own customs and immigration service as well as those of foreign countries.

"We know about the hundreds of different items of regular and emergency equipment aboard the plane, including the antidote for snake-bite, where it is and how to use it. We know how to administer oxygen and when, for in wartime Clippers fly high. We make sure that blackout regulations are enforced at home and abroad, and that no photographs are taken by passengers in flight....

"Wartime missions bring widely diverse groups together aboard the Clippers, from diplomats, cabinet ministers and Latin American generals to U.S. business executives, physicians, scientists, engineers and contractors, the great and the near-great and the merely average traveller. So far as passenger service goes, we make no distinction between them. To be sure, we get a thrill from seeing in the flesh some world famous personage whom previously we have known only from newspaper accounts. It is fun, too, to chat with radio and movie stars like Bob Hope and Frances Langford, when they fly to some military establishment to entertain the boys....

"The qualifications for landing this job were so stiff that no one in our original group is quite sure even yet how she managed to make the grade. Looks, charm, brains, poise, discretion, unblemished health and a character record free from the taint of even a minor traffic violation—these were some of the requisites of Arthur Nugent, who is in charge of the flight service department of Pan American's Latin American Division. It goes without saying that no one of us is conceited enough to imagine that she embodies all these traits of Mr. Nugent's ideal flight stewardess. No girl so perfect ever lived, except in the mind of man.

"'You will be paid while going to school,' we were told. 'After you have passed your examinations—if you pass—you will be paid on the same basis as the men. You will have the same chances of promotion—and just as much will be expected of you. So don't use your sex as an excuse for failure to deliver. Never let anyone in this company hear you say: 'You can't expect a woman to do that....Don't let the amount of things you have to learn in the next few weeks scare you...your instructions boil down to a few simple rules. Keep neat, use common sense at all times and try to hold your tongue. Be good listeners. Don't argue. Don't express opinions on controversial subjects and don't wisecrack with the passengers.'"

At the end of her address, Louise admitted: "There are times, towards the end of some particularly busy day, when the job seems rather on the tiresome side. Where, we ask each other, is the high adventure we hoped to find? But at dawn, as we gather in the Operations Room for a 5 a.m. take-off, and the loud-speakers rattle off the news of six Clippers leaving within the hour, and the flight crews come and go in brisk, business-like succession, everything seems worthwhile and wonderful again.

"After the war, who knows? That Pan American's initial experiment with stewardesses has proved practicable and will continue for the duration is indicated by the fact that a new class of 12 girls has finished training and is ready for flight assignment. In the postwar era, when the Clippers again girdle the globe on the commercial air routes, it is expected that larger and faster aircraft will carry both a male purser and a stewardess in the flight crew."

Louise concluded her address by confiding to the trainees: "Not long ago one of the girls visited a fortune teller. 'You may think that you are travelling a lot now,' the palmist told her. 'But it is nothing, absolutely nothing, to the travelling you will do and the places you will see later on.'"

The first seven had no idea how true that prophecy would be.

Pioneering In Alaska

Alaska in the 1920s was as remote and as alien a place as anyone could ever dream of visiting, but it had a firm hold on the American people's imagination, largely as a result of articles in *The National Geographic*. Many an armchair traveller dreamed of seeing the aurora borealis, of panning for gold, of setting foot on the Mendenhall Glacier, of fishing by the light of the midnight sun in summer, or riding with teams of huskies in winter; but very few had the chance to go to Alaska. It was a land of ice fields and glaciers, Eskimo villages and fishing ports, mining stations, and military installations. It was a land of meteorological extremes.

Weather and remoteness were never factors that deterred Juan Trippe. Instead, he saw the potential they offered. As early as 1925 he stated, "A territory where people pay four hundred dollars for the privilege of walking behind a dogsled for ninety days is a good prospect for an airline," and proceeded to form a company, Alaskan Air Transport, which consisted of one ski-equipped DH-4, one pilot, Ben Eielson, and absolutely no cabin attendants. Eielson, whom the Eskimos called 'The Moose-Ptarmigan,' carried mail to remote communities, and this source of competition enraged the dog-team drivers, who protested. The postal authorities ruled against Trippe and his fledgling airline, and Ben Eielson was literally left out in the cold, operating as a bush pilot on his own. But that is another wonderful—and ultimately tragic—story.

In 1931, the year when the Lindberghs landed at Point Barrow and Nome on their way to Asia, the long fingers of Pan American were already reaching back into Alaska. In 1932, Juan Trippe bought out two struggling little airlines, which had managed to wangle mail contracts out from under the noses of the dog-team mushers. He called his new subsidiary Pacific Alaska Airways. Its Fairchild 71s and 100s carried one pilot and up to ten passengers—but no cabin attendants. This fleet later included Lodestars, Electras and Norsemen—and still no cabin attendants.

Alice Hager, the sole female aviation journalist of the time, describes what it was like to travel on Pacific Alaska: "They stacked their passengers at first on top of the mail sacks, stuffing them in headfirst under the cabin roof and hoping they wouldn't all slide down at once into the tail if the plane happened to hit rough air. Usually the passengers were in so tight they couldn't have slid anyway, much less have turned over."

At the end of the War, Pan American upgraded its Alaska fleet with C-47s bought from the military. These aircraft underwent a metamorphosis and reappeared as elegantly-furnished DC-3s. A publicity handout declared, "The new DC-3 Clippers are equipped with upholstered chairs, quilted cabin lining, hot air heating systems, and are designed especially for sub-zero flying weather." With the success of the stewardess program in Miami, Pan American wanted one on board each of the Alaska DC-3s, but were dubious about how well the young women would handle the extreme conditions of flying in Alaska. They were unwilling to hire new, unseasoned staff because it was such a pioneering effort, so they cast about among their ground personnel for "girls who were tough, girls who could take the weather, who were self-

From left to right, the original Alaska seven: Barbara Fowler, Peggy Whiteside,
Lois Thompson, Phyllis La Sota, Virginia Smith, Mary Myers, and Marcia Black.

disciplined and had great fortitude." They found seven adventurous, eager
candidates: Marcia Black (a championship skater from Eastern Canada who
appeared in the film *Lady, Let's Dance*), Barbara Fowler, Phyllis LaSota,
Mary Myers, Virginia Smith, Lois Thompson, and Peggy Whiteside.

Apart from a willingness to endure the hardships of flying to Alaska,
Pan American also required that their Alaska stewardesses "be between
5'2"and 5'5", 120 lb or less, have personality rather than glamor, and be of a
bland temperament." They warned them that they would encounter miserable
conditions—snow and ice, constant turbulence, and weather that could go as
low as 50 degrees below zero. However, they promised to return them to their
previous jobs should the Alaska flying experience prove to be too arduous.
There was no need for that assurance because the first seven met the challenge
with courage and resourcefulness, in spite of the fact that none of them had a
bland temperament.

Lois Thompson (Blanchard) was one of the eager volunteers. She
already had Alaska experience, having worked for Pan American in Fairbanks

during the War, sending weather in code to airplanes. She already knew what it was like to work for an around-the-clock operation in what was in practice still an Eskimo village. She knew how treacherous the Alaskan weather could be, but she had fallen under the spell of the North. When she was given the opportunity to fly to other parts of Alaska, she jumped at it.

Along with the six other 'cold weather women,' she underwent rigorous medical examinations and high altitude tests, during which they were sealed in an altitude chamber at Sand Point Naval Air Station in Seattle and 'flown' up to 30,000 feet to measure the effect on them of flying in unpressurized cabins. These tests were followed by a six-week training, which included courses in the geography of Alaska, first aid, swimming, physical fitness, psychology, poise, aircraft familiarization, meteorology, the Link trainer (a rudimentary flight simulator), handling of ship's papers, civil air regulations, and, most important, passenger service. The original seven also had a part in writing the Alaska flight service manual and, because of her knowledge of Alaskan weather conditions, Lois was responsible for designing the cold weather uniform: black ski pants, fox fur-trimmed parkas, and mukluks (Alaskan fur boots).

Stewardess service from Seattle to Alaska began on 3 December 1944. Lois was the first of the seven to 'fly' Alaska.

"I was terribly nervous about my first flight, and it turned out to be the most turbulent flight I ever had. Even Charlie Krause, who was checking me

Lois Thompson checking tires and footgear. (The aircraft is a Grumman Widgeon.)

*Peggy Whiteside, Lois
Thompson, and Phyllis
La Sota show off their
cold weather gear.*

out, agreed, and he was an old timer who had worked on the flying boats. But I got through it." Lois obviously came through with flying colors. Her supervisor reported that, in accordance with company regulations, she had an "efficient and businesslike manner, was friendly and affable with passengers, and handled children excellently."

Lois continues: "The DC-3 held 21 passengers. We worked alone, just one stewardess on each flight, and we served hot meals instead of the box lunches which were standard on the Lodestars and handed out by the co-pilot. We had a small galley in the back with large hot thermoses containing the food in fitted wells. The menus were delicious. We often served filet mignon with mushroom gravy. One day I said to my roommate who had followed me in on a flight "Wow! That was a great meal today," and she responded "Yes, but I had one passenger who fussed about the dessert." I replied "That was Yorkshire pudding; you should have put gravy on it!"

"It was a long haul in one day. The journey from Seattle to Fairbanks with its various stops took 12 hours, and we served food on every leg of the flight. We started at 6 a.m. and ended at 6 p.m. with a feeling of accomplishment and exhaustion, having 'run' all the way to Fairbanks. We flew all year round. The weather was so bad that lots of times we would lay over where we didn't intend to, or else we'd go part way and have to turn around and go back and wait for a break. Some of the most useful pieces of equipment we had on board were the packs of cards and the cheese and crackers for all those unexpected layovers in places like Gustavus, places which were nothing, where you would sit for hours and hours with a load of impatient passengers, waiting for the weather to change. We had a lot of icing, we had rough engines, and we lost engines. Nowadays you fly and they cut off an engine and you still fly. Up there, when you got a rough engine, it was something to be frightened about."

Another member of the first Alaska seven, Phyllis LaSota (Ritter), wrote about flying in Alaska in these words: "Because of the constant turbulence, food service was an exercise in dexterity and balance, with intermittent airsick bag service. We dished up hot foods onto plates served on trays, with part of the menu in lidded containers. The tray was placed on a small pillow on the passenger's lap. The Alaska flying public was the most congenial, gracious, fun, appreciative, good sport, unpretentious, remarkable-without-showing-it passengers with whom to be blessed. We were invited to homes, entertained royally, and often could remember who took coffee, tea, or milk on ensuing flights."

Lois adds: "In 12 hours of personalized service, you really came to know your passengers. That was the beautiful part of it. You knew how many kids they had, if and where they were married, why they were going to Alaska. We carried mostly Alaska residents and U.S. businessmen. Flying from the U.S. to the Frozen North was not affordable for the average person, but everyone within Alaska travelled by air with the daring and respected bush pilots."

However, once they had landed, the first seven did encounter other visitors to Alaska. **Virginia Smith (Hart)**, another member of the first seven, recalls: "We were flying into Alaska when Soviet Air Force pilots were still in evidence on the streets. Under President Roosevelt's Lend-Lease Program, the U.S. provided Russia with Lockheed P-38 fighter planes, and the Russian pilots flew them out of Nome and into Russia over the Alaskan-Siberian Highway. They were the cream of the Soviet Air Force and formidable in their big coats with yellow epaulets, and most appeared square-jawed and hostile. They were, however, invited to the officers' quarters at Ladd Field and we occasionally shared some group get-togethers, with an interpreter from Fairbanks."

Time and again as they describe their experiences, these three women from the first seven recognize the role that turbulent weather and bad visibility played in their lives. Lois explains: "The ride was rough because the cabin was not pressurized and because we flew at between 12,000 and 13,000 feet, through the clouds, not over them. The landing was rough, too, especially on the dirt runway at Weeks Field, Fairbanks, where night landings were made possible by hand-lit oil pots defining the runway.

"Juneau was particularly difficult and treacherous, sitting at the base of two mountains. Yes, we had some real tricky deals going in there. You could only go in during daylight, and there was lots of turbulence between those two

Virginia Smith delivers a special passenger.....and considers a giant leap.

mountains. When you looked out the window, you felt sure that the wing tips were going to touch the mountains, which looked just like giant ice cream cones. It was gorgeous, but it was so turbulent. We tried to eliminate the snack service between Juneau and Whitehorse because most of the time people needed oxygen rather than food. You spent a lot of time administering oxygen to the passengers, and you yourself needed it because you were racing up and down that aisle and pretty soon your cheeks were getting all red and you'd have to go and suck on the oxygen bottle.

"We had some hair-raising experiences when we were thankful for flying with an ex-bush pilot, someone who had a sixth sense about where he was going and was experienced in the ever-changing challenges of weather and equipment. Those guys would fly low enough to find their way by the logs on the river. I had one of those hair-raising experiences leaving Annette Island. It was marginal weather, but we took off, got a rough engine and sudden icing conditions. We could not return to Annette because by that time it had closed in. Our first alternate was Juneau, but we were not permitted to land in Juneau after dusk, and it was after dusk. We could not make it to our second alternate because of our engine failure. This was one of those times I was happy to be with a former bush pilot. He trimmed the rough engine and told me we were going into Juneau in spite of the prohibition and to prepare everyone for it. It was turbulent, it was terrible, coming in on one engine between those two mountains. The food jugs broke loose and everything that I had really battened down broke loose. As we approached, I could see the landing strip and the fire-trucks waiting for us. It took real experience and good judgment getting that airplane in, but he did it. He was a very, very good pilot."

Virginia adds: "Pan American originally pioneered the Arctic as a training ground for pilots, and from all accounts the only place rougher weather could be encountered was over the Hump in China. Winter turbu-lence was a fact of flying in Alaska. One day after I had served lunch and was stowing the buffet in the galley next to the DC-3 door, a loud swish of air had me grabbing for an overhead luggage bar. I glanced out of the open door down to an endless expanse of seething ocean. It was estimated that one could survive for about 15 minutes in that water. Fortunately, all the passengers were seated. I reached for the intercom, and in a minute the engineer strode down the aisle, having hastily donned his white coveralls, announcing, 'Here comes Snow White.' With that, he anchored himself to the luggage rack with the ditching rope, managed to get a noose around the door handle, and pulled it into place with great difficulty."

Just a few minutes before the door blew open, a little boy of the 'holy terror' type had come into the galley and had emptied the silverware drawer onto the galley deck, thinking this was a great game. Virginia wisely drew a halt to these antics, and escorted him back to his seat, forbidding him to leave it until the 'plane arrived at its destination. Her gentle firmness probably saved his life.

Indeed, the winter weather in Alaska was nothing short of treacherous. One member of the courageous first seven, Mary Myers, lost her life in a crash on a mountain north of Ketchikan. Lois was luckier, but only just.

One February afternoon, as the DC-3 took off from from Juneau for Seattle, Lois was well aware that the weather looked ominous. "My room-mate was on the 'plane ahead of me, and both her captain and the one I was with decided they would go look at the weather and, if necessary, use the alternate, Vancouver, Canada.

"The pilot ahead decided Seattle was too socked in and landed in Vancouver, but my pilot decided to head for Boeing Field. It was miserable weather, getting dark, raining, dreadful visibility. As we descended over the port of Seattle, there was no way of seeing where we were, but I could tell that they were letting the flaps down and going through all the preparations for landing. Suddenly the pilot gunned that airplane. Even today I can still feel that moment that shouted 'DANGER!' He gunned that airplane and then away we roared. I had no idea where we were going. Nervous.

"Then I felt us coming down again through this awful weather. I looked out and saw a runway and a cross runway go by. When you see the cross runway, you know that you have used up quite a bit of runway already. We were at Bow Lake! There was no way of our knowing the condition of that runway because it was brand new. The airport facility was still under construction, in fact, and there was nobody on duty to help us except one security guard. Somehow the captain got hold of the guard and told him to turn on the north/south runway lights; instead he turned on the east/west lights. The pilot had no advice on ground conditions; it was icy and we used up too much runway. We went off the end, which was elevated over the highway. I watched a big transformer go right underneath the wing, and with that we dropped down off the runway, a deep drop, and the severe impact collapsed the landing gear. So now we're on our belly, going at a fast pace through all this rutty, weedy area. We break off a telephone pole, go through a barbed wire fence, cross the highway on our belly—no traffic, fortunately— and slide over into a large field. The thing that stopped us was running into a big stump.

The DC-3, the big stump, and the effective whitewash job.

"It was pitch dark and pouring rain outside, and everything was on a slant. I kept trying to find the flashlight, but it had broken away from its position and all I could lay my hands on were plastic dishes and trays, which had been strewn all over the cabin. The radio operator appeared, flashlight in hand, with a frightened expression on his face because he had no idea about the fate of the passengers. Reassured to find that everyone was alive, we tried to open the door, but it was sprung. We were in a desperate hurry to evacuate, and we tugged and pulled and finally got it open enough for people to squeeze out. They were all trying to find their belongings even though we had to move them away from the airplane as fast as we could because we were afraid the fuel tanks might explode. We got everyone out, but even then nobody wanted to leave the site because of their possessions.

"There were several children on board, but what was more trying was one of those difficult men, the sort you can tell is going to be difficult just by looking at him. He had refused to fasten his seat belt all the way down, and finally when it was real rough and soupy and scary as we were coming into the Seattle area, I said 'If you don't fasten your belt, I will get the captain.' He did thank me after we landed, but he was the only one who complained of a bad neck afterwards.

"The radio officer went out on the highway and thumbed a ride to Boeing Field and told Pan American where we were. Until that time, nobody knew. They sent a bus for us; when it arrived, we were all lined up by the highway, shivering from fright and cold. A Pan Am fellow with a big bucket of white paint leaped out, and the first thing he did was to paint out the name 'Pan American' from the airplane. They didn't want that crashed plane sitting in the middle of a field announcing its affiliation.

"I had a date that evening, waiting for me at Boeing Field where we were meant to land. He had a long wait. Pan American tried to call the next of kin because they knew that the news would come over the radio, and they wanted to inform them that there were no injuries, but they had the wrong 'phone number for my parents. When I finally arrived at Boeing Field, muddy and soaking wet, the day was still not over. There were details to be completed and passengers to take care of. Finally, my date drove me to my parents' house, and I thought my mother would die when she saw me looking like that. She thought that I had half-way drowned, but fortunately they hadn't heard the news. I told them all about the crash, and then I changed clothes and went out for the evening to try and calm my nerves and to feel thankful for coming safely through the ordeal.

"In the aftermath, the investigators never did dwell on the landing lights as an issue, rather they focused on poor judgment. I agree; it was poor judgment. The pilot said 'Let's go ahead and try it.' The weather deteriorated as we approached Seattle and we were in trouble. That runway at Bow Lake, which is now Seatac, was not ready to be used, but how lucky we were that it was there. Even though visibility was zero and the runway was icy, it was there, and we survived.

"A couple of days later, an entrepreneur tucked a dolly under the plane's tail, picked up the nose with a truck, and towed it two-and-a-half miles to a site on the highway where he planned to refurbish it and open it as a restaurant called The Crash Inn. But Pan American took the 'plane back and put a stop to that."

Lois was shaken up by the crash landing and the company gave her a month's leave for routine investigation and calming of the nerves. It would have been fortunate if her first flight after that last experience had been a smooth one, but in Alaska, in a DC-3, that was a rare occurrence. "It was a terrible trip. We got into really bad weather in Whitehorse, and we had to hole up there. It was 50 below zero. The heat was off in the little hotel, and I remember the rime ice, like you have on the coils of a freezer, on the mirror in my hotel room. We were joined by another flight that had been turned around to go back to Seattle, and the stewardess warned me about a passenger that I would be inheriting when we finally continued to Fairbanks. She was just looney, on dope at a time when dope wasn't even in the picture. I learned that on the previous flight she had pestered the stewardess for morphine because she knew the captain carried it with his emergency equipment."

Lois listened to her friend's warning and told her captain about the woman. "He was a real firm captain who said 'She's not going to give me any of that business.' Well, the woman went berserk and chased me into my room, just wild, chased me all over the place, thinking I could get the captain's briefcase. Finally, I escaped from her and ran back to the captain and demanded that something be done about her, that he call the police or get a doctor to sedate her. They did take her to a doctor's office and got her calmed down that night. But from then on for the next four days we would try to make the run to Fairbanks with full tanks and maybe five passengers—only that many could go on board because we had to carry so much fuel—and she'd be right there, ranting and raving, begging to get on board. But she had to wait her turn like everybody else. We'd go clear up to Fairbanks, circle around in the fog, use up as much fuel as we dared, and then come back. When you have fog up there it is like a layer cake. It sits right over the town, and you can see smoke from fires spiraling up out of it, but you cannot penetrate it unless you're lucky and find a hole.

"Finally, on the fourth day, the captain said 'I'm going through,' and I thought 'Oh boy, I've been through that.' Up we go, and we circle around and around, drone, drone, drone, and all of a sudden WHOOMPH! he found a hole and we plunged down through it.

"Then we were in Fairbanks doing the same thing, sweating out the ice fog. Passengers and crew would go to the airport every day, bag and baggage. That was my first time out after the crash and it was a really trying experience. Even now, when I fly somewhere and I hear the flaps come down and the engines throttling back, if they push them forward a little, it all comes back to me—that pilot gunning the engine in the murk."

On 6 May 1947, two months after the crash, Lois assisted Joe Amarok, the Nome Eskimo leader, in christening *Clipper North Wind*, the first of Pan American's new DC-4 fleet in Alaska. The Eskimo chief was dressed in full ceremonial furs and, instead of champagne to christen the airplane, they used water from the Bering Sea contained in a walrus bladder. The following day, Lois notched up another first: she was the first stewardess to work the Alaska run on the brand-new DC-4s.

The natural wonders of Alaska and the ingenuity of its native population constantly revealed themselves to the first seven. Phyllis recalls "In the summer, we would swim at midnight in the broad daylight or go fishing or panning for gold. In the winter, we would ski or ride in dog sleds." Virginia recalls catching a 35-pound halibut and then taking it down to one of the canneries in Juneau to have it cleaned and packed to take back home. She remembers watching Eskimos "stripping the skin from the blubber of whales. The two inches of blubber beneath the skin is called muktuk and is considered a delicacy. It is cut into small squares and served up like fudge!" She remembers watching King Islanders arriving at Nome in their 'umiaks' (skin canoes), having paddled across the open waters of the Bering Sea. Once ashore, they propped the umiaks up on the sand and sat underneath on fur blankets, carving whalebone for sale to tourists. She

Lois Thompson and Barbara Fowler bring Christmas to Alaska (back in the days when air mail was 5¢).

remembers "sitting down at an old upright piano in the tacky lobby of the Nordale Hotel in Fairbanks, playing some ragtime tunes for a group of miners from out in the tundra. They were a grizzly, hardened group, accustomed to the rigors of the bush, where mining and fur trapping were their source of livelihood. But what an appreciative audience they were, and what stories they could weave if encouraged." Virginia also remembers the sound of huskies howling in excitement at the first snow in fall, but most of all she remembers: "Nature's theatre, the aurora borealis, that unbelievable phenomenon, that light show extravaganza of all Creation, the northern lights. I gazed in awe hundreds of times at the ever-changing ribbon of pastel sashes ascending and descending in a rhythmic motion, arcing overhead."

Lois looks back with awe at the first seven's grit and with pleasure at the cameraderie of the Pan Am experience in Alaska in the 1940s. "I guess we had a lot of stamina. It was truly rugged flying in those days. And it was rugged on the ground too. If you objected to walking a block to the outdoor john in the middle of the winter, you didn't belong there."

The first seven obviously belonged there, held fast in the spell of the North during their adventurous years of pioneer flying in Alaska.

Guinea Pigs In San Francisco

With the Japanese surrender, following the bombing of Hiroshima and Nagasaki on 6 and 9 August 1945, respectively, Pan American resumed its commercial operations across the Pacific. By this time, it had already successfully included women on its Caribbean, Latin American, and Alaskan routes. Now it was time to see how they handled the long Pacific flights. Although the weather would be less threatening and the flying less dangerous than in Alaska, the first stewardesses would need, above all, endurance for the 18–20 hour flights between San Francisco and Honolulu. As it had already done so successfully in Alaska, Pan American looked at the talent it had in its own ranks for use as guinea pig stewardesses in the Pacific. The spotlight fell on **Mary Lyman (Talbot)** and **Beverly Mogensen (Cowden)**.

"Bev and I were working in the office one day when Mr. Holmes came in and announced that Pan American had decided to try having women on board the flights from San Francisco to Honolulu. He asked us if we'd like to volunteer. I didn't think about it too long because it sounded like fun," says Mary. She and Bev worked in Pan Am's traffic department at Treasure Island, taking reservations, meeting the airplanes, seeing passengers off on Pan

American's two regular flights a week across the Pacific, or soothing them when bad weather made it unadvisable for the flying boats to carry passengers and the flight crew took off bearing just mail.

"I thought 'What on earth am I doing?'" says Bev, when she was approached about the experiment. "I loved my job in the traffic department; it was a wonderful situation, working for such a young airline. But I told my mother and she said 'My goodness, Beverly, go for it. If only I could have done something like that.' That took care of that, and off I went." (Right here I would like to pay a tribute to the many mothers, like Bev's and mine, who with unselfishness and a vicarious spirit of adventure encouraged their daughters to fly rather than restraining them.)

Bev continues: "They gave us a bit of training before the guinea pig runs, and then the pursers gave us further training once we were on board the Boeing 314s. A lot of those pursers were from the American President Lines and had experience working on ships, so they were very service-oriented. Some of them were quite wary about having us on board. They couldn't have been nicer, but they were definitely wary, and they did make us work very hard. They had to make sure we could really handle it. I'm left-handed, not too skilful with a knife, and on my first trip I cut my finger badly; I still have the scar. Blood was all over the place, and I could feel Roy Donham, who was

Beverly Mogensen and Mary Lyman during training.

the head purser, thinking 'Oh my, my, what have we gotten ourselves into?' Anyway, he fixed me up and my finger stayed there, so we were all right."

Mary describes her first flight: "After the main meal service, the purser said he would go and have his hour's rest and all I had to do was finish the clean-up and carry the bag of garbage to the hatch in the tail of the airplane, but he cautioned me not to open the hatch. 'Don't worry, I won't do that,' I said. In those days, they just dumped the garbage in the ocean. We had served mashed sweet potatoes with the ham, and they hadn't gone over too well. There were tons left over, which we stuffed into this great big trash bag. I picked it up and, of course, it exploded, covering me from head to foot with yellow goo. I spent my entire rest time trying to clean up my uniform. I only had one. It was navy blue and was what I wore in the traffic department. Pan American had asked us to use our traffic uniform because they didn't know whether they were going to keep us on the line, and we didn't want to have to buy something for five experimental flights.

"Those flights seemed endless, and we served every meal you could think of: breakfast, lunch, dinner, cups of coffee, cups of tea, a snack here and a snack there" continues Bev. "Flying to Honolulu could take as much as 20 hours. We flew between 6,000 and 8,000 feet in a non-pressurized cabin. There were terrible headwinds; sometimes they were so strong that we would get as far as equi-time and then have to turn round and go back to San Francisco. I had one 18-hour flight from San Francisco to San Francisco. Although the noise was terrific in those flying boats, they were glamorous in their own way, and we had elegant furnishings including white linen, attractive silver, lovely plates.

Mary adds: "We served meals at a table to 12 passengers at a time. Soup, salad, entrée, dessert. After the meals, people would want to sleep and the hardest job for us was making up the bunks on the flying boats. They were always heavy, and by 1945 they were old and difficult, and we were glad we had a male steward to help us."

Bev continues: "We used to rest in the honeymoon suite; we never had honeymooners in those months when the War was ending. All our passengers were military officers or civilians working for the government. I remember something really cute: when I was flying with the purser, Tommy Quotzoe, he would wake me up from my rest with a cup of tea."

After they had each flown five experimental roundtrips to Honolulu and had proved that women could endure the long Pacific hauls just as well as men could, Bev and Mary returned to work in the traffic department. Pan American hired the first official Pacific stewardesses about a year later, when the War was completely over and they had started to replace the old flying boats with

Beverly Mogensen (far left) and Mary Lyman (facing, far right) during emergency training.

long-range, land-based aircraft. Bev and Mary were invited to become members of this group, and they were joined by seasoned stewardesses from Miami, Brownsville, and Alaska, as well as a few new hires. They were all given a six-week training and sent to work on DC-4s. Hope Parkinson, who came from the Miami base, was the first official stewardess to fly out of San Francisco.

The flight from San Francisco to Honolulu on the DC-4 took ten hours instead of the Boeing 314's 18–20 hours, and from Honolulu the stewardesses continued west as far as Manila and Shanghai or as far south as Auckland and Sydney. The stops between Honolulu and Manila continued to be Wake Island, Midway, and Guam. Bev describes a layover on Wake: "It was a fabulous place, with a huge lagoon, where we water-skied and played all kinds of funny water sports. We slept in Quonset huts, which had rats running around the ceilings. There were no women on the island, so we always had a rapturous welcome. When we got to Guam, we sometimes had to stay at the station manager's house because there was not enough room in the Quonset huts for all the crew members. It was that kind of family operation in those days. In Fiji, where we stayed in little thatched huts, the wake-up call was a handsome, great Fijian tickling our toes."

After flying for 18 months, Mary and Bev called it quits because they were both about to be married, Mary to George Talbot and Bev to Bill Cowden, both Pan Am employees. San Francisco's prototype stewardesses left Pan American the same day, married within a month of each other, both produced three sons, and have remained friends ever since.

Atlantic Firsts

In 1942, Dottie Bohanna became the first airline stewardess in the world to cross the Atlantic. At the time, she was working for American Export Airlines, which later became American Overseas Airlines until it was bought out by Pan American in 1950. But who was the first stewardess across the Atlantic for Pan American? Madeline Cuniff claims that honor. Like Mary Lyman and Bev Mogensen in the Pacific, she stepped out of her job on the ground and proved for Pan Am in October 1945 that a woman could do a splendid job on the Atlantic flying boats. Her pioneer efforts brought results. In 1946, Pan Am's first Atlantic training group of eight stewardesses started work out of LaGuardia.

Like Ellen Church and all the earliest stewardesses, **Dorothy Cecilia Bohanna** was a nurse. She also trained student nurses, one of whom left the hospital to join the airlines and encouraged Dottie to do the same. Tempted by the challenge, she quickly wrote to T.W.A., United, and American, and

Mary Lyman and Beverly Mogensen fold their wings.

made her choice of airline in her own unorthodox way: "I didn't like the paper that United used for their reply. I was very unimpressed. T.W.A. had great stationery."

In 1940, Dottie was hired by Transcontinental & Western Air (T.W.A., now Trans World Airlines), a solely domestic airline in those days, and flew out of Kansas City for two years. Her first flight as a stewardess was on a DC-2. "It was so small, just 14 passengers, and you worked alone. I was quite nervous because the company threatened that if we received three 'brown letters,' which were letters of complaint that they sent out on brown stationery, we'd be out. The most frequent complaint was that meals were cold. I had a problem; when I first started flying, I used to get airsick. It was a rough ride in the unpressurized DC-2s and DC-3s and we flew at about 7,500 feet. The galley was in the tail, which was always rougher. Our meals were put on in thermos jugs, one full of meat, one full of vegetables, and one full of potatoes. You would set up three trays at a time, then dish out the food, cover it quickly, and rush it out to the passengers. Then you would start all over again.

"On my first flight, which was a day flight, I had it all under control. I would get three meals dished up and delivered, then I would rush back to the john and throw up. Then I would come out and set up three more meals, and so on. When we arrived in New York, I found the supervisor and said, 'I can't keep this job because I was airsick all the way across the country. I was able to get the meals out this time, but suppose I couldn't time it right? The meals would be cold, I would get lots of brown letters, and I would be out on my ear. I'd rather resign.' He told me that I would have to return to Kansas City to resign. I prayed and prayed that I would get through the next flight. Going back, it was a night flight, and it was wonderful. Everything was smooth and I didn't get sick—nor did the passengers. But each time I took the day flight to New York, it was a different matter, and each time the supervisor suckered me into doing one more trip."

Just after Pearl Harbor, Dottie learned that a steamship company, American Export Lines, was just about to start operating a flying boat service called American Export Airlines (A.E.A.) across the Atlantic and wanted to hire six nurses as stewardesses. (After World War II, A.E.A. was purchased by American Airlines, providing American with the trans-Atlantic division known as American Overseas Airlines.) Intrigued by the idea of working on a flying boat and going overseas, Dottie applied. At her interview, she found herself describing the work of an airline stewardess to her interviewer. Having worked with steamships up until that point, he had no idea what it entailed. He immediately recognized Dottie's competency, and she was hired on the spot.

"We did a Newfoundland survey first with only pilots and company officials on board," says Dottie. "When the time came for people to sleep and for us to set up the berths, I found to my surprise that for the lower berth we had to drag the mattresses from the stern of the airplane, where they were stored, through the cabin—in front of the passengers! I was appalled and reckoned that we had to find some way of doing it on the ground. I spoke to the vice president for operations and he invited me to figure out how. The next day, I went out to the airport, but the aircraft was being serviced and the head of maintenance didn't want any females getting in his way. He and his men thought females were going to be a bunch of trouble. I went for the boss, and together we boarded the plane and spent about four hours figuring out how we could make up those berths on the ground. Then I taught the men how to do it, so they didn't have to suffer our interference."

After the first survey flight, the government found out that A.E.A. was planning to use nurses as stewardesses on board its aircraft. They tried to call a halt, insisting that the nurses were being withheld from vital duties in the hospitals or in the military. A.E.A. argued that the flying boats could, at any time, be turned into hospital ships, bringing the injured back home from the war front. The argument was successful. On 20 June 1942, Dottie Bohanna took off on the first passenger trip across the Atlantic.

"Yes, I was the first stewardess across the Atlantic. I just happened to be in the right place at the right time. We flew from New York to Foynes, in Ireland, and B.O.A.C. took the passengers on to England. From Foynes we flew to Bathurst in Gambia, and then on to Belém, and from there to Trinidad. We had no armaments, and we only flew at night so that the Germans could not see us.

"We were too young and stupid to be frightened during the War. One time we went in to North Africa four days after the invasion. At that time, there was no Air Transport Command and no Naval Air Transport Service, just us. So we followed the troops in. Our captain was given an envelope with our destination when we left Foynes, but was not permitted to open it until we were a certain distance from Ireland. Our destination turned out to be Port Lyautey in Morocco, where we had a rapturous welcome. I stayed in the captain's quarters on board the *Fort Biscayne*, the naval ship under the command of Captain Turner, because they couldn't put me in the barracks with all the fellows. Flying in to Port Lyautey actually made our lives easier because the flight from Foynes to Bathurst could take 20 hours; the stop in Port Lyautey gave us a break."

Even though Dottie claims that she was never frightened during the War, she had every reason to be. She remembers one particular evening in

Port Lyautey when she and the Sikorsky crew were down at the dock, preparing to take off. They heard the drone of an incoming aircraft and watched, mesmerized, as what appeared to be the spectre of an airplane came into sight. Riddled with bullets, falling apart in front of their eyes, it managed to alight on the water. They learned from its battle-scarred crew that there were Focke-Wulf fighters nearby, and were all warned to return to the barracks for the night.

Thinking back on that time, Dottie says, "As a child, I was taught that I had a guardian angel. Well, my poor guardian angel had a heck of a job."

"I was in love with the flying boats. I would go anywhere in them, and I never tired of them. My eyes would be fixed on the windows on every take-off. When you started in the water and then you'd get up on the step and the water rushed past the windows, and that ZOOM as you'd go sailing along and all of a sudden you're airborne and you knew you were off to Europe. In a land plane, on our Boston trips, I never bothered to look up." (The step is a step-like projection across the keel of a flying boat, which facilitates separation of the craft from the water.)

A.O.A.'s flying boats were long-range Vought-Sikorsky VS-44s, and could go from New York to Ireland nonstop. "Pan Am had to stop at Newfoundland and sometimes Shediac, New Brunswick, and they couldn't carry many passengers. What they did have was luxury. Our 'plane was more serviceable and not real formal because it was wartime. We had a steward and stewardess on each flight, and we dovetailed our work: the steward was in charge of the galley and the food, and the stewardess was in charge of the cabin and the passengers. We were equals, absolutely equal.

"Early on, A.E.A. liked the alliteration of the words 'steward' and 'stewardess,' and that is what we were called. When the fellows decided they wanted to be called pursers, like Pan Am, they asked if the women would like to be called 'purserettes.' I nearly died laughing. Stupid me, and the other girls were just as dumb. The fellows knew that on Pan Am, the purser was the guy in charge, and when Pan Am bought us that really meant a difference in our paychecks."

In 1950, after years of wrangling between Pan Am, T.W.A., and American, Pan Am bought A.O.A. for $17,450,000. "I was out on the Korean airlift when we became Pan Am," recalls Dottie. "We were flying from Wake Island to Tokyo when the captain notified me that I had to put a sign up on the partition between the front and back of the airplane, right by the entry doors, saying, 'This aircraft is now the property of Pan American World Airways.' I posted that sign with tears streaming down my face. I was heartbroken. We had a Pan Am navigator, Black Bart, who had been added to our crew, and he didn't dare come near me the rest of the trip. I was so upset. We all felt terrible.

"I found the transition extremely difficult. My ideas of service differed from my new co-workers' many times, and because I was not a purser, I had no authority. I decided to quit, but Ted Emmons, the flight service superintendant, kept talking me out of it. 'Just try one more flight,' he'd say. I was exasperated. Finally he said, 'How would you like to fly the President's Special?' 'Are you kidding?' I said, 'If I'm this unhappy when they pay a regular fare, how do you think I'll feel when I know they're paying extra?' (The President's Special was the super deluxe service on board the Boeing Stratocruiser from New York to London and back and from New York to Paris and back. These flight operated only at weekends, and no children were allowed on board.)

Ted Emmons had recognized how valuable Dottie was to the airline. He recognized what a hard worker she was, how practical she could be about solving problems on the aircraft, and how competent she was. He had no intention of letting her go.

Dottie continues, "He insisted. The President's Special crews were hand-picked and stayed with each other. I was put with Tony Volpe (see page 82), who was great, and I was never so excited in my life. I loved every minute of it. When I returned to New York, I went back to Ted and said, 'Sign me up.'"

Working on the President's Specials meant plenty of days off for Dottie. Not being a believer in idle hands, she went back to nursing at Mercy Hospital in Rockville Center, Long Island, in her spare time, where she was soon in charge of the men's private floor. "It never occurred to me that my work on the airline would contribute to my nursing the way my nursing contributed to my flying. But I found that, because I was so used to making sure that passengers were happy, I did the same with my patients. On the aircraft I might soothe a passenger who had an overdone steak, but in the hospital I found myself in a position to make a terminally ill patient's passing much more comfortable.

"I began to appreciate my airline job all the more when I realized how lucky I was to be able to fly away for the weekend and have dinner in Paris with the boys before coming back and being a nurse again. In a four-bedded room, there might be two patients who were there from the previous week, and when I'd walk in, one of them would say, 'Hi, Miss Bohanna, how was Paris?' The new patients would say 'Paris, France?!' in disbelief. And the old timer would reply 'She was working here Thursday, she went to Paris for the weekend, and she's back here already.' They looked forward to my coming back and it cheered them up to hear all about my trips."

Dottie Bohanna cuts the cake at her retirement party.

Dottie Bohanna flew for 40 years, the last 30 of which were with Pan American. When she retired on 31 October 1980, she was renowned for her competence, her integrity, and her professionalism. Dottie was also remembered with envy because she never needed sleep and was possessed of far more energy than colleagues half her age. She had a résumé full of records and commendations: during her time with A.E.A. she was the first stewardess ever to cross the Atlantic; she was Pan Am's first female In-Flight Director on the 747s; and at the time she retired, she had enjoyed an uninterrupted flying career longer than any other stewardess's, a career which was conspicuously free of emergencies. As Dottie herself is inclined to say, "That was my guardian angel working overtime. I always seemed to be in the right place at the right moment."

Opal Hess, whose name is often mentioned in the same breath as Dottie Bohanna's, also set longevity records with Pan Am. She was a registered nurse who started flying with American Airlines in 1935, but left to get married. She resumed flying, this time for American Export Airlines in 1943. Like Dottie's, her career with Pan Am started when A.O.A. was bought by Pan Am in 1950, and she also retired from the company in 1980. Between 1967 and 1971, she was responsible for the publication of *Wing Tips,* a magazine for flight service, by flight service. Opal is currently at work on a book of memoirs of her flying during World War II.

Many of the early stewardesses were pilots who had to pass on to a future generation their hopes of a seat on the flight deck of a commercial aircraft. It was unthinkable that a woman could enter that world, even though women had proved themselves capable of extraordinary feats of skill, daring, and strength in the air. But by compromising and becoming a stewardess instead of a pilot, Ellen Church had opened up a new career for women who wanted to leap beyond the quotidian. If they wanted to fly, if they wanted to see the world, if they wanted to escape from what was expected of them— early marriage or jobs as secretaries, teachers, and nurses—the airlines offered them the opportunity. Pan American not only offered them an opportunity to fly, it offered them the world.

Like Ellen Church, **Madeline Cuniff** was a pilot. Born and raised in Alabama, she studied at the University of Alabama, where she majored in physical education and minored in English. She was greatly influenced by her Shakespeare professor, Hudson Strode, author of many travel books, who opened her eyes to the world outside Alabama. After she graduated and started teaching, she soon became restless, and when she learned about the adventures of Amelia Earhart, she began attending air shows. Suddenly she realized that she could not spend the rest of her life teaching in Alabama; she was determined to fly, one way or another.

Seeking adventure and wider horizons, Madeline Cuniff left Alabama for New York in 1939. She moved in with her sister, who worked for American Airlines and encouraged Madeline to do the same. However, her professor's descriptions of foreign countries were still lodged in her mind, and instead of seeking work with a domestic carrier, she joined Pan American World Airways in July 1940. The company promised her the opportunity to become the first trans-Atlantic stewardess. Madeline continues: "After spending two months of training in the Pan Am kitchen at LaGuardia airport and in the galley of the Boeing 314, my dream of being the first trans-Atlantic stewardess for Pan Am was delayed because of the War. Instead, the idea of a Passenger Service Department was conceived and three of us were assigned to start it, A. Paul Wollam, Torrence Thornton, and myself. Our work entailed checking in departing passengers for their flights and assisting and interpreting for arriving passengers. Later, Pan Am hired a special group for intelligence work, and I trained and worked very closely with this group.

"One of the highlights of 1941 for me was meeting Jacqueline Cochran, a top female pilot, who was forming a squadron of women in Texas, thanks to the support and encouragement of General Hap Arnold. Cochran sponsored me as the first female to join the Civil Aeronautics Patrol and to enter their training program. I earned my pilot's license, Number 9-7229-41, on 21 June 1941. She also sponsored me for the Ninety-Niners, an organization for ace women pilots, which had been formed by Amelia Earhart.

"I continued working in Passenger Service until 1945. With the termination of World War II, Pan American decided to continue with its original plan of assigning me as their first trans-Atlantic stewardess."

But first, Madeline had to cut her teeth on some Bermuda flights, which, in flying over part of the ocean, using the same equipment, provided an ideal training environment. Here she describes the experience of setting out for work on the first of these: "I donned my beautiful new Pan American stewardess uniform one lovely fall day, went to Pan Am at LaGuardia, marched down the wharf with the all-male flight crew and boarded the most elegant airplane in the world, the Boeing 314, for Flight 130, leaving for Bermuda at 10:00 a.m. On this, my first flight, I was assigned to serve the cocktails and luncheon while the purser worked in the galley. Shortly after we took off, I made sure that the passengers were comfortably settled, including the honeymooners in their own suite at the rear of the aircraft, complete with champagne and caviar and a sign on their door which said 'Please do not disturb.'"

The luncheon service was elegant. The entrées came on board partially cooked and were completed in the ovens on board, and the cabin crew added 'frills' to the partially prepared salad and appetizers. The meals were served course by course at tables in each compartment, and Madeline says that each table setting included "Limoges china and sterling silver (or reasonable facsimiles!); linen cloths and napkins were a must.

"When we reached Darrel's Island (in Bermuda), the governor came out in his launch to meet us, and a calypso band was waiting on the banks to celebrate our arrival. Pan Am in Bermuda considered having a stewardess on board like having a new ambassador! It made me feel like a Hollywood leading lady, and I loved every minute of it.

"The work on those Bermuda flights was hard," Madeline continues, "but weather was the most important factor for those seaplanes. Sea swells were always measured. [The passenger flying boats did not as a rule take off in swells higher than three feet.] If the flights were delayed, which they often were because of the swells, I would take care of the passengers on the ground. We would go on tours of the island, on picnics, on shopping expeditions, to dinner dances at the Belmont, and to golf tournaments."

In October 1945, after Madeline had proved how competently she could handle work on the 314 to Bermuda and how graciously she dealt with passengers on the ground, she was once more approached about working on a trans-Atlantic crossing: "I was so excited about that first flight; wouldn't you be? I remember marching out to the end of the ramp as the loudspeaker announced the dramatic departure of the flying boat. The public was surprised to see a female stewardess march down with the 13 male crew members of a trans-Atlantic crew.

"The purser with me on that flight scrutinized my every move, making me nervous. He was very, very jealous. He would sit there and watch me do all the work, never taking his eyes off me. The male pursers didn't like having us on board. They did half the work for twice the pay." Nevertheless, Madeline passed that acid test with flying colors. About her passengers, she comments: "In those days, everybody who flew had top priority. Many of our passengers were military, but others were working on special missions for the president, and once in a while we'd have a honeymoon couple."

In common with her Bermuda experience, Madeline discovered that her job did not end with the Clipper's arrival at any given destination. She found herself at work almost 24 hours a day. "Tours, entertainment, card games, anything that would distract the passengers' attention from the Clippers' delays was essential. We were almost always stranded in Shediac and Botwood, in Canada, because of the high swells. The men on the ground in Shediac would say 'Why don't you help us by taking the passengers to see the fisheries?' And I'd take them off on a sightseeing tour. In Botwood, I would take them to the airport shop to buy fur gifts. While I was away from home, I didn't sleep much at all; I don't know how I survived. Sometimes on the airplane, I would try to slip down to the dressing room for a nap, but it was never enough.

"The flight from Botwood to Foynes was a long one, and besides serving meals, I would arrange bridge tournaments and other games. We had one called 'Navigation,' which our navigators would explain to the passengers, and there would be a prize for the person who came closest to figuring out the arrival time in Foynes. The navigators would sometimes invite passengers to the flight deck and show them the 'Bubble' where the celestial navigation took place.

"We would often be delayed at Foynes, waiting for flights to return to the U.S. (those flying boats required an awful lot of servicing) and several times I organized golf tournaments for the passengers and crew. I played, too, and shot somewhere in the 80s. We always had such a delightful time in Ireland. We stayed in Adair, where Lady Adair, who was very charming, would invite us for lunch."

When the flying boat service was discontinued, Madeline found herself more and more involved with stewardess training and passenger service.

However, with the advent of the Stratocruiser, she was back on board again, doing publicity for that magnificent aircraft. "We took the airplane over to London, to show our fabulous double-decker Stratocruiser to the dignitaries there. From there we took it to Detroit and Chicago and showed it to businessmen there. We took it to Boston, Rome, Brussels, Shannon, and showed it off there."

Once the Stratocruiser publicity work was completed, Madeline was offered a choice: she could continue to devote her time to training stewardesses, or she could become the manager of passenger service on the ground. She decided in favor of the latter because it would provide her with more variety. "I had studied teaching and was good at training people, so I really enjoyed setting up passenger service for various parts of the world. I trained the ground staff for Mexico and Central America at our base in New Orleans when we opened the run to South America. Later I set up a training school for ground crew in Miami."

Madeline Cuniff worked for Pan American for a total of 44 years, the last of which were spent managing the Clipper Club at Kennedy Airport. In that capacity, Madeline continued to entertain and to comfort weary travellers, visiting dignitaries, the rich, the famous, (and the infamous) with her own particular brand of Southern hospitality. She retired in 1984, and lives in Fort Lauderdale and New York.

Madeline Cuniff and Joanne Carson appear on the Joan Rivers Show.
(Photograph by Raimondo Borea.)

"Nowadays, I do volunteer work with the scholarship program at the University of Alabama and I have worked with the Whitbread round-the-world race. It is the most difficult yacht race in the world, and Fort Lauderdale is the only place the yachts stop in the United States. From my apartment, which looks right over Port Everglades, I can see them arriving. Every ship, every small sailing boat, that comes into Port Everglades sails right under my terrace. I bicycle to mass in the morning at St. Sebastian's down the street, and then I come back and greet the people off the ships, then I swim my laps. In recent years, I have become very interested in boats. I guess I always was if you consider the seaplanes to be boats."

Madeline's enthusiasm for life and her pride in her career with Pan American is undiminished. She says "I think life is so beautiful. I enjoy every minute of it. Age is not important to me, life is. I leave you with the words of Leonardo da Vinci: 'When once you have tasted flight you will always walk the earth with your eyes turned skyward; for there you have been and there you will always be.'"

By 1946 Pan American had stewardesses working in all divisions—Latin America and the Caribbean, the Atlantic, the Pacific, and Alaska—and continued to hire women at an increasing rate. In fact, during the 'sixties they ceased to hire men at all, apart from the Cornell University hotel school students who were brought in during the summer to help with the heavy loads. This women-only hiring policy changed in 1972 after Celio Diaz, Jr., who wanted to work as a steward for Pan Am, filed a sex discrimination suit under the Civil Rights Act of 1964. The jury ruled in favor of Diaz, and Pan Am once again started hiring male cabin crew. Diaz, however, was not hired because he did not fulfil other criteria.

When examining the characters of Lois Smith, Lois Blanchard, Mary Lyman, Bev Mogensen, Dottie Bohanna, and Madeline Cuniff, common denominators become apparent: a sense of adventure, true courage, humor in adversity, and eagerness to take a first step into unknown (and sometimes hostile) territory. During an era when jobs for women were predictable and restrictive, Pan American offered an amazing opportunity to escape the mundane. Young women from small towns all over the United States woke up to the call. And not just from the United States; in 1946, Pan American hired Sophie Hansteen (Hange) and Liv Mangschou (Aigeltinger), the first of its European flight attendants, and they were soon joined by others. This was the beginning of a long hiring relationship between Pan American and northern European stewardesses. The company needed young women who were at least bilingual; it also seemed to be particularly partial to blue-eyed blondes.

Round The World

...the vast aerial chariot, gleaming like pearl, planed above the highest buildings... an incomparable artistic achievement, travelling in space like a guiding light in the orbit of the sun, it was immeasurably resplendent.... Irresistible and swift as the wind, capable of ranging the firmament, containing many apartments and furnished with innumerable works of art, captivating to the mind, stainless as the autumnal moon.

Rishi Valmiki, *The Ramayana*

By 1947, three years after the first group of women was trained, Pan Am stewardesses had won a place in the public's mind; they were perceived as glamorous world travellers, young women who spoke at least one foreign language, and who were as at home in Hong Kong as they were in the United States. Which of these young women would be chosen to be the only female crew member to work on the flight that was the fulfillment of Juan Trippe's dearest dream, a flight that would encircle the globe?

Pan American adored publicity, especially when there was something new to spring on the public, and the company avidly sought the media spotlight for its historic moments. The company's greatest publicity blitz of the decade was the one surrounding the first commercial round-the-world flight on 17 June 1947.

Clipper America was a brand new Lockheed Constellation 749, perhaps the most graceful-looking aircraft ever manufactured. It cruised at around 300 m.p.h., it was pressurized so that it could fly as high as 20,000 feet, and in Pan Am's configuration it carried 54 passengers. It was the perfect aircraft for Juan Trippe's perfect moment. To ensure the maximum visibility, he planned a publicity bonanza by inviting some heavy duty members of the press who also happened to number among his best friends: Thomas H. Beck, Chairman of the Board, Crowell-Collier Publishing; Paul Bellamy, Publisher, *Cleveland Plain Dealer;* Erwin D. Canham, Editor, *Christian Science Monitor;* Gardner Cowles, President, *Des Moines Register;* Earl Barry Faris, Editor-in-Chief, International News Service; Marshall Field III, Publisher, *Chicago Sun;* Frank Gannett, Publisher, Gannett Newspapers; Mrs. Oveta Culp Hobby, Executive Vice President, *Houston Post;* Roy Howard, President, Scripps

Howard Newspapers; J. Loy Maloney, Managing Editor, *Chicago Tribune;* M.T. Moore, Board Chairman, Time-Life-Fortune Publications; Ralph Nicholson, Publisher, *New Orleans Item;* Paul Patterson, Publisher, *Baltimore Sun;* Mrs. Ogden Reid, President, *New York Herald Tribune;* Francis H. Russell, Director, Office of Public Affairs, Dept. of State; James G. Stahlman, President, *Nashville Banner;* and Clayton Knight, a well-known artist. He also brought along with him Mayor Lapham of San Francisco and three Pan Am Vice Presidents.

As crew on the 13-day, 22,170-mile journey, the Constellation would carry three captains, one navigator, two radio officers, and two flight engineers. Purser Raymond Tunstall would be in charge of the cabin, and Flight Service office was abuzz with rumors about which stewardess would accompany him on this historic flight. Finally, the spotlight focused on Alice Lemieux.

Alice Lemieux (Jacobsen) was born in Westbrook, Maine, in 1921. Because her father was French-Canadian, she spoke French at home. She loved the language and took 'Parisian' French in high school with an eye to European travel, but World War II intervened and she decided to aid the war effort by working as a personnel counsellor in the Pratt & Whitney airplane factory in Hartford, Connecticut. After the War, she left for New York to work for American Airlines on the ground, but she soon learned that Pan American was looking for stewardesses who spoke a foreign language. Immediately, she took herself over to Pan Am's Flight Service Department. One look at Alice was enough for the recruiters. That very evening, while she and her friends were eating dinner in their boarding house, the doorbell rang and it was Western Union with a telegram from Pan Am saying that she had been hired and inviting her to report for a physical a couple of weeks later. She started work in January 1946, and during the next 18 months, Alice Lemieux proved her efficiency and graciousness aboard. She was also hard-working, enthusiastic, and easygoing.

In addition, Alice was a reporter's dream. Not only did she hold the job that every young woman in the United States coveted, she had the face to stop any man in his tracks, she resembled Hedy Lamarr, a movie star the public was crazy about at the time, and the camera adored her. The company was well aware of how much attention the press had paid to her in previous public relations ventures. With all the fanfare of a Hollywood première, Pan American announced its choice of stewardess for the round-the-world inaugural, and the press went to town.

Alice Lemieux

Alice expresses complete surprise that she was chosen for the honor of working on the round-the-world inaugural: "My superior telephoned me at my apartment and asked me to come in to the office and talk to him. My immediate response was 'Oh, my heavens, what have I done?' I knew there was going to be a trip around the world, but everybody assumed that a certain gal who was always chosen for special trips would be on it, so I never gave it a thought. When they told me I had been chosen, I was so excited that I was practically in tears. I asked them why they had picked me and they replied 'First, we think you are one of the very best. Second, you photograph real well.'"

On 15 June 1947 Vincent Adams in the Brooklyn Section of *The New York Times* wrote: "Three women will be aboard the *Clipper America* when it takes off Tuesday from LaGuardia field for the world's first globe circling commercial flight, and the busiest of these will be Alice Lemieux, 26, of Jackson Heights, Queens, one of the prettiest and most capable stewardesses at Pan American. The two week, 21,000-mile flight is something stewardesses dream about while puddle-jumping from New York to Bermuda. With a passenger list composed of 25 leading publishers, the plush red carpet will be out at all the stops. Already scheduled is a tea with Prime Minister Clement Attlee, cocktails with the American ambassador, and a banquet with General MacArthur in Tokyo. In between are official luncheons, formal dinner parties, guided tours to historic spots and innumerable receptions, and petite Alice is wondering just how she is going to get enough clothes to last her two weeks and still remain within the 66-pound luggage allowance. Now after two weeks of intensive shopping and countless hours of her own needlework, Alice is loaded down with 12 white blouses, two uniforms, several summer frocks, an evening gown, suitable footgear, swimming suit and other raiment. The Constellation has everything on board except a laundry, and ground stops will be so brief she won't have time to get to the cleaners. But the boys at the airport are laying even money Alice comes through with colors flying."

Other correspondents dealt even more closely with the details of her wardrobe. They described the pink, non-crushable linen (surely an oxymoron?) dress which she made herself and the pink flowers she would wear in her hair for a reception in Istanbul. They described the green and white piqué dinner gown with its sweeping skirt and black velvet ribbon sash, designed by Emily Wilkins, which she would wear at General MacArthur's dinner party in Tokyo. They waxed lyrical about the important short white coat, spectator sport shoes, shiny patent leather pumps, white piqué hat, and tiny black silk turban that she carried with her. They even described how she spent three evenings washing and ironing a dozen blouses for the trip.

This intense scrutiny from the press did nothing to calm Alice's nerves as she prepared for the flight. She had been required to study the passenger list so that she could call the passengers by name the moment they boarded, and she had recurring nightmares about getting their names confused. However, a few practice runs on board the Constellation with veteran purser, Ray Tunstall, acted like a charm to soothe her. Ray was often chosen for inaugurals and other special trips because of his years of experience and his expertise. She and Ray had flown together many times and their in-flight service was smooth and professional.

There was a carnival atmosphere at the airport as the hour for take-off approached, and the mayor of New York, William O'Dwyer, presided over the departure formalities. After the take-off, at 2:17 p.m., the Constellation was escorted for 150 miles by four Navy Corsairs and 14 Army P-51 Mustangs.

On board, Ray and Alice set to work. Alice had no trouble remembering the names of the passengers, all of whom were delighted by her gentle and courteous service.

The flight to Gander and on to Shannon was calm and uneventful, but between Shannon and London, one of the engines 'acted up,' and had to be shut down, which meant a 35-minute late arrival, a fact that the London press was quick to note: "With an equipment Jules Verne would never have thought of, consisting mainly of Panama hats, a 30-pound ham, and a big purple orchid, a party of 21 American editors and publishers from New York arrived at London Airport yesterday. London was their third stop on a whirlwind global journey. They arrived at 1 p.m., half an hour behind schedule. With a groan for the pouring rain ('Doesn't the sun ever shine over here?') the party, which included two women, stepped from the Pan American World Airways *Clipper America* to enjoy a 12-hour visit to England, en route for Turkey, India, China, and Japan. Mr. Juan Trippe, president of Pan American, brought the ham for Mr. Attlee, who received the party at 10 Downing Street." The prime minister was no doubt pleased to supplement the meagre meat ration that was in force at the time in a Britain still recovering from the devastations of World War II.

Each night the Constellation flew east and arrived in a new country the next morning, and at each destination Juan Trippe and the press team were royally entertained by local dignitaries. They would return to the airplane at day's end and the long journey would continue. When they came aboard after a day of receptions and sightseeing, Alice and Ray served them soothing drinks and made sure that they were tucked comfortably in their sleeperettes. All through the night, Alice and Ray stayed alert, ready to answer any needs, ready to offer refreshment or conversation to those whose internal clocks were having trouble converting to the relentless time changes.

Although the press claimed that Alice attended all the receptions and banquets given for the Clipper's passengers, this was far from the truth, although Pan American publicity encouraged this notion with press releases such as: "The globe-circling flight has not been all work for the attractive stewardess, since the Clipper has flown only at night, with parties and receptions the order of the day. Accompanying fellow crew members and American newspaper executives who are passengers on the Clipper, Miss Lemieux has met dignitaries in London, Istanbul, Karachi, Calcutta, Bangkok, Shanghai, Manila, and Tokyo. In Tokyo, she attended a reception given by General Douglas MacArthur and heard MacArthur declare that Japan should be supervised for a generation, perhaps with the aid of American bomber and fighter planes."

This was absolute rubbish! Alice did not go to Downing Street to meet Clement Attlee, nor did she hear General MacArthur recommend vigilance. The trip for Alice was not at all the same trip that the press trumpeted. Here is her account of her days and nights:

"We were always invited to go along to the banquets, but usually did not because that was the time we desperately needed to sleep. The passengers could sleep on the airplane, but we could not. However, we served hardly any meals on board because of all the banquets the passengers attended ashore. We mostly served breakfasts, cups of coffee, and lots of cocktails. Ray would fix the drinks and I would serve them. I got to know what every passenger drank, and they drank a lot, that crowd."

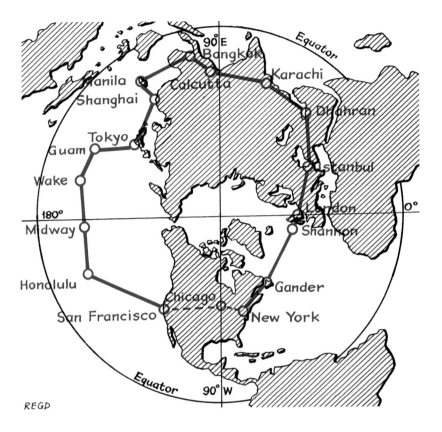

REGD

Route of Clipper America *on the inaugural round-the-world flight from 17 to 30 June 1947, the world's first such itinerary flown as a regular schedule.*

It was a gruelling 13-day journey with the Clipper passing through time changes on each leg. Because she continued to be the prey of photographers, the trip was especially demanding for Alice, who needed to appear dewy-eyed and adorable at each destination. Her appearance had to be immaculate, and no matter how tired she felt, her demeanor had to be charming. She smiled, and she smiled, and she smiled. And at every stop, she was weighed down with bouquets and showered with gifts, which included a Japanese sword from Tokyo, silver chopsticks from China, a black and silver bracelet from Thailand, a huge silver coin from Dhahran, and a silver cigarette case in Chicago.

Even though she did not attend the reception given by General MacArthur, Alice claims that the arrival in Japan was the high point of the trip for her. As the Constellation parked at the terminal in Tokyo, Alice looked out the windows and saw what appeared to be the entire U.S. Army of Occupation. The passengers disembarked one by one, followed by members of the flight crew. Alice was the last to leave the cabin. As she stepped out of the door and onto the aircraft steps, a huge shout of joy went up from the crowd. Thousands of American men in uniform welcomed Alice as only they know how. That one small figure in blue with its incredibly lovely face represented for them all the femininity they were missing —their wives, their sweethearts, their sisters, their friends, and the women of their dreams.

After Tokyo came the long Pacific legs to those islands, Guam, Midway, and Wake, where Pan American had created airports out of practically nothing but crushed coral. There the rapturous welcome came primarily from Pan Am employees, but once the Clipper reached Honolulu, the hoopla continued. Alice was showered with flowers, laden with leis, and once again adored by the camera.

Finally they reached San Francisco, and at last Alice anticipated an opportunity to display the formal gown she had carried all the way around the world with her. It was not meant to be. Alice describes what happened: "My bags were missing. Somehow Mayor Lapham got wind of this and said to me 'Instead of going to the hotel, I want you to come and stay at my house because my mother's nurse is your size, and I am sure she will be able to fix you up with some clothes.' So I stayed with them and got royal treatment, and sure enough the nurse and I were the same dress size, and she lent me a green and white print gown. It was lovely but I had to wear my black uniform shoes with it because she had bigger feet."

The passengers disembarked in San Francisco because Pan American was still an exclusively international carrier and was not permitted to carry people between points in the United States. After a fuelling stop in Chicago,

Alice Lemieux, with Captain Hugh Gordon (left) and Captain Gordon Maxwell (right), before taking off on the first round-the-world commercial passenger flight in airline history.

Alice Lemieux announces lunch.

the *Clipper America* completed its round-the-world circuit. On Monday, 30 June, at 4:58 p.m., the tower at LaGuardia Field picked up Captain Hugh H. Gordon, III, reporting their arrival. At 5:05, the Constellation burned rubber, and nine minutes later was on the blocks. It was 13 days, three hours, and ten minutes since the take-off from LaGuardia field. A crowd of newspaper photographers and reporters, newsreel and television cameramen were lying in wait. As had been the case all around the world, their eyes and cameras were focused on Alice Lemieux.

A year later, when Alice was on leave in Maine, she received a telephone call from Flight Service. "Oh, oh, what have I done now?" she thought again. But they were calling to say that the passengers who would be on board Pan Am's proving flight to Johannesburg had requested the same cabin crew that had been on the round-the-world inaugural. They were the same members of the press who had flown on *Clipper America*, and they were were determined to have another opportunity to fly with lovely Alice Lemieux.

Life Raft in the Desert

Round the decay
Of that colossal wreck, boundless and bare
The lone and level sands stretch far away.

Shelley, "Ozymandias"

The fanfare and triumph of the first round-the-world commercial flight could not obscure the fact that all was not well with the beautiful Constellation. The engines of the original Model 49s had a nasty tendency to overheat, causing frequent cylinder changes and, depending on the location of the cylinder, lengthy delays. (In 1946, a Constellation with Vivien Leigh and Lawrence Olivier on board made a forced landing in Connecticut because an engine was on fire.) On 18 June 1947, the second day of her history-making flight around the world, Alice Lemieux received the frightening news that a Constellation had gone down in the Syrian desert.

Anthony Volpe was born in Juneau, Alaska, but moved to Italy with his parents when he was six years old. He returned to the United States when he was 18, with two goals in mind: to learn to speak English again and to join an airline. He had always been fascinated with aviation, and recalls frequent visits to LaGuardia to observe take-offs and landings. His friend Phil Casprini (see page 33), a purser with Pan American, recognized Tony's potential and referred him to the company's personnel department. During Tony's interview he was asked how he stood with the draft. Dutifully, Tony contacted his board. "Where have you been?" they asked. "You should have been drafted a year ago." It was July 1942. A month later Tony was sent to Spokane for training and then served two and a half years in Europe. He left the Army in November 1945 and immediately made contact with Pan American. He started flying a month later.

Tony Volpe

Tony worked for the company for 35 years, most of the time in flight service as a purser or supervisor, but for three years as an assistant manager of the 'Copter Club on top of the Pan Am Building in Manhattan. During his career, he made hundreds of safe Atlantic crossings and round-the-world flights. However, on one occasion, while the members of the press circled the globe on *Clipper America*, revelling in the wonders of aviation, relaxing on board as Alice Lemieux and Ray Tunstall catered to their every need, Tony was coping with an aviation nightmare on *Clipper Eclipse*.

He describes the incident: "I was working on a New York/Karachi/ New York pattern, and we incurred several mechanical delays along the way. The first delay was in Shannon, where we awaited the incoming aircraft which had had mechanical problems in Gander. Eventually we left Shannon for Istanbul. Shortly after passing Paris, I noticed quite a bit of smoke in the galley, and it was not coming from the ovens. In the galley, there was a rack which housed the electronics and radio transmitters. Apparently there was an electrical short, so the unit was shut down, and the flight was diverted to Rome.

"We overnighted there, and the next morning I went shopping with Captain Hart, acting as his interpreter. I recall stopping in a leather goods store, and the sales lady assisted the captain in selecting a birthday gift for his wife. We returned to the airport, and walked out to the aircraft with the flight engineer, and he started the standard pre-flight inspection. I went to check if the crew luggage had been loaded, and walking past the Number 3 engine, I spotted a small puddle. I told the engineer; he came over, put his finger in the liquid, and said, 'We have a problem. This is hydraulic fluid, and a hydraulic leak is difficult to trace.' That meant another delay, and lunch in the airport restaurant."

During the delay, a Pan Am representative made arrangements for passengers and crew to visit St. Peter's. Tony and **Jane Bray (Wessman)**, the stewardess, rounded up the passengers. (Jane was from Memphis, and well-known for her Southern hospitality. When cooking lobsters, she always slipped a measure of bourbon into the water as they boiled so that "they would die happy.") Tony continues: "We were taken on a special tour of the dome by a Vatican guide. This was not usually available to the public. After climbing endless steps, we finally entered the dome, and walked completely around it. Hundreds of feet below you could see the main altar. The acoustics up there were fantastic. If you whispered against the mosaic wall, a person on the opposite side of the dome could hear the whisper as clear as a bell.

"We finally left Rome for the long trip to Karachi, and arrived in the middle of the night. I was looking forward to a few hours of rest during the short layover time." But it was not meant to be. It was nearly morning; it was June; and Karachi was sizzling.

"The hotel was near a mosque," Tony says, "and we were subjected to regular, amplified calls to prayer from the nearby minaret. The hotel room, which I shared with the engineer, was very noisy—the hallway outside sounded like a main thoroughfare. The ancient ceiling fan creaked slowly around, creating additional hot air instead of cooling the room, and the curtains were too short, and let the sun slice in. It was not a restful layover. Karachi was our turn-around destination, and we set off for home that same evening, after the minimum layover time, still feeling exhausted, but hoping to have a glimpse of *Clipper America* on its round-the-world flight." The brand-new *Clipper America* was a more advanced Constellation than *Clipper Eclipse* on which Tony and Jane were working, and *America* was equipped with larger engines which were far less likely to overheat.

Tony continues: "I felt my spirits lifting at the thought of leaving the heat and sand behind. As I approached *Clipper Eclipse*, I noticed that my Air Force B4-type bag, containing my personal belongings, had not made it into the cargo compartment and was standing at the foot of the stairs. Rather than cause a delay by re-opening the cargo door, I picked up the bag and stowed it in the rear coat room."

The passengers struggled across the tarmac, carrying heavy tote bags and drooping from the heat and the frustration of waiting for the incoming aircraft to arrive in Karachi. Once they were on board, everyone heaved a sigh of relief. The interior was comfortable and they were finally setting off for their destinations.

The Constellation set off down the runway. On and on it went, utilizing the whole length. "It seemed forever before we left the ground," says Tony, "but weight was not the problem, the intense heat was. When we finally left the ground, it seemed an eternity before we reached cruising altitude. If the weather is hot, you can't take off at high gross weight, and you have to cut down the payload for every extra degree of heat. We just kept chugging along, chugging along, slowly, slowly climbing, inch by inch. Shortly after we were airborne, Jane and I started to serve refreshments. One of the pilots came into the galley for a cup of coffee, and I asked him why we were still climbing. He replied that the Number One engine was overheating and they had to ease back on the power."

Because of the delay in Karachi, there were only 26 passengers on board (one American, the rest British and Indian), so Tony and Jane were able to give them the opportunity to stretch out on the vacant seats. Once they had settled down, Tony told Jane to take her rest while he prepared some refreshments for the flight crew. "When I entered the cockpit to deliver them, I noticed both engineers monitoring the instrument panel and discussing the readings with the captain. It was quite evident the cockpit crew was concerned about the overheating. Shortly, Captain Hart shut down the engine and pushed the red button to feather its propellers." (The purpose of 'feathering' is to reduce the drag. The propeller blades are rotated on their axes so as to point forwards and slice into the wind rather than offer resistance.)

"Meanwhile, we were getting closer to Baghdad," continues Tony, "and we tried to reach the tower there, but after repeated attempts and no response, the captain decided to land in Damascus, the nearest alternate. I checked with one of the pilots for the estimated time of arrival, so that I could plan the breakfast service. 'You have plenty of time,' he said, 'we are flying on three engines on reduced power and we're way behind our flight plan.'"

The passengers were sleeping peacefully, unaware of any problems, so Tony began work on the time-consuming documentation. "In those days there was so much unnecessary red tape," he says. "We had to complete so many forms: cargo, passenger, general declaration, health, and customs, plus making sure the passengers completed theirs. Then I sat down next to Jane. I was going to awaken her and take my rest time, but all of a sudden, the forward cabin lit up." Number Two engine had caught fire, and Tony saw flames and sparks shooting past the window. Immediately, the seat belt and no smoking signs came on. Tony leapt up and woke Jane and they hurriedly made sure that the passengers' seats were upright, their seat belts fastened, and that no one was smoking. The third officer, Gene Roddenberry, entered the cabin with another "No smoking" reminder, and seated himself in a vacant seat in the rear of the cabin. Tony and Jane joined him in their usual places in the rear of the cabin, Jane by the window and Tony on the aisle. Suddenly, the burning engine fell off, the aircraft bounced in the air, and everything was black again outside for a couple of minutes. Then the wing started to burn, partially illuminating the cabin and creating an eerie aura. Captain Hart had no alternative but to decide on an emergency landing in the desert below, where the terrain was flat and the sand appeared to be smooth. The frightened passengers sat quietly, not uttering a sound, as the aircraft went into a steep descent.

Jane continues: "We kept going down and down and down. I don't know how many minutes it was; it seemed like a lifetime. But I knew that nothing was going to happen to me fatally. I don't know how I knew, but I just knew." During those minutes, Jane thought about her father who had recently had a stroke. She was convinced that news of a crash would kill him. Then she took a look at her watch; it was 12 o'clock Greenwich Mean Time.

Tony recalls, "I wasn't scared. I was too scared to be scared. Jane was holding on to me tightly, and I said 'Don't worry, honey. Everything will be fine.'"

The engines were unusually quiet as the aircraft circled and then went into its final approach. Suddenly there was a smooth, skidding bump and swerve. The aircraft swung a complete turn on the ground, and came to an abrupt halt with its nose digging into the sand at the original point of impact. The cabin was ripped open just behind the trailing edges of the wings, and the cockpit and galley areas were immediately engulfed in flames. Even so, a few of the passengers in the front section were able to jump out the opening. Tony recalls: "The whole front end was burning. It was an inferno from the wing forward, the cockpit, everything. After making such a spectacular landing, those brave men up front never had a chance."

Jane continues: "We opened the rear door, and we just started shoving passengers out. We pushed them, threw them, kicked them, anything to get them out because they were still groggy with sleep. We had to get them out and away from the airplane because it was going to explode. All you could hear was our voices shouting 'GET AWAY FROM THE AIRPLANE.' We dragged them, we pulled them, we *had* to get them away from the airplane. A lot of people were burned, had broken legs and cuts. They were very sick and very hurt."

Three of the four passengers at the rupture point died instantly. Tony, Gene, and an uninjured passeger assisted the fourth to safety away from the airplane, but he died shortly thereafter. Then they went to the aid of a heavy-set Indian woman, who had remained frozen in place, her hands gripping the arm rests. They pried her fingers open and gently but firmly eased her from her seat and assisted her out of the cabin.

As soon as all the passengers were off and had been directed away from the airplane, Tony, Gene, and Jane rushed on board again and tossed every-thing out of the coat room that was not nailed down: the first aid kit, the ship's brief case, the water thermos, paper cups, a bundle of blankets, some pillows, Tony's B4 bag (the only piece of luggage to survive the crash), and, as a last thought, the life raft. There was no food; the galley was in flames in the front of the aircraft, flames that were beginning to spread to the rear section. Jane continues: "We were in such a hurry, and the life raft was stuck to the wall because of the heat, but we got it out."

Once on the ground, Gene Roddenberry, now the senior crew member, began calmly directing activities around the crash site. He assembled the survivors together. "They appeared to be calm and were deep in their own thoughts," Tony adds. "We used the passenger manifest and took a roll call, putting a check mark beside the names of those who answered. If they didn't answer, we assumed that they had perished."

Jane continues: "After the airplane blew up, we went back to see what had happened. The oxygen was in the galley, behind the cockpit, and it had exploded and ignited. We couldn't find any more officers. Seven brave men, all dead at their posts. We couldn't do anything for them. They didn't suffer because they suffocated." At this point, Jane, Tony, and Gene had the dreadful experience of turning their backs on their fellow crew members, heroic men who, by their airmanship, had made it possible for others to survive.

Suddenly, out of the darkness came the sounds of voices shouting, of horses' hooves, and the soft, deliberate footsteps of camels. The flames from *Clipper Eclipse* had attracted the attention of some Bedouins a few miles away. "They kept pointing to the sky and then away from us. They must have been indicating the flaming engine as it fell," Tony says. They had arrived to offer help. One of them spoke some French and Tony was able to communicate with him; he learned there was a small village near the crash site where telephone service was available. They had crashed about 30 miles from Al Mayadin in northeast Syria, a small city with a hospital, close to the Euphrates River. Gene wrote a note for the Bedouins to carry and asked them to telephone from the village for assistance. They circled around, thoroughly inspected the accident site, removed some souvenirs, and then took off on their camels and horses, racing through the night with the dreadful news.

The night air was cool and some of the injured passengers felt the chill. Tony and Jane handed out blankets to make them more comfortable. Tony, however, found the cool air a welcome antidote after the intense heat and humidity of Karachi.

At daybreak, there was the drone of aircraft in the distance; it was a Syrian Air Force squadron on a training mission. Tony quickly inflated the life raft so that Gene could remove the flares it carried and light one. Up it went into the sky, and was immediately spotted by one of the Syrian pilots, who circled and then landed on the sand, much to the surprise and joy of the survivors. Gene was able to communicate in English with him, and the 'plane took off again for Al Mayadin, bearing a radio message.

By this time, the sun was well over the horizon, and the burned and injured passengers were beginning to suffer the effects of the heat. Tony offered sips of water from the thermos, and Jane handed out Charms, candies that were part of the life raft survival kit. "You'd be surprised how much energy that stuff gives you," says Tony.

"Jane was so wonderful," he continues. "In those days, the stewardess had to wear uncomfortable high heels all the time, and when she jumped off the 'plane, she sprained her ankle. But that didn't stop her; she hobbled around with a swollen ankle, giving aid to the injured survivors. With her Southern charm, she offered words of comfort and assured them that help was on its way. Jane adds: "It didn't hurt at first, and I had to get around. We had some interesting passengers who were uninjured, and they helped me with the first aid." (Three were uninjured. One of these, Captain Michael Graham, a former Royal Air Force pilot working for Indian Air Services, had previously been shot down or crashed ten times in combat. On arrival in the States, he received a telegram from Bombay: "Greetings darling indestructible Michael, you lucky kid." Signed: "Sandra.")

Tony's seat belt severely bruised his ribs when the aircraft swerved around, but that did not stop him either. The sun was rising high in the sky and the desert air was no longer cool when Tony realized that he could make a tent for his injured passengers if he erected the life raft's nylon shade. The uninjured survivors helped him lift the seriously wounded passengers into the raft, and soon they felt the benefits of Tony's ingenuity as they rested under the shade.

Towards the middle of the day, when the thermos of water had been exhausted and the injured passengers were in dire need of medical attention, a whirlwind of dust appeared on the horizon. It was a small caravan of jeeps and vans arriving to transport the survivors to Al Mayadin, about an hour's drive away. After assisting the passengers on board the more comfortable vehicles, Jane and Tony climbed on board an open-top jeep. As the last vehicle in the caravan, it was subject to the clouds of sand whirling up from those ahead of them. "The dust was terrible," Tony recalls. "I remember Jane's beautiful blonde hair was stiff with it. Our eyes and noses were full of it. Our mouths were full of it. We were already so thirsty, and although it didn't seem possible that anything could make it worse, that dust made us thirstier than before."

At that point, Tony experienced the classic mirage. The scene changed. Out of the dust appeared a shimmering blue lake with green palm trees surrounding its edge. Tony imagined himself scooping up a handful of water and wetting his parched lips.

In those days, Pan American had a few DC-3s and instructors based in Damascus to train Syrian pilots. Shortly after the survivors reached Al Mayadin, one of the DC-3s arrived there to fly the survivors to Damascus, where the more seriously injured, including Jane, were taken immediately to

*Jane Bray receives a
welcome-home kiss from
her sister. Michael Graham
(bottom left) and Tony Volpe
(far right).*

hospital. Jane remembers the kindness of the consulate wives who made a special point of visiting her that night. "They brought me some clothes because mine were so bloody, and that made me feel a lot better."

In spite of the horrors he had lived through, an exhausted Tony Volpe finally secured a good night's sleep in the hotel in Damascus. To ensure his rest, he first made a visit to the bar, where he had a couple of screwdrivers to relax himself. The bartender, who had learned about the accident and wanted to commiserate with the crew, was overgenerous with the vodka, and Tony had no trouble at all sinking into well-earned oblivion. Jane, meanwhile, was presented with a pair of crutches before she fell asleep.

Clipper Eclipse was nothing but a few charred fragments when Alice Lemieux on *Clipper America* arrived to her rapturous welcome in Tokyo.

✈ ✈ ✈ ✈ ✈

Gene Roddenberry left Pan American shortly after this incident and returned to his home in Los Angeles to pursue a career in Hollywood. A visionary writer even during his days as a Pan Am pilot, he became the author and producer of the *Star Trek* series. The Trekkers among you may be interested in the letter shown opposite. It includes three paragraphs from a letter Gene Roddenberry wrote to Richard O'Leary, Pan American's superintendant of flight service.

PAN AMERICAN WORLD AIRWAYS SYSTEM

ATLANTIC DIVISION, NEW YORK AIRPORT STATION, LA GUARDIA FIELD, NEW YORK   .

August 7, 1947

Mr. Anthony Volpe
Pan American World Airways System
LaGuardia Field, New York

Dear Mr. Volpe:

We are quoting below a letter that we received from Mr. E. W. Roddenberry,
(3rd Officer), Jr. Pilot:

> "As the senior surviving crew member of Clipper 88845 which
> crashed at Mayadine, Syria on June 18, 1947. I wish to file
> with your department this report commending the personal
> courage and professional ability of both Tony Volpe, Purser,
> and Miss Jane Bray, Stewardess.
>
> Were this the military service, with which I am more familiar,
> I am certain they would by this time have received decorations
> commensurate with the valor and merit they demonstrated.
> However, the company and the public are well aware of this
> fact and I request that this report be placed in their personal
> files as a matter of record.
>
> It would be easy to cover several pages pointing out incidents
> in which one or the both were involved which would prove
> their courage again and again. In the performance of rescue
> and medical aid they demonstrated beyond coolness and ability,
> a high degree of training of which your department can be
> proud. Rather than continue at length, I direct your attention
> to the survivors reports of the accident and to the many letters
> since received from passengers and their families further
> praising these actions."

We would like to add our commendations and tell you how pleased we are
with the way you conducted yourself.

R. E. O'Leary
Flight Service Supt.

REOL:pfc

The System of the Flying Clippers

Berlin

For a while Berlin remained a phenomenon, existing on sheer nerve, like a trainer's head in a lion's mouth.

Fodor's *Germany*

On 24 June 1948, all traffic to and from West Berlin was blocked by the Soviet administration in East Berlin. This interdiction on the movement of goods and passengers effectively cut off the Western sectors of Berlin from the rest of the world. The great Berlin Airlift began the next day on the orders of General Lucius Clay, the American military governor, and for the next 11 months, in approximately 200,000 flights, essential provisioning was brought into the city by French, British, and U.S. aircraft. All carriers were required to fly below 10,000 feet in three narrow air corridors between Berlin and and the rest of West Germany, corridors which were vigilantly monitored by the U.S.S.R. American Overseas Airlines (A.O.A.) provided the U.S. airline assistance during the Airlift. Pan American's relationship with Berlin did not officially begin until 1950 when the company acquired A.O.A., whose employees included several who had worked in beleaguered West Berlin during the blockade.

Fred Stecher, from Siegen in West Germany, worked for the Control Commission for Germany (British Element) at Gatow before he joined A.O.A., and he describes conditions in Berlin during the blockade: "There was nothing to be had in the city, no food, no fuel, and we were completely cut off from the outside world. Electricity was rationed to a few hours a day, and candles were almost impossible to find. We were totally isolated.

"At work, I made out manifests, and I was extremely busy because we had a flight every two minutes. They brought in everything, including coal and salt, and in all those flights of DC-3s and other small aircraft, we never had an accident. We worked closely with personnel at the other two airports, and I often visited Tempelhof. The approach to Tempelhof was very difficult because the flight path was right between high-rise apartment houses. When the pilots came in, they flew right over a cemetery, then between the buildings, going so low and slow that they almost hit the ground, but during this low approach they would throw candy and chocolates out the cockpit window

91

Fred Stecher and the Stratocruiser.

to the kids down below. The kids called them '*Chocolaten Bomber*' or '*Rosinen Bomber.*'"

At a young age, Fred had taken gliding lessons and quickly acquired his soaring license. The job at Gatow airport only served to whet his appetite for flying, and he desperately wanted to find work with an airline. He approached a friend who worked for American Overseas Airlines at Tempelhof Airport. "I really got on their nerves because I went over there not once but twice a week," says Fred. Eventually his persistence paid off, and he was offered a job as a cargo loader for A.O.A.'s DC-4 aircraft. "I wasn't fussy. I enjoyed cargo loading, and later on I was glad because I understood the way an airline is run, from checking the baggage, where it goes, how it's loaded, and what the baggage compartment looks like. Most flight attendants never know that. But I wasn't unhappy when a job came up in reservations. We were just three people in reservations, for a big city like Berlin, and we sat on chairs at a round table, which had charts for each day's flight on a carousel. We had to spin the carousel to make bookings. Very primitive."

Lufthansa, Germany's national airline, was prohibited at that time from flying into Berlin because of the city's unique political position, an enduring hangover from World War II. This, combined with the purchase of American Overseas Airlines on 25 September 1950, opened the way for Pan American to initiate its Internal German Service. On that day, Fred became a Pan American employee; he continued working at the ticket counter, steadily moving towards his goal of a job in the air. "I was still determined to fly, but at that time Pan American only hired females, Scandinavian females, to work on the I.G.S. A little later they started hiring German girls, but still no men."

Fred's dream of flying finally came true at the end of his second vacation in the United States. On both occasions, he presented himself at the Flight Service Office in New York. On his second visit, he was asked, "Can you start training tomorrow?" Fred could and did. He packed up and left Berlin in less than 24 hours, and soon became one of Pan Am's valued pursers, working on the 'President's Special' Stratocruiser flights—Flight 100 to London and Flight 114 to Paris—and on the rest of the Pan Am fleet.

One of the Scandinavian stewardesses mentioned by Fred was **Gwen Persson**. She was not entirely Scandinavian, having been born in Britain to a Welsh mother and a Swedish father. However, when she was six months old, the family moved to Copenhagen, where Gwen was educated. She continued to visit Britain during school vacations, and learned to speak English and a little Welsh.

Gwen was in her teens when the Germans occupied Denmark, and she describes that experience: "Tanks rolled up and down the streets. We had to be home by 8 p.m. for the curfew. There were all kinds of restrictions. You couldn't even leave a window open in the summertime. We couldn't move at all; we couldn't go to Sweden; for five years we couldn't leave Denmark at all. My mother and I had to be very, very quiet because we had been born in Britain. When the Germans left, I was 19 years old, and I said to myself, 'I am going to get out of here at last.'

"My nose has always been in newspapers, to this day, particularly their employment sections. I was always looking for a wonderful job and dreaming about escape. One day, an advertisement jumped out at me. It announced that American Overseas Airlines was looking for a couple of stewardesses to fly inside Scandinavia. They asked us to come to a downtown hotel in Copenhagen for an interview. It was just what I was looking for."

When Gwen arrived at the hotel, the lobby was teeming with young women. "Thousands and thousands of girls were there," Gwen continues. "Two guys from A.O.A. in New York interviewed us and then flew on to Sweden and Norway and went through the same routine there. They only took four girls—myself and Ruth 'Chris' Christensen from Denmark, plus one from Norway, and one from Sweden. They made three different visits to check us out, and the whole process took 18 months.'

Gwen believes that she was chosen because of her British heritage and the interviewers' automatic assumption that her English would be stronger than the other applicants'. (Like the rest of them, Gwen also spoke the three Scandinavian languages and German.)

The chosen four were flown to New York on 1 January 1949 for six weeks of training, and then based in Stockholm. They flew, in DC-3s, from Stockholm to Helsinki, and in DC-4s from Stockholm via Copenhagen to Iceland and then to Ireland. A.O.A.'s New York-based crew would take over the flights from Iceland to New York. Gwen continues: "This was because the union would not allow us to go all the way to the United States. We were A.O.A.'S very first foreign nationals; we opened the door, but the union would not let us all the way in at that point.

"After a year, the union decided that even Stockholm was illegal. The American cabin crew didn't want to disembark in Iceland and sit there for a week; they wanted to go on to Sweden. That's when A.O.A. got the idea of moving us Scandinavian girls to Berlin to fly within Germany.

"Because everything had been bombed in Berlin and there was nowhere for us to stay in the city, A.O.A. made a special deal for us to live in the officers' club, right next to Tempelhof Airport. We didn't suffer any deprivation because our lodging and meals were provided."

Then rumors started flying concerning Pan American's plan to buy A.O.A., rumors that became more and more persistent. Finally, the stewardesses were warned, "We do not know what Pan American wants, how long you are going to be with us. We just want you to be prepared for the worst."

At first after the purchase, Pan American kept the status quo in Berlin, and Gwen and the other three were shortly joined by a few Belgian and Dutch stewardesses. Shortly afterwards, however, Pan

Gwen Persson (left) and Ruth Christensen (McNiven) during their A.O.A. days.

Am decided to hire German stewardesses exclusively. Gwen continues: "It was a purely economic decision. They figured it would cost less money; we had a cost-of-living allowance because we were not in our own country and we lived in the officers' club. The German girls would be able to live at home.

"Pan Am didn't know what to do with us. They finally decided to offer us three months' employment to train the German girls and a one-way ticket to visit the States which had to be used in three months. Just a one-way ticket and no promise of a job on arrival! But I thought, 'Why not?' I wanted to travel. Here's another thing: I was able to obtain a visa for the U.S. right away. Because I was born in Britain, my quota for the visa was large. Had I been under the Danish quota, I would not be in America today."

When Gwen arrived in New York, she visited Pan Am and asked them to hire her back. They turned her down, citing union regulations. "Then I joined a little fly-by-night outfit; I can't even remember its name. They had one DC-3, which they flew to St. Louis and back. I was to be their sole stewardess. They didn't have a uniform, and when I told them I still had my A.O.A. uniform, they said, 'Put it on.' So I did, and I made one flight for them to St. Louis and back. On my return, I had a call from Pan American. The union had made an exception and the company was now ready to hire the Berlin stewardesses who had taken up the offer of the one-way ticket to the United States."

Gwen's career as an international flight attendant had just begun. Now she would truly be able to see the world beyond the curfew of her teens.

As soon as Pan American had consolidated its Internal German Service, the 30 or so stewardesses they hired in Germany were based at first in Frankfurt. In the early years, they deadheaded (flew as passengers from one city to another to pick up a working flight) into Berlin, whence, in unpressurized DC-4s, they would fly for five or six days at a stretch to other major German cities, four or six legs each day. Later, when tensions eased somewhat, the I.G.S. base was moved back to Berlin. "Some people thought it wasn't safe and were afraid, but we did it and nothing happened. I had no problem with it at all," says **Ingrid Gabrielli (Lubienicki).**

Ingrid was born in Austria. In 1955, when she decided she wanted to become a flight attendant, Austria had no airline and she had to look around for other options. She found Pan American's Internal German Service. It was challenging work. She explains that the I.G.S. stewardesses had to work extremely fast because all the flights were so short. Good teamwork was essential, and senior flight attendants would often 'bid down' in order to stay with a particularly competent junior partner. The flights were often bumpy because of the 3,000 metre (9,000 feet) altitude limit, and this added to the challenge. In spite of the rush to complete a meal service in a bare minimum of time, most of the stewardesses enjoyed working on the I.G.S. team and serving passengers who flew in and out of West Berlin on a regular basis, people who always sat in the same seat, people they came to know. (In fact, in 1965, after Boeing 727s were brought into service in the I.G.S., the stewardesses had to work even faster, often serving 128 passengers and the cockpit crew in the 35 minutes between Berlin and Hannover.)

For the most part, the short hops between German cities meant rather predictable flying. However, lightning can strike anywhere. Ingrid recalls that on a flight between Berlin and Cologne, there was a sudden tremendous THWACK! —a horrendous noise—and the aircraft dropped like a stone before levelling off. "I thought it was the end. I really thought my last hour had come," says Ingrid. The laden tray she was carrying sailed out of her hands, and everything loose in the cabin flew up in the air and scattered all over the cabin.

In the cockpit, Captain Lodesen immediately recognized what had happened, and his quiet, reassuring voice came over the public address system, saying, "Please do not be concerned. We were just hit by lightning, but nothing serious has occurred; all devices are functioning." The aircraft continued to Cologne, and landed safely, but the passengers were extremely shaken up although there had been no injuries and no panic at the time. "We kept smiling and smiling," says Ingrid, "and everyone stayed calm." When she disembarked, she saw the huge hole that the lightning had made in the rudder, and realized how very lucky they had been.

Like Fred Stecher, Ingrid was impressed by the approach to Berlin. "It was almost like flying down a street with houses left and right, and when you approached in the evening, you could peer into the lighted rooms and check out what was happening." On one occasion, Ingrid had a special bird's eye view of Berlin: "The door opened unexpectedly as we were circling. I called the first officer, but then I thought, 'Oh oh, this is urgent. I'd better do it quickly myself.' I grabbed a husky passenger, and made him anchor himself and hold on to me so I wouldn't fly out. It was so strange to be looking down and seeing the houses flash directly beneath me as I reached out for the door."

That bird's eye glimpse was one of Ingrid's last views of Berlin. With the advent of jets and the increase in trans-Atlantic travel, Pan American needed multi-lingual cabin crew to fly out of New York, and started to lure stewardesses away from Berlin. Ingrid immediately transferred, to take advantage of the travel opportunities.

The Pregnant Whale

[The Stratocruiser] looked as ponderous as the Constellation looked graceful. It seemed to bore its way through the air, defying apparent theories of clean aerodynamics. It was, in fact, as fast as the Constellation, and set up many point-to-point records. The feature for which it is best remembered is the lower deck lounge, fitted out as a cocktail bar, a welcome diversion during the long trans-Atlantic flights. Largely because of the bar, the Stratocruiser was invariably used by the airlines for luxury or first-class service.
R.E.G. Davies, *Pan Am: An Airline and its Aircraft*

"The Boeing 377 was a wonderful gift to the passenger; it was the best airplane for the passenger ever invented. It had four beautiful Pratt & Whitney engines and a gorgeous interior, even though the exterior looked so ungainly. The crews called it the Pregnant Whale," says **Grace Burtt (Walker)**.

"It was like a hotel, decorated mostly in blue and white. There were 87 lounge seats, and 12 upper and 12 lower berths could be provided for overnight flights. There were also two staterooms up forward, and a cocktail lounge downstairs. Even the two restrooms, one for men and one for women, were large and luxurious. People could go in there and change their clothes to get ready for bed," says **Mickey de Angelis**.

Grace continues: "The cocktail bar seated 14 people, and it was very popular, especially at night on those trans-Atlantic flights, which took between nine and 11 hours going over, longer coming back. There were armrests between those 14 seats, and on one flight a famous (huge) tennis champion asked if he could sleep in the lounge. 'Not possible,' I said, shaking my head, 'Those armrests are permanent.' 'No, they aren't,' he said, grasping two of them and yanking them straight up and out of their fittings.

"But the Stratocruiser had flaws as far as flight service was concerned," Grace adds. The galley was in the tail of the airplane, which fishtailed terribly, and passengers in the front could not understand why, if there was any sort of turbulence, we could not serve meals. We literally could not stand up.

"There were two bunks in the cockpit for the flight crew to rest on. There were none for the cabin crew, but on the lower level, at the back of the

Mickey de Angelis

cocktail lounge, going into the tail, was a cargo compartment whose door was never locked. We used to take blankets and pillows and slip in there to sleep on the mailbags when it was our turn to rest. It was dark and cold, a wonderful place to sleep if you had blankets, although I wonder why we weren't bashed to death against the roof of the cargo compartment in all that turbulence. But we weren't; we were young and fearless."

✈ ✈ ✈ ✈ ✈

Grace Burtt Walker was born and raised in Ferndale, Michigan, a small town just outside Detroit. She attended Hillsdale College and majored in music (voice), but found her studies disrupted by World War II. Wanting to serve her country, she left college to attend the Hartung Flying School in Rosedale, Michigan. After a year of ground school and flying lessons in Piper Cubs, she won her pilot's license. She applied to and was accepted by the Women's Air Service Pilots, and was all set to go to work for them when the war ended and the WASPs were disbanded.

In 1946, she went to Japan as an employee for the U.S. Government, and worked in Tokyo for two years. However, flying was still in her blood and she wrote to Pan American from Japan for an application to become a stewardess. On her return to the U.S., she passed her interview and language test in Japanese and was assured of a job on the West Coast. However, Grace wanted to fly the Atlantic, and so she returned home to Michigan and went to Berlitz to brush up her college French. The reward for her efforts was a telegram from Pan

Beauty in the eye of the beholder.

Am inviting her New York. In two days she packed up her belongings, said her farewells, and set out for more interviews and language tests. She became a member of the September 1948 class at Pan Am's training facilities at LaGuardia Airport.

Mickey de Angelis was born in New York. In 1942, he was playing baseball professionally, having spent a season in Nova Scotia, followed by the winter season in Panama. One day, after returning to New York, he was out practicing, and was hailed by an old high school friend, a Pan American employee who asked, "How'd you like to fly? There's a steward's opening." Mickey replied "I don't know anything about food." "They have a class. They'll teach you," his friend rejoined. The ballplayer thought it over, and then flew to many bases and made countless short stops during his 33-year Pan Am career.

Some of the Rich and Famous

The rich and famous loved the Stratocruiser. Mickey recounts his encounter with Errol Flynn on a flight from London to New York. "The station manager in London said to me, 'Take care of him if you can; he's had a rough trip so far.' So I made him comfortable and served him a beautiful dinner. Then the captain said, 'Do anything you can for him. Why don't you give him a stateroom?'

"I went up to Mr. Flynn and said, 'I know people will probably bother you, so how would you like the stateroom, compliments of Pan American?' He said 'That would be great. I'd really like some rest.' I made up both berths in the stateroom for him, so that he could have his preference, and told him they were ready for him any time. Then I went down to relieve the stewardess in the bar and told her, 'See that Mr. Flynn gets his berth all right.' It wasn't two minutes before she was back again saying 'You'd better go upstairs. He says his berth isn't ready.' I was puzzled. I quickly filled up the guests' drinks and then excused myself and went upstairs with the stewardess walking behind me. I walked into the stateroom and said 'Mr. Flynn. Having a problem?' 'Yeah. The berth isn't ready,' he replied. I pulled the curtains back and said 'Look, it's ready. What's wrong?' He said 'She isn't in it,' pointing to the stewardess. He winked, and she ran out of there, saying 'I'm not going back in that place.' He apologized and said 'I hope I didn't scare her,' and I said 'You sure did.'"

"One of the few problems we had with the 'plane was that not everybody who wanted them could have bunks," Grace recounts. "And Pan Am would sometimes oversell. One time Jack (H.J.) Heinz, was on board. He was a constant passenger with Pan Am, and we all adored him, a real gentleman, attractive, funny, and considerate. After dinner he said to me 'I have Bunk 11.' I was horrified because I knew it was taken. I said 'Oh dear, Bunk 11 is already occupied.' 'No problem,' he said. 'Just bring me an extra pillow; I'll sleep in my seat.' He took everything in stride. People were different then, they really were.

"There was another time coming out of Frankfurt during the Airlift, when I saw someone coming up the gangway, wearing jeans, a T-shirt, and a leather jacket. He looked very familiar, and I thought he was a Pan Am mechanic I recognized from Gander. He asked if he could sit in the lounge, and I said 'Sure, but don't tell anyone.' Then I started hustling coats back and hanging them up, and the next thing I knew he was back again, asking 'How soon can I get a drink?' I said 'Hey, you know the rules. I can't serve you liquor until we're airborne. Either go down there and sit and be quiet, or come up and help me.' So he came up and asked what he could do. I said 'Stand back by the coat closet. I'll collect the coats, tag them, and then you hang them up.' He worked pretty hard, but I insisted that he work harder because we had a lot to do.

"A passenger came up to me, laughing, and said 'You certainly have a good helper, even if he is famous.' I swung around. 'What do you mean famous?' 'Don't you recognize Montgomery Clift?' he asked. I was so embarrassed. It was amusing for Mr. Clift but, believe you me, I waited on him hand and foot after that. He had been filming *The Big Lift* on location in Germany.

"The only time Winston Churchill ever flew on a commercial airliner was on a Pan American Stratocruiser," says Mickey. "I was fortunate to be chief purser on that flight. The whole of the first-class section was partitioned off for him and his entourage, which included his bodyguard and his nurse. We served him a seven-course dinner, and when we came to the entrée, I said 'Sir, what is your preference? Filet mignon or lobster thermidor?' and he responded 'I'll have the lobster, then the steak.'

"I went all over the Far East on the Stratocruiser with the Eisenhower press charters. The press were really great, and they loved that airplane because there was plenty of space to stand around talking. The most interesting thing is that the press always landed first. I said to one guy 'I guess you have to get your cameras ready to take pictures of the president getting off the airplane,' and he said 'We're there first in case there's an accident.' It made me feel strange to be taking these fellows around, fellows just waiting for an accident."

Grace recalls: "They were always having inaugurals for the Stratocruiser. Pan American was so proud of that airplane; I was even on an inaugural to Cairo, a place that was not a Pan American destination. I flew in from London, had a very brief layover in Rome, got back on the aircraft, and flew on to Beirut. We just had enough time there to change uniforms and pick up two extra pursers before taking off for Cairo. The flight was jam-packed with press who were scrutinizing the airplane.

"We tried to serve 114 people a deluxe meal in just two hours of flight time in an aircraft designed for far fewer passengers. It was impossible. I remember looking out of the window and seeing the Pyramids for the first time in my life. I fled up to the cockpit and said 'Captain, captain, don't land. We're not ready.' We had just served the meals (the passengers had been quite serious about the cocktail service). The captain circled the city until we could land without too many trays on too many laps.

"During the flight, people kept saying to me '*Joyeux Anniversaire,*' and I thought 'Why are they saying that to me? It's not my birthday.' When we landed in Cairo, finally, and disembarked, I was surrounded by photographers wanting to take my picture. I thought it was because of the new aircraft and I kept pointing to it, but they really did want me for something the publicity agents had trumped up. It was, in fact, 15 May 1950, and was the 20th anniversary to the day of Ellen Church's first flight, and I had been chosen to represent all the stewardesses in the world rolled into one, for that particular day.

"We had worked so hard and I looked terrible. It seemed like years since I'd had a shower. My uniform was soiled, and the heat was fierce. But I pulled myself together and was handed a huge horseshoe of beautiful flowers. Huge. As I received it, I crashed to the ground under its weight. The flowers were actually nailed to a heavy wooden framework, and I just couldn't hold it. It was so funny. Finally, they managed to prop the horsehoe on a counter, put me behind it, and took my picture. I didn't see the Cairo papers, but the one in Beirut had a caption that said 'Miss Burtt has been flying for 20 years.' It certainly felt as though I had.

"We were on the ground for about four hours, and we gave free rides over the city to anyone who wanted them. The first time, it seemed as though everybody in Cairo crammed onto the airplane. Women were holding two or three children, couples were sitting on each other's laps. I set off for the cockpit to tell the captain that something was wrong, but was intercepted by a man who said 'Would you take my card to the captain and ask him to come back here?' I looked at the card; he was an F.A.A. inspector. We went to the cockpit together and brought the captain back. He was furious with the purser and the ground crew who had let all these people on. Half of them disem-

"I crashed to the ground under its weight."

barked and waited for the next flight. For the next four hours, we loaded people on and off the airplane and flew round and round over Cairo. The airplane was a huge success. Everybody loved it, even if their flight on it was just that little circle over Cairo. Finally, we returned to Beirut at the end of the day. Everything was a blur at that point."

Mickey and Grace were chosen to work on the President's Specials, the deluxe, trans-Atlantic flights that I have already mentioned. They both recall the passengers' astonishment at the level of service provided, the seven-course menus with seven choices of entrée, the variety of wines and liqueurs, the elegant gifts of orchids and perfume for the women and cigars for the men.

"In spite of all that elegance," counters Grace, "we were still wearing that dreadful uniform from Smith-Gray, whose main business was making uniforms for the military. I felt it was important to do something about it. I had noticed that in Paris all the Pan Am ground crew and ticket counter women looked smashing, even though they were apparently wearing the same uniform as we were. I thought 'You can't tell me that every French woman has a perfect figure.' So I said to one of my friends, 'Mireille, how come your uniforms look so feminine and ours look like Naval officers'?' 'Oh, we have to take them to our local dressmakers for fittings once Pan Am gives them to us,' she answered, as if it was the most obvious thing in the world. I asked the name of her 'local dressmaker,' and on my next flight, I walked over to the very French lady's nearby apartment to see what she could do for me. I put my uniform on and said 'Please taper it like Mireille's.' The dressmaker looked at me and exclaimed 'Sacré bleu! Jean, Jean, viens ici.' Her husband came running, took one look at me, threw up his hands and said 'Sacré bleu!'

"They pulled that uniform apart; took the padding out of the shoulders and put it at the hips, inserted a tape at the waist, and cut the voluminous skirt down, drastically down, so that it was almost a straight skirt with a pleat in front.

"It was a wonderful success. I took every uniform I had to that dress-maker. At first I didn't tell anyone what I was doing, but my roommates noticed how good I looked and said 'How come?' I told them about my French dressmaker, and immediately they started bidding Paris. All of a sudden the company caught on—they couldn't help but notice; it was a stunning change. Out came a ruling: 'Uniforms will not be modified. They must be worn as produced by Smith-Gray.'" But it wasn't long after that we started having designer uniforms.

"I was always a trouble-maker with Pan Am because I would write my ideas to Mr. Trippe or anyone in Pan Am's top management. The company was then still small enough for a single voice to be heard. For instance, I asked for a map in the seat pocket. In those days, the flight to Gander was especially long and dull, no matter how many magazines or newspapers you had, no matter how good the company was. It occurred to me that it would be entertaining if we had a map showing where we were flying, with a little bit of text about the countries. The responses to my proposals were pretty typical of a corporation: 'That's a nice idea, and thank you for writing, Grace.' But I think management kept everyone's ideas and suggestions and reviewed them. Two years down the line, a wonderful little map suddenly appeared in the seat pockets. Then I started agitating for cheaper fares and tourist class because I did so want people like my family to travel, ordinary Americans, and to be seen by people in other countries. I wrote and nagged and talked to people about this. I'm not solely responsible for the initiation of tourist class in Pan Am, but the company always claimed I was."

Coming in for a landing in New York, Grace noticed that someone had taken her seat. Looking around for an alternative, she saw a handsome man beckoning her to him. He said, "Come here. I survived the Pan Am crash in the desert, and as my reward, all the stewardesses get to sit on my knee." It was the intrepid Michael Graham.

✈ ✈ ✈ ✈ ✈

The age of mass transportation was about to begin. On 1 May 1952, Pan American inaugurated its all-tourist 'Rainbow' service between New York and London on the DC-6B. However, the Stratocruiser kept working, and was the last of the piston-engine aircraft to be retired from the North Atlantic prestige

Grace Burtt

routes. The beloved, snub-nosed airplane, which came off the same production line as the B-29 and B-50 Superfortress bombers, is still remembered by air passengers as being the epitome of luxurious flying in much the same way that the *Queen Mary* is remembered by those who sailed the oceans.

Ditching by the Book

Brute power was not the answer or the most important element; instead it was control, and balance.
                                                  Oliver Jensen, *Wind and Sand*

Although **Katherine Shiroma (Araki)** was born in Honolulu, her parents came from Okinawa, so she grew up speaking both Japanese and English. She joined Pan American upon graduating from the University of Hawaii, and was a member of the first group of Japanese-speaking stewardesses, young women who were hired expressly for their language ability on Pan Am's Tokyo flights. All of Japanese ancestry, five of them hailed from Oahu and two from the mainland. They flew exclusively between Japan and the United States, and were based in Honolulu. By 17 October 1956, Katherine had been flying that route for two years.

Clipper *Sovereign of the Skies* was one of eight Boeing 377 Stratocruisers that Pan American acquired when it merged with American Overseas Airlines in 1950. Shortly after the merger, *Sovereign of the Skies* was moved to the Pacific, where it performed efficiently over the long stretches of water. By 17 October 1956, it had flown 19,800 safe miles, and there was no indication that any of its four engines might give trouble on the 2,395-mile flight from Honolulu to San Francisco.

A four-man cockpit crew was ready to fly the airliner: Captain Richard Ogg, First Officer Lee Haaker, Second Officer Dick Brown, and Flight Engineer Frank Garcia; the cabin was staffed by three competent young women: Purser Pat Reynolds and Stewardesses Katherine Araki and Mary Ellen (Lynn) Daniel. Just 24 passengers would be aboard that night: 13 Americans (including a Naval officer, Commander Strickler, and a pair of two-and-a-half-year-old girl twins), three Japanese businessmen, four Filipinos (including two doctors and a three-year-old girl), a student from Taiwan, an Indonesian, a Dutchman, and a French doctor. However, there was a surprisingly large animal load in the belly of the aircraft: two dogs, 3,300 canaries, and a parakeet called Tippy.

Fourteen of the passengers had already made the long flight from Tokyo, and a mere ten more embarked in Honolulu to make the total of 24. Again and again, Katherine repeats: "It was a surprisingly empty 'plane. Really, it was such a light load. It was a blessing."

The Clipper was half an hour late leaving. As soon as the passengers boarded, Katherine started work in the tourist-class section, settling 13 passengers into their seats in the forward section of the aircraft. One passenger handed her several leis to store in plastic bags in the refrigerator. Lynn Daniel welcomed the 11 first-class passengers to the luxurious rear section. Then, as Purser Pat Reynolds began the emergency announcements, the two stewardesses showed the passengers where their life jackets (called Mae Wests in those days) were located and demonstrated how to use them. Little did they realize how important that demonstration would prove to be.

The *Sovereign of the Skies* took off at 8:26 p.m., and as soon as the seat belt and no smoking signs were switched off, some of the passengers descended the flight of stairs to the cocktail lounge, where Pat fixed them the drinks of their choice. Lynn and Katherine started preparations for the dinner service: braised sirloin tips in the tourist section, and the 'Aloha Champagne Supper' in first-class. The menu included rock Cornish game hen with wild rice farci, served with Belgian spring carrots and baby Brussels sprouts, washed down with Champagne Brut-Almaden.

The Clipper had reached its initial cruising altitude of 13,000 feet when, as so often happens just at the moment when the meal service is ready, it hit some rough weather. This did not last long, but it was enough to put a few of the passengers off their food. The cabin crew were soon able to resume the meal service for those who wanted to eat. Then it was time to prepare the cabin for the night. Because there were just 13 people in the 35-person tourist section, Katherine was able to remove some armrests so that her passengers could stretch out for a decent night's sleep. The French army surgeon, Dr. Marcel Touzé, knocked back a couple of sleeping pills just to make sure.

In the first-class section, Lynn and Pat let down four berths, two for the twins and their parents, one for Hendrik Braat, the Dutch businessman (who donned his pajamas) and one for the Navy commander, Kenneth Strickler (who stretched out in his slacks and Hawaiian shirt). The other first-class passengers made themselves comfortable by pulling out the leg rests of their sleeperette chairs. The stewardesses handed out pillows and blankets and dimmed the lights. Soon the cabin was silent as the Clipper flew steadily across the ocean.

Before leaving Honolulu, Captain Ogg had received instructions to climb to a second cruising altitude of 21,000 feet just before the half-way point between Honolulu and San Francisco. He was also aware that the Coast Guard weather ship, the *Pontchartrain*, was in the vicinity of the half-way mark. Just before climbing to 21,000 feet, he made contact with the captain of the *Pontchartrain*, Commander Bill Earle, who confirmed for him that the weather ahead was clear. The *Sovereign of the Skies* started the climb, then leveled out on reaching the new altitude.

Twenty-three minutes later, a deafening whine penetrated the cabin, there was a sudden dip, and the aircraft started vibrating violently. Pat Reynolds fled up to the cockpit. As soon as Captain Ogg caught sight of her, he shouted "Pat, Number One engine may catch fire. Go back to the cabin and watch it."

This is what had happened: the propeller on that engine had gone out of control because the governor had ceased to function. The terrifying whine was caused by the propeller spinning wildly, and this in turn dragged the aircraft to the left, straining the engines. Lee Haaker was at the controls, and immediately started to descend to a lower altitude, while Captain Ogg tried to feather the propeller, a manoeuvre which was unsuccessful. He pressed the emergency switch which activated fire extinguishing foam onto the engine and told Frank Garcia to shut down the oil supply to it, freezing it. Then he contacted the *Pontchartrain:* "Ocean Station November. Ocean Station November. This is Clipper Niner-Four-Three. We are having engine trouble and may have to ditch alongside. Please prepare to assist."

In the cabin, the passengers were immediately awake and alert, waiting for instructions. Captain Ogg's calm voice came to them over the public address system: "Sorry to disturb you. We have an emergency and the possibility of ditching. Just to be on the safe side, I would like you to put on your life jackets and fasten your seat belts. Please follow instructions from your stewardesses."

The stewardesses switched on the cabin lights, helped the passengers into their life jackets, and reminded them of the rules for ditching. Katherine intoned the instructions to each of her passengers: "Put your seats in an upright position. Remove your shoes and glasses and any sharp objects you may have in your pockets. Pull your seat belts as tight as possible. Do not inflate your life jacket until you are outside the plane. No smoking please." Calmly and attentively, the passengers complied with her directions.

In two minutes, everyone was ready.

Below them, the *Pontchartrain* came to life. Until that night, the sailors had passed an uneventful (frankly, boring) three weeks of duty, and it was nearly time for them to switch with another weather ship and steam home; they were ready for some excitement.

The ship's radar center picked up the *Sovereign of the Skies* and charted her course. The decks swarmed with activity as the sailors manned their stations and fired star shells into the sky. Commander Earle gave the order to throw flares down on the water to illuminate a landing strip. Katherine describes what the *Pontchartrain* looked like from the air: "It just lit itself up so we could see it. You know, when Christmas comes and all the lights are on—it looked just like that. It was so reassuring."

On board the Clipper, with the threat of fire diminished by the foaming and with no necessity for immediate ditching, Captain Ogg began to hope that he could still feather the propeller and make it to San Francisco after all, but suddenly the propeller disengaged from the engine and started windmilling, causing considerable drag. Almost immediately, Number Four engine started sputtering and it, too, failed.

Even with one engine windmilling and the other at a standstill, Captain Ogg still felt he had a shot at reaching San Francisco without ditching. The Stratocruiser was certainly capable of flying on two engines. But with the added drag from the windmilling propeller, did he have enough fuel? The four men started calculating, and all came up with the same conclusion: there would be no fuel for the last 200 miles. They would have to ditch; the question was when they should ditch. Ditching in daylight is, to say the least of it, problematic. Ditching at night is suicidal because it is almost impossible to judge how far an aircraft is from the water and the swells. The crew started calculating again, and then they agreed that they had enough fuel to circle the *Pontchartrain* until daybreak. Captain Ogg informed the passengers of his decision, reassuring them that the Coast Guard cutter was standing by, and adding that he had learned that the water temperature was 74 degrees and the sailors had taken a dip the previous day.

Katherine reminds us: "Before this emergency, there had been another ditching off the Pacific Northwest, and Captain Ogg was on the hearing panel for it. He had learned that it was vital to move everyone forward over the wings in a ditching. Until then, we normally would stay back in the tail. We were so lucky that he knew this."

The stewardesses stowed the sleeping berths and moved all the passengers to seats over the wings. They instructed them to keep a sharp lookout for the three children in case they should be separated from their parents during the ditching; the children were seated so that they would be first out. Then they tossed all the hand luggage down into the cocktail lounge on the Stratocruiser's lower level, and stowed the galley equipment in the aft restrooms. When everything was secure, they went over the ditching instructions another time, and made sure that everyone was barefoot. In the calm that ensued, the stewardesses offered orange juice and Chiclets. Most of the passengers remained awake, a few dozed; Dr. Touzé's sleeping pills were still at work, so he drifted off into a sound sleep again. The Clipper droned in eight-mile circles around the *Pontchartrain* for three hours until dawn finally broke.

It has always been a mystery why the great ocean is called 'Pacific' when it is remembered by sailors instead for its huge rollers and giant storms. On the morning of 18 October 1956, however, it lived up to its name. Katherine describes it: "It was a beautiful, clear day, and I have never seen the ocean that calm, not a swell, nothing. It was like a lake on a still day. We were so fortunate that conditions were right."

She continues: "It's good to be young and naïve because I never really felt we were in danger. I thought we'd just go sliding in and stop, and then be picked up. We all thought we'd have time to grab our purses as we left, so we put them in a little compartment by the door."

With daylight on his side, Captain Ogg was ready to finalize plans for the ditching. Over the radio, Commander Earle assured him that conditions were perfect and that rescue boats had already been deployed. At last the long, tense wait was over. The captain's voice came over the public address system. The crew would ditch the aircraft in ten minutes' time. He would give a five-minute and a one-minute warning. He reminded the passengers to follow instructions to the letter. Then he began practice runs over the area where the men of the *Pontchartrain* were laying a foam runway.

While the stewardesses recited the ditching instructions a final time, Commander Strickler hurried down to the cocktail lounge, found his uniform case amidst the jumble of briefcases and overnight bags, and quickly changed into his uniform. When he came back upstairs, he found the stewardesses making sure that all the passengers had pillows on their laps and knew to clasp their hands under their knees. He sat down as they were checking all the seat belts one last time and ascertaining that the three children were safely held between their parents' legs. On the final approach, the adults would curl their bodies over them, acting as human shields. At the one-minute warning, the stewardesses finally sat down. "The atmosphere was so calm, and we were fortunate that there was no one excitable among the passengers or crew," adds Katherine.

The Clipper descended, lower and lower, and finally hit the water at a perfect angle, once gently, and once again with terrific force, a blow which must have instantly killed all the livestock in the belly. "They warn you in training that the impact of a 'plane on water is like hitting a brick wall. They're right. That's exactly what it felt like. Even with my seat belt on, I lunged forward and scraped my knees," recalls Katherine. Henrik Braat's seat belt snapped, and Commander Strickler swung up and then down onto the arm of a chair, gashing his head. One of the Filipino doctors flew through the air, inadvertently kicking another passenger en route, and landed several feet away. The 'plane swerved sharply and the tail section of the aircraft snapped off.

This dramatic sequence vividly illustrates a classic 'text-book' example of the result of applied discipline by an experienced cabin crew. As described in the accompanying chapter, this Stratocruiser had to ditch ignominiously into the

Pacific Ocean. The fuselage broke in half after the aircraft hit the water with terrific force. Every person on board was saved by the Clipper's life rafts and boats from the Coast Guard rescue boats.

Quickly, Pat Reynolds directed the opening of the wing exits and the deployment of the life rafts. With three rafts in the water, the passengers began their orderly exit. The flight crew extricated themselves from the cockpit, whose door had been jammed on impact, and found that the passengers were already stepping down from the wings into the rafts. At this point, with all the passengers out except one, Katherine was faced with a serious problem: "We had this tall, elderly woman on board, and the captain and I tried to push her out the door, but we couldn't get her through. Because of her age and height, it was hard for her to move and she couldn't figure out where to grasp a handhold to pull herself out. So I finally said to her, 'I'll go out and pull you while the captain pushes.' So I climbed out and gave her my hand and pulled as hard as I could, and between us we got her out, pulling and shoving."

Then it was Katherine's turn to step down into the life raft containing most of the women. Unfortunately, on that particular raft, only one of the air chambers had inflated, and when a male passenger, who had jumped into the water, swam up to it and was assisted aboard, the raft began to sink. However, help was close to hand. "The Coast Guard rescue boats, which had been launched before the Clipper went into the water, manoeuvred and came up real close," Katherine says. "We were submerged by the time they reached us, but the sea was so calm. We were so lucky."

The rescue boats hurried the dripping passengers to the *Pontchartrain*. Katherine vividly remembers clambering up the rope ladder to the ship and being wrapped in a warm blanket and offered some coffee. Then she turned to look back at the *Sovereign of the Skies*. She recalls: "The plane stayed completely afloat for 20 minutes, and the Coast Guard was even able to rescue some of the baggage that floated out. I had one of those old Pan Am bags with a zipper, containing my makeup, and that floated up. At least we could have some cream and some lipstick, and the officers and men of the cutter loaned us some clothes for the days we were on board. The crew of the *Pontchartrain* were wonderful. They took care of us all. And we were in constant interaction with our passengers. They all needed someone to talk to, to listen to their concerns, and to assure them that everything would be O.K."

Katherine continues: "Before docking in California, our Pan Am flight service boss came on board and, I couldn't believe this, but he had uniforms for us! He said 'We had so much trouble outfitting you three because you're so small.' So we came ashore in full uniform and shoes, ready to face the press and the crowds of relatives who were meeting passengers from the 'plane. It was so emotional."

Katherine was greeted by an enormous bouquet of roses, a gift from her husband and his instructors at the Naval Center in Newport, Rhode Island, where he was in training. Later that day, she flew back to her base in Honolulu, to replace her belongings and documentation, before returning to San Francisco for the hearing.

The cause of the accident was given as mechanical failure. Katherine continues, "Just a couple of years ago, I had a letter from the engineer who reminded me that I was the only one who testified that there was oil on the wing. They needed somebody in the cabin to verify that, and he said I was the only one to do so. He was very grateful that somebody out there had noticed it too.

"I thought we were a very competent and highly skilled crew. Our training was invaluable. In fact, one day I met a United Air Lines stewardess at a party and she said 'Did you know that the ditching you experienced is used as an example in our training for over-water emergencies?' So everybody learned from it.

"It was a ditching by the book. So fortunate."

Surprise Swim
In Jamaica

it is a cool harbour...
soft for ships, cloud, high, in shadow
prows cut their white teeth towards it
                    Edward Kamau Brathwaite, "Harbour"

Meanwhile, back in the Caribbean, Pan American had updated its fleet, replacing the steady, sturdy DC-3s with twin-engined, 40-seat Convair 240s. As R.E.G. Davies points out in *Pan Am: An Airline and its Aircraft,* "Though still thoroughly reliable, [the DC-3] was seen by Pan American and its clientèle as the airline equivalent of a steam locomotive in an era of diesel and electric traction." Passengers in the pressurized cabin of the Convair 240 flew comfortably from island to island.

In September 1951, a powerful hurricane swept across Jamaica, wreaking havoc, and smashing boats and piers in Kingston Harbour. Two days after the hurricane, small boats were still picking up debris, although the actual approach over the water to the airport at Palisadoes [later Norman Manley airport] had been cleared. It was a beautiful day with excellent visibility, and the water was as flat as glass. As the Convair 240 made its approach, the 29 passengers and four crew members could see people at work in their boats collecting the flotsam left behind by the wrath of the storm. Little did they realize that in a few seconds they would join those boats when the Convair set down about 800 feet short of the runway in 25 feet of water.

Robert Betancourt was born in Havana, Cuba, of a U.S. mother and a Cuban father. He came to the United States when he was six, and has lived there ever since. When he returned from service in World War II, he visited his parents in Miami, idling his days away until his brother-in-law, Nicholas Miranda, a purser with Pan American, prodded him into action, saying "Why don't you come down to the office here? They're looking for fellows and you'll have no trouble being hired since you're a high school graduate and a veteran." Bob went along, was interviewed, and hired on the spot. He started training the following week. He thoroughly enjoyed flying from island to island in the Caribbean, and his career was without serious incident until that September day in 1951. Bob describes what it was like:

"It was very smooth and we didn't feel any bump. Then all of a sudden we realized that something had gone wrong. Water was pouring into the cabin and there was a terrific rattling noise. People started crying out 'What's happened?' but there was no real panic. Dick Abbot, the purser, was sitting in the back of the 'plane by the door, and shouted up to me, in the jump seat in the galley, 'Bob, are you all right? We've landed in the water.' I yelled back 'Yeah, I'm O.K. We'd better go.' He opened the back door, threw out the raft, jumped in the water, inflated the raft, and helped people down into it. The passengers could step right into it, and most of them went out the back door with him. I took the rest, maybe three or four, including an unaccompanied ten-year-old boy and the co-pilot, through a hole where the wing had torn off, and we swam around to the raft. I was in the water for about five minutes, holding on until we got everyone, including a pregnant lady, into the raft.

"We were very lucky that those boats were out picking up debris, because one of them came straight to our aid, and we got everyone ashore very quickly. It wasn't until we were aboard the life raft and the boat that we noticed the 'plane sinking. Finally, there was just one wing sticking up out of the water. There were very few injuries, certainly none of them was serious, and they were all taken care of at First Aid in the terminal. I received a cut on my ankle when the galley equipment came loose and something hit my foot. I had a three-inch gash, but I didn't notice it until I was in the raft."

After the preliminary investigation at the airport, the crew stayed in Kingston at the airport manager's house until the Civil Aeronautics Administration (C.A.A.) had completed their investigation. Bob was given 30 days off when he returned to Miami. Like all those who have been through the trauma of a crash, he wondered what his reaction would be when he resumed flying. He continues:

"Here's an interesting item. I remember it very distinctly. They assigned me a trip, saying 'Hey, Bob! Guess what? You're going back to Kingston.' And I said 'No! I don't believe it.' They responded 'We think it's the best deal for you. It's a cargo plane with no passengers.' So I did it, and it turned out all right. I was very nervous, but there was nothing on board but bags of rice. When we landed at Palisadoes Airport, I saw pieces of the Convair still there, all rounded up. My first flight after the accident and I was right back where I

*Bob Betancourt
shows the way.*

had left off! It was very good in a sense and it certainly cured me of any nervousness. After that I was fine.

"There was a C.A.A. hearing at the courthouse in Coral Gables. At the time of the landing, the co-pilot was at the controls. They blamed him. Pilot error."

Bob's wife, Martha, likes to tell the story of what happened five years later: "This is something. A few of the Pan Am stewards were learning to become barbers and they were taking their training at the barber college in downtown Miami. We all used to take our children there to have their haircuts so that these guys could practice on them. We took the boys down one time when Bob was home from a flight. I was sitting waiting for them while Bob was chatting to some of the guys. The fellow sitting next to me leaned over and said 'Miss, do you know that man over there?' And I said 'Yes, that's my husband.' He replied 'I think I know him.' So I said 'Well, you may think you know him, but I don't know from where because I don't know you.' I thought that would keep him quiet, but he kept on looking and looking at Bob, and finally he asked 'What does he do for a living?' And I said 'He's a purser for Pan Am.'

"He jumped out of his chair and shouted 'Oh, my goodness, was your husband ever in an accident?' 'Yes,' I said 'a few years ago.' 'Where?' he asked. 'Off Kingston Bay.' And then he said triumphantly 'Yes. That's it! I want you to know that I was one of the crew on the boat that came to the rescue. I have never forgotten seeing his face in the water. I have never forgotten his expression as he was swimming and struggling to get all the passengers into the lifeboat.'"

Martha adds: "I get goose pimples every time I think about it."

L'Avventura del Quadrimotore

*L'aereo americano DC7... a rientrare a Roma dove ha atterato
felicemente metendo in salvo i 42 passageri.*
   Il Messaggero di Roma, 29 December 1955

L' *Avventura del Quadrimotore* is the story of an almost-ditching, a perfect piece of flying, and some exemplary behavior in the cabin. It is also the best documented chapter in this book because **Artha Gruhl (Hornbostel)**, who hails from Madison, Wisconsin, is a writer and historian herself. She believes in keeping scrupulous records and, better still, scrapbooks. In preparing this chapter, I have had the good fortune to work closely with Artha and with her scrapbook. Not only did she save the Civil Aeronautics Board (C.A.B.) accident report but, true historian that she is, she had the presence of mind to scribble down the messages to the tower in Rome, which she found lying on the Pan Am Dispatch counter in Rome during debriefing. I have also read the many letters of commendation she received from passengers, and have seen the pressed yellow rose, one of many, many flowers that she and stewardess Eva Fredin received in Rome.

As always, it is fascinating to follow the route by which cabin attendants find themselves on the Pan American team. You may remember reading that Al Tuinman was a chef at '21,' Madeline Cuniff and Grace Walker were pilots, and Mickey de Angelis was a professional baseball player. Eva Fredin was a Swedish Olympic Games Swimming Bronze Medalist in 1952, and Artha was a ballerina.

In 1950, while Artha was dancing with Ballet Theater in Chicago, she was spotted by Dame Ninette de Valois who whisked her away to dance with Sadlers Wells in London. Forced to retire at the early age of 21 because of a knee injury, Artha returned to the United States and went to college. After graduating and being accepted at Radcliffe in their fine arts masters program, she felt the world closing in on her. Her time in London had given her a thirst for travel, and Pan American had flown her between London and the United

In transit with Artha Gruhl.

States. She suddenly recognized that by working for Pan Am she could have the whole world as her classroom.

Civil Aeronautics Board
ACCIDENT INVESTIGATION REPORT
Released: May 31, 1956

PAN AMERICAN WORLD AIRWAYS, INC., DOUGLAS DC-7B,
N 776PA, NEAR VENICE, ITALY, DECEMBER 28, 1955

The Accident
A Pan American World Airways DC-7B, N776PA, lost No. 3 powerplant because of engine fire while in flight near Venice, Italy, on December 28, 1955, about 1930 GMT. The aircraft returned to Rome, its last point of departure, and landed without further difficulty. The 42 passengers and six crew members were not injured.

History of the Flight
    Pan American World Airways Flight 65 of December 28, 1955, origi-
nated at Tehran, Iran, for New York, New York, with several stops scheduled
including Rome, Italy, and Brussels, Belgium. The flight segments from
Tehran to Rome were routine. Flight 65 departed Rome at 1818 on an IFR
(Instrument Flight Rules) flight plan to Brussels which specified a cruising
altitude of 19,000 feet. The crew of six consisted of Captain A.D. Reedy, First
Officer W.J. Box, Third Officer J.B. Sorenson, Flight Engineer L.C. Thayer,
Purser Miss Artha Gruhl, and Stewardess Eva Fredin. Cruising altitude was
reached without incident at 1842 and the flight proceeded in clear weather.

"When we prepared to leave Rome on *Clipper Nonpareil*, the passenger
agent was gaily singing 'Arrivederci Roma,' as he waved goodbye and shut
the door," says Artha. "The flight was completely routine at first. We had 42
passengers from many nations on board, including six Turkish soldiers, a
Greek Orthodox priest and his family, an Arab woman traveling alone, and an
American colonel. Eva was working in the galley and I had just served six
first-class meals. Suddenly there was a high whine from an engine and a sharp
descent as I was pouring white wine into Colonel Chaffin's glass. I have had
difficulty pouring wine ever since." Artha grabbed hold of his arm-rest, and
held on for dear life.

At 1912 No. 3 engine and propeller overspeeded and the tachometer
needle swung rapidly past the highest calibration 3,200 r.p.m., to full deflec-
tion, where it remained. The captain immediately reduced power on all
engines, then disengaged the auto-pilot, and the flight engineer attempted to
feather the No. 3 propeller, without success. At the same time the copilot
noticed a momentary flicker of the fire warning light for the power section of
No. 3 engine. Airspeed was reduced from 200 knots to 140 knots and descent
was started.

It was a terrifying moment but in the seconds that ensued, Artha and
Eva were able to grope their way to seats in the lounge and buckle themselves
down. Through the windows, they watched as Number Three engine caught
fire. Tongues of blue and orange flame streamed over the wing, followed by
brilliant white balls of burning magnesium. In the dark December night, there
was no way of concealing this horrifying vision from the passengers, a vision
which was completely invisible to the captain in the left hand seat in the nose
of the aircraft. Nor was there any way of deadening the high-pitched squeal
of the engine.

The first officer, who had been in the cabin, came forward and reported a fire in No. 3 engine. As No. 3 propeller was windmilling at a high speed, an attempt was made to "freeze" the engine by shutting off its oil supply. Accordingly, the firewall shutoff valves were closed. One bank of CO_2 was temporarily held in reserve. During these actions the flight engineer was intermittently depressing the feathering button. The discharge indication on the ammeter showed the feathering motor to be operating but the propeller did not feather and continued to windmill as before. Fire warnings were still lacking in the cockpit with the exception of the momentary flicker immediately following the overspeeding.

Artha and Eva cautiously unbuckled their seatbelts and started battening down the cabin. Eva rushed to the galley and began stowing all loose items. Artha removed trays and replaced tray tables, running to and from the galley. They left the cabin lights on so they could see what they were doing and in the hopes of distracting the passengers as much as possible from what was happening on the wing. "As we were desperately trying to strap everything down, a man suddenly showed up in the galley," says Artha. "My training came to the fore and out popped the standard question: 'Is there anything I can do for you, Sir?' He wanted to be reseated; he had apparently been frightened by the behavior of the Arab woman sitting next to him and wanted to be closer to the door. I managed to find a place for him in the lounge, but I noticed that he returned to his original seat later on."

Zone 2 and zone 3 fire warnings from No. 3 engine then appeared. This was followed by increased fire at the No. 3 engine area, whereupon the second bank of CO_2 was discharged to that engine. The red warning lights and aural alarm still operated after this second use of CO_2. About this time the flight engineer noticed an intense white fire through a rupture in the cowling near the air scoop of No. 3 nacelle.

Once the cabin was battened down, Artha began to think about the emergency landing routine. She immediately enlisted the help of Colonel Chaffin because she had recognized that not only did he appear to be fit and strong, but the fact that he was in uniform would instill confidence in the passengers. "This was particularly true in the case of the Turkish soldiers, who were obviously ready to panic," Artha continues. "I instructed Colonel Chaffin in the use of the emergency evacuation slide, a mechanism with which he was already familiar. He, in turn, instructed his terror-stricken seat partner how to operate it, in order to distract him from the emergency, and so that they could be first out and in a position to handle the slide on landing and assist people as they came hurtling down."

In spite of the drama that was being played out right in front of their eyes, most of the passengers remained calm. One or two women wept quietly but uncontrollably and the Greek Orthodox priest wrung his hands, tore his hair, and prayed loudly while his four-year old son watched him in amazement.

Suddenly, the DC-7 shook and struggled as though it were being buffeted by winds from all directions. Artha looked out the window for the flaming engine; there was nothing but darkness. She rushed forward to announce that the fire was out. As she started speaking, Mrs. Bode in seat 3C, right next to the Number Three engine, called out: "Look again, stewardess. The engine is gone!" She was right; it had torn free of the wing and, still flaming, had plummeted like a meteor to the ground below.

Up in the cockpit, Captain Reedy had been making preparations to ditch before the engine dropped off. From an altitude of 5,000 feet, he could see by the light of a bright full moon that the flat shore and shallow water at Ravenna offered him an ideal location. The shallow water would not only extinguish the fire but would provide a relatively easy access to the land for the passengers. He contacted the tower in Rome: URGENT - CL65/28 DITCHING DUE NO 3 ENGINE AND REQUESTING BOATS WHEN IN VICINITY VENETO APPROX 2819182Z.

Captain Reedy descended to 500 feet, and then came the sudden buffeting as the engine broke off. The airspeed dropped to about 90 knots, and he immediately applied power to the remaining three engines. To his amazement, the aircraft started to climb. Soon he had reached an airspeed of 140 knots and was climbing at 150 feet per minute. He headed for Milan, but soon changed course to Rome when it was clear that nothing else on the wing had caught fire and the DC-7 was flying with reasonable stability.

There was a sudden change of atmosphere in the cabin. The flames had disappeared, the high-pitched whine had ceased, the aircraft was steadily ascending, and the passengers began to relax a little. Captain Reedy came on the air from the flight deck and reassured them that everything was under control once again. He estimated a flight time of 45 minutes back to Rome.

A shepherd observed the still burning engine on the ground near Venice and notified the State Police, who guarded the engine and propeller until arrival of PAWA personnel.

Artha and Eva dimmed the cabin lights and handed out blankets and pillows before serving coffee and complimentary liqueurs. Artha describes the passengers' reactions: "They remained remarkably quiet and calm during the emergency even though they were all extremely frightened. With a few exceptions, they kept their fear and reaction to themselves while on the plane. Those in seats 2C, 2D and 3C, 3D received the full impact of the emergency as they were seated next to the flaming engine. The gentleman in 3D remarked afterwards, 'I had no emotion. I was just spellbound.' Mrs. Bode, in 3C, was thoroughly frightened but remained calm. After I put the lights out, she started to remark on everyone's conduct, and then began to cry. I spent some time with her until she was under control. Coffee and a bourbon brought her spirits back."

Because the cockpit crew did not know if the fire had caused any damage to the landing gear or if the loss of the weight of the No. 3 engine would skew the landing in any way, Captain Reedy asked Artha to get the passengers into brace position. The Pan Am staff in the Rome Dispatch office received another message: CLEARED ROME REQUESTING CRASH EQUIPMENT STAND BY AS MAY NOT BE ABLE TO GET GEARS DOWN OR HOLD THEM DOWN.

Artha continues: "We were just two minutes from landing, and I glanced out the window and saw the lit runway and the straight approach. Eva and I quickly instructed the passengers in the brace position: 'Bend over tightly, grab your arms under your knees, keep your head down.'

"The passengers all responded quickly as I went up the aisle, all but the Greek Orthodox priest. His wife and son were neatly tucked down, but he kept popping up, and I kept running back trying to pop him down again. No one saw this hilarious scene except Eva, who was coming forward after bracing the back compartment. We both slid into seats in the lounge at the same moment and then realized that we were already rolling down the runway because Captain Reedy had put that Clipper down so softly. Out the window we could see two fire trucks racing alongside.

"There was no sense of relief after we landed; we were too keyed up, or maybe it was shock. When the passenger agent who had been so gaily singing 'Arrivederci Roma' on our departure opened the door again on our arrival, he was as white as a sheet. I heard him muttering 'I'll never sing that song again.' What really struck me first was the overwhelming stench of burned metal and rubber that floated into the cabin as soon as we opened the door. I learned later that, despite the gear holding up on landing, the tires were still so hot that sticks and stones and rocks became embedded in the hot rubber as we rolled along.

"After the ladder was pulled up to the main cabin door, it took nearly five minutes to deplane the passengers because they were, surprisingly enough, in no great hurry to leave. As there was no longer any reason for a quick evacuation, we did not hurry them. Once they were in the terminal, Eva and I stayed with them until arrangements had been made for them to continue their flight or to remain in Rome. All of them were well under control, quite hungry, and most were eager to go on. Only seven of them chose not to board the DC-6 for Brussels that night."

The voracious Roman press fell in love with the incident. Both Artha and Eva were beautiful, photogenic heroines, and Captain Reedy was a modest, appealing American hero. *L'Avventura del Quadrimotore* became an overnight *paparazzi* feast. Artha describes what it was like to be in the spotlight: "In the hotel, very early the following morning, we were asked to come down to discuss the flight. We thought we were going to be questioned by Pan Am personnel, and just drew on any clothes that came to hand before proceeding downstairs. Believe me, it wasn't just discussion, and it wasn't just Pan American. We were completely outnumbered by the Roman press, and in the end Pan Am had to rescue us and whisk us away for a quiet lunch. In the evening, Eva and I went on Italian television with Captain Reedy. It was a hilarious interview. The young woman interviewer talked in rapid fire English, repeated it in Italian for the viewers, and then we would answer her in English, which she would then translate. Captain Reedy was completely her opposite; he's a very laid back, quiet, shy person. When she would ask him a question, he would say 'Well, now...' and there would be a long pause, which drove her out of her mind. But he would give steady and straightforward answers to her questions."

Two days later, Artha and Eva took Flight 65 from Rome to Brussels, and flew home to New York on New Year's Eve. Artha recalls that they were far too tired to be worried about getting back on a 'plane at that time, although later on she would have some delayed reactions. Looking back on the adventure, Artha explains: "We all knew what to expect of each other, and we just behaved in the standard method of operating with Pan Am at that time. Our training was so excellent, and even though we flew with different crews all the time, we could expect the same reaction from them all."

Captain Reedy, writing to all the crew members individually in February after the accident, echoes her sentiments: "Our recent hair-raising experience is getting a little blurred by time already. I know that none of us would care to repeat it. But you should find considerable satisfaction in the knowledge that you behaved very well in a very tight spot.

"From time to time people have congratulated me on doing a good job that night. I do think a good job was done. But I am anxious for everyone, and particularly for the rest of the crew, to know that it was anything but a one-man show. I am the front man for a team, and I am very grateful it was such a good team that night."

Artha concludes: "There was a feeling in those days that nothing bad would ever happen to Pan Am."

Here Come the Jets

And in one stroke, the 707 cut the size of the world in half.
Jeffrey L. Ethell, *Frontiers of Flight*

I mmediately after the Second World War, Charles Lindbergh made a trip to Germany to tour abandoned aircraft factories, looking for and finding evidence of the production of jet fighters. He also discovered Willi Messerschmitt in his cow barn (his house had been requisitioned by U.S. troops), where Messerschmitt declared that he had been on the verge of producing a passenger jet in the final years of the War. Given a different set of circumstances, he believed he could have delivered it within four years.

At a time when no work at all was being done on jet engines in the United States, the British surged ahead, producing turbojet engines in 1947, and by 1949 they had completed a prototype of the Comet, a gorgeous-looking jet airliner which could fly at 500 miles an hour and as high as 40,000 feet.

With such visible evidence of competition, engineers at Lockheed, Douglas, and Boeing began scurrying to design a jet aircraft. They were aware that Juan Trippe was not interested in the turboprop aircraft that other airlines were purchasing from the British; he wanted to leap from piston-powered aircraft straight into the jet age, and he leaned hard on the U.S. companies, promising a bonanza to the one that produced a jet airliner that offered economic advantages in the shape of a large payload. His dream of providing the American public affordable, speedy flights at half the cost was about to be realized.

The British Comet flew under an evil star. Three of the aircraft were involved in runway accidents, and three others exploded mysteriously in mid-air, killing all on board. Painstaking work on the wreckage of one of them, salvaged from the Mediterranean Sea, revealed that the cause of the explosion of that particular Comet was metal fatigue from repeated flexing as the aircraft's fuselage alternately expanded and contracted under the forces of its pressurization system. This resulted in a small crack which catastrophically ripped open. Not surprisingly, all the Comets were grounded.

Trippe leaned harder on the U.S. companies, and finally Douglas and Boeing came through with what he wanted, in the shape of two aircraft which were remarkably similar: the DC-8 and the Boeing 707. On 13 October 1955, the order was placed for 25 DC-8s and 20 Boeing 707s. The Boeing, however, would enjoy the more brilliant success, as its design was further advanced than that of its rival, enabling it to gain a head start into airline service.

With the jets, every statistic was either doubled or halved. They flew at nearly 600 m.p.h. instead of the 300 m.p.h. of the fastest piston-engined aircraft; they reached their destinations in half the time; instead of 60 passengers, they carried more than twice that number; and instead of three flight attendants, the 707s and DC-8s carried six.

Tony Volpe, whom you will remember from the crash landing in the Syrian desert, was on the proving flight of the first 707 across the Atlantic. The airplane carried members of the Federal Aviation Administration (F.A.A.), Pan Am's chief pilot, several other pilots who were being trained on the 707, and various vice presidents of the company. No paying passengers were on board the flight from New York to Rome, a flight which might well have been designated a 'stop flight,' as opposed to a 'non-stop flight.' The Boeing set down at every airport and every alternate along the way: Gander, Keflavík, Shannon, Paris, Rome, and at each stop the F.A.A. would examine the landing strips and emergency and maintenance facilities.

For the flight attendants, the first surprise of the flight was the incredible roar of the 707 speeding down the newly lengthened runways. Those in the jump seats in the aft cabin were astonished by the noise and vibration. They had been told about the remarkably quiet ride of the jets, but the take-off was terrifying for the uninitiated. They had to agree, however, that it all changed once they reached cruising speed and the 707 glided smoothly towards its destination.

Tony clearly recalls the excitement of the proving flight: "Taking off from Kennedy to Gander with a light load of fuel, the aircraft climbed like a jet fighter, pinning us up against our seats. That was a thrilling experience. Another thrill was our arrival in Rome. As we came in over the airport, the 'plane dove and flew real low over the runway, and then pulled right up. Those early jets used to have a water injection that gave the engine an additional boost. leaving a trail of black smoke. The thousands of people who were watching were amazed when we did that."

For the cabin crew, it was not merely an exciting trip; it was a flight of adjustment and experiments. All equipment on board was new, and everything needed modification. As chief purser, Tony worked to streamline the first-class service, and he spent all his spare moments writing suggestions in the purser's log, suggestions, for example, about the recalcitrant coffee machines and ovens. Most important, he monitored the cooking time for the roast beef and various entrées. When working properly, the ovens cooked twice as fast as the ovens on the piston aircraft, and consequently, many modifications had to be made for the first-class meal preparation on the 707. The economy service was also upgraded, and even boasted a choice of entrée; this was a far cry from the 'Sandwich War,' which started in 1955 with the first tourist flights, at a time when the airlines were striving to be true to the notion of economy and the meal service involved a simple, cold plate.

Tony remembers that Tex Johnson, Boeing's chief test pilot, was on board, a friendly, personable man who solicited comments and an overall impression from the flight attendants. When Tony mentioned the troublesome coffee maker, he commented, "Boeing had nothing to do with designing the galley and its equipment. I am sure Pan Am and the coffee maker's vendor will solve the problem." Hmmm.

"We enjoyed the flight so much because it was such a great adventure to be on board a jet," Tony concludes. "We did many, many experiments as we served the meals. It was quite primitive at first and the service required many modifications." As was so often the case, flight attendants from other airlines profited from the experiments—trials, errors, successes—and from the modifications suggested by Pan Am's trail-blazing cabin crew members.

Ingrid Gabrielli's backward glance at the 707 proving flight is not as affectionate as Tony's. She was on board from London to Hong Kong, and, once again, the aircraft landed at many stops and their alternates. Ingrid describes her experience on that interminable journey: "The company told us that it was an incredible honor to be chosen to work on this trip. Afterwards I realized that we were workhorses. Believe me, they flew that 'plane into all the airports you can possibly find between London and Hong Kong and back again. We had no layover, so they put mattresses in the rear of the 707 for the pilots and the cabin crew to rotate and take a little break. It was a killer, it was a haze, it was incredible. We were four cabin crew: Mario Domenici, Eva Fredin, Gisela Wright, and myself, and we were working out the details of the first-class service, testing everything. There were 44 first-class seats on board.

"We made a touchdown at almost every airport we came to. In some places, we offered courtesy flights to the local press, flights in which the 'plane would take off and circle around for a few minutes. During those few minutes, we hurriedly served canapés and drinks. I was scared stiff of the galley and couldn't stand to go near it, but Eva stayed in it all the time. She was an absolute genius in the galley, she was excellent, she was something else. She tested eggs, she tested how to prepare the first-class meals, and how

Publicity for the Jet Age.

to present the service, she battled with the coffee machines. She never stopped.

"Everything went very smoothly and the comments we received were fantastic," Ingrid continues. "When we landed, people would be in hysterics, not believing what they saw. The 'plane was overwhelming, just fabulous, and completely different from a propeller 'plane."

The crew laid over in Hong Kong for 12 hours, and then set off on the return trip. "We touched down at all the airports that we had missed on the way out. Finally, in Lisbon, we were given some time off and told that we could fly wherever we wanted for a week, after which we had to report back to Frankfurt to pick up the inaugural flight from there to Karachi. Pan Am gave us tickets to wherever we wanted to go. I hurried home to Innsbruck to tell my family all about the experience."

Ingrid learned to love working on the jets, and her charm and competence assured that she was chosen for other special flights. In 1959, she found herself on the White House press charter that accompanied President Eisenhower to Kabul, Tehran, and New Delhi; in 1960, by which time Pan Am cabin crews were handpicked for the Sukarno charters, she flew around the world with President Sukarno. "He had his favorites, and he had to be handled carefully," says Ingrid, "but it really wasn't a problem." Ingrid remembers, in particular, flying with him to Acapulco, where the crew had luncheon with the president of Mexico; accompanying him to Cuba, where they met Fidel Castro; and the extraordinary hospitality that was afforded the Pan Am crew on arrival in Indonesia.

The first U.S. jetliners were a success, and the public raced to buy tickets. The jets flew with full loads immediately and for months thereafter. Juan Trippe was right. He had doggedly insisted on a large, commercially splendid jet aircraft, and he got what he wanted.

Dr. Johnson

When Death's pale horse runs away with persons on full speed,
an active physician may possibly give them a turn.

Dr. Samuel Johnson, *Sayings*

I t is time to take another look at **Ted Johnson** because time and again in his long career he was called on to deal with medical emergencies in flight, relying on his almost uncanny medical intuition and his calm and reassuring manner. "I never lost a passenger on the airplane," he says. "I always got them through the flight, although they might die afterwards. Once I had a merchant seaman try to commit suicide on a 707 between Honolulu and Tokyo. He was missing from his seat, and I checked the johns for him. One of the doors was locked, and there was no response when I banged on it. So I opened it up. I saw blood everywhere, but mostly I remember the expression in his eyes, pleading. Blood, tears. I started wiping the blood off with towels, and lifted up his chin to wipe... 'Jesus Christ, he's slit his throat. Get help,' I called to one of the stewardesses. Just ahead, she found a surgeon, who came back. 'We have to get him out of the john,' he said. We spread some blankets on the galley floor and laid him down.

"'He's lost so much blood, we must get some liquids into him. Boil some water,' the surgeon continued. And I thought 'How in hell are you going to get liquid into him when he's cut his trachea?' But I went along with him and boiled the water. Then he realized, 'We can't give him a drink; there's no way to get it down.' I said 'I knew that, but I thought I'd get you calmed down.' I had already accepted that there was nothing I could do. We wrapped some gauze around him. Then I went up to the cockpit, and told the captain what had happened.

"We diverted to Wake Island, and arrived there in about three hours. There were three doctors on the island, not one of them a surgeon, so the one from the flight operated on the passenger, with the assistance of a nurse from the island. The man had not only slit his throat, he had tried to disembowel himself, to rip himself open, using the dullest knife possible. We found the weapon later when they emptied the johns, along with several $100 bills, all torn in half. We learned that he was Chinese, returning to Malaysia. In his suitcase, we found a picture of his family—the most beautiful wife and children you have ever seen in your life. The probable reason for his suicide

129

attempt was that he had learned his family was in the hands of the communists. He had flown all the way from Rio de Janeiro without a break.

"We installed a berth and took him on to Tokyo, after the operation in Wake. A nurse accompanied him. When he came back on board, he looked up at me, and the gratitude in his eyes was so heartwarming. I had been wondering whether I had done the right thing. I wish this story had a happier ending, but, sad to say, he died three weeks later.

Ted continues: "In spite of flying for 41 years, I've never had to evacuate an airplane. I've come very close. Starting to taxi in San Francisco once, preparing to leave for Tokyo, I was sitting in my seat, clear forward, and I saw a man get up and open the rear left door, and disappear. I picked up the 'phone and told the cockpit that a man had just jumped out the rear end. They slammed on the brakes. I ran back and found that he'd fallen off the chute and it had landed on top of him, pinning him to the ground. His injuries included a broken arm and leg. He was a deportee.

"But that kind of thing was easy enough to deal with. It's when you have allergies, heart attacks, epileptic fits, appendicitis on board that the going is difficult. I've had them all. For instance, on a Stratocruiser once from Hong Kong to Tokyo, a night flight, a woman was having a good time in the bar. Then she came up from the lounge while we were serving dinner, very allergic, terrible breathing problems, blotches coming out all over. I gave her oxygen. She passed out. I gave her a whiff of ammonia and some artificial respiration, and she came back. This happened several times. I worked on that woman all the way to Tokyo, where we were met by an ambulance. The next day her husband called me in my hotel room and said 'I just want to tell you how grateful we are. The doctor said that if you had not kept her from passing out, she would have stopped breathing for ever.' She had eaten some nuts, along with a drink or two, and those nuts were what caused it.

"You are often aware that certain passengers are trouble before they manifest it. On a flight from London to Los Angeles, I spotted this woman as I walked down the aisle. I could tell she was turned on by me. Vibes. After I had finished the service in first-class, I walked back again, and she was showing signs of epilepsy, swallowing her tongue, the whole thing. I got her out of her seat and put her on the flight attendants' seat in the back, where she started coming on to me in between episodes; she insisted we have sex right there, and then she'd pass out and I'd have to slap her face to keep her breathing. A British doctor finally came back to help me, but he said, 'You're doing all I could do,' and confirmed that it was a pre-epileptic phase, exacerbated by drinking. My God, I was exhausted by the time we got to Los Angeles."

Ted Johnson (far right).

Wartime emergencies, suicides, allergies, heart attacks, childbirth labor, appendicitis, drunks, and epilepsy compounded with nymphomania—Ted dealt with them all, efficiently and courageously. It is no wonder that he was often referred to as 'Dr. Johnson' by many of his colleagues and his grateful passengers.

Ted Johnson was employed by Pan American for a total of 41 years, always running a tight ship and providing the most professional service that the company could offer. In the course of his career, he worked on most of the important inaugural flights out of San Francisco, he trained other flight attendants, was a check purser, in-flight director, and union negotiator.

Angel Teacher

Until his death in January 1961, at the age of 34, Dr. Thomas A. Dooley had devoted his life, his medical skills, and his fund-raising abilities to improving conditions for Asian refugees through his organization, MEDICO. After he died, his brother, Malcolm, invited Dr. Verne Chaney to go to Asia as Medical Director of MEDICO. Chaney, a thoracic surgeon who had served in the Mobile Army Surgical Hospital (MASH) unit during the Korean War, and was much decorated for his valor, had already acted as a consultant to MEDICO. He accepted Malcolm Dooley's invitation and never returned to private practice. In the fall of 1961, with the support of Tom Dooley's mother, he established the Dooley Foundation and has been its prime mover ever since.

On a trans-Pacific flight in 1961, Verne Chaney watched the Pan Am stewardesses as they were hard at work. The glimmer of an idea was forming in his head. When the meal service was over and the passengers settled down for the night, he got up to stretch his legs. He walked to the rear of the aircraft, where he found stewardess Marleane Thompson tidying up the galley, and they began to talk about the Dooley Foundation. Marleane was already acquainted with it from films she had seen on television, but she was fascinated to learn more from the charismatic Dr. Chaney. A few days later, he telephoned her in San Francisco to discuss his new idea: inviting volunteer flight attendants to work in Asian refugee centers for two or three months at a time. He had already interested Pan Am Vice President, Sam Pryor, in the project, and he needed a couple of flight attendants to initiate the program. Marleane convinced him that she and her roommate, Marge Burgy, were precisely the spearheads he was seeking. They wrote a persuasive letter to Sam Pryor, asking him to allow them a two-month leave of absence without pay. Their wish was granted.

Marleane Thompson (Mitchell) was born in North Dakota and has carried her strong midwest childhood with her ever since. She first became aware of Pan American when she moved with her parents to Seattle, and as soon as she was old enough, she applied to become a stewardess. It was 1957, and competition for Pan Am stewardess jobs out of Seattle was fierce. She went through seven interviews, and was one of five young women finally selected from the entire Pacific Northwest and Canada zone. She started work the day after her 21st birthday and flew on the Stratocruisers out of Seattle before transferring to San Francisco with the advent of the jets.

✈ ✈ ✈ ✈ ✈

In 1961, refugees were streaming out of Tibet into India and Nepal, where they were held in large camps until they could be registered and redistributed throughout other parts of northern India. Families were often split up, parents sent to build roads in mountain areas, children placed in full-time day-care and schools. Verne Chaney had decided that Dooley-Intermed could help ease resettlement problems, in spite of the fact that he had no programs in either India or Nepal. He made a sudden decision to send Marleane and Marge to India instead of locating them in Vietnam as they had expected. He told them: "You girls just go there, contact a refugee center, and I am sure that they'll just love to have you work there." On 1 November 1961, Marleane and Marge arrived in New Delhi on their way to Darjeeling—the first volunteers in the AirIntermed stewardess program.

Marleane Thompson

Marleane relates, "Immediately upon arrival, we had our first rounds with red tape and opposition to our presence. We were told by the Indian Government that conditions were too rough and 'untidy' in the refugee schools and that we would not be happy working there. We were given a hundred reasons why we should not go, but the underlying factor was that they thought two American girls simply could not stand the living conditions, let alone 'the dirty little children.' We persisted and, eventually, in exasperation, they said: 'Send the girls to Darjeeling. It is a beautiful trip.'"

Their sudden, unheralded arrival at the refugee camp in Darjeeling caused quite a stir.

"Who are you?" the officials asked. "What are you doing here?"

"We have come to help," Marleane responded.

"What can you do?" they asked.

"We are willing to do anything, but we know that we can teach English and public health," Marleane replied boldly.

The officials found this interesting, but said they had been receiving a lot of help in that particular refugee center. However, there was a pressing need for staff in the refugee school nearby. This turned out to be the school where Marleane would work for the next four months.

"We were introduced to the Tibetan principal, three Tibetan teachers and one Tibetan lama, who were in charge of the school. Two of the teachers spoke simple English, but none of the children did. The principal asked two things of us: to teach them English and to help keep them alive through the winter.

"We found a home in a sweet, modest hotel. Darjeeling is at 8,000 feet, and was an Indian hill station; in the old days the British would go there in the summertime to cool off. It's a gorgeous, beautiful place, but in the winter it is bitter, bitter cold. The 200 children we worked with were camped on a hillside in an old two-storey army stable, which doubled as their school and their living quarters. There was no heat at all, and many of the rooms were in danger of collapsing. There were window frames but no windows. The children slept, ate, played, and had classes all in the same space on the floor. Sometimes their bare hands and feet were blue with cold, and they would sit on their hands in class to keep them warm. When it was too cold to sit or stand, one of the Tibetan teachers would lead the children in a foot-stomping song and dance. There was a steady stream of runny noses, which were continually wiped on over-used sleeves.

"We worked six days a week, sometimes seven, and our day was broken into two parts. In the morning, Margie and I taught English, with 50 children in each group. They sat on the floor in rows of ten, and we stood at the head of the class. Since pencils and paper were almost non-existent, we used a

Marleane Thompson and friends in Darjeeling.

makeshift blackboard and copied the Tibetan teachers' style, using rote memorization and singing, starting with the alphabet. I can still hear those little voices chanting: A = ass, B = boy, C = cat, D = dog, E = egg.

"In the afternoon, we opened a dispensary in an abandoned room to try to treat the immediate illnesses. An English-trained Tibetan doctor visited the school once a week, diagnosed the cases, and left medicines and instructions for treatment. The most common problems were intestinal parasites, ear, nose, and throat infections, tuberculosis, malaria, diarrhea, skin ulcers, and lice. We were also hit by a wave of mumps.

"Margie and I spent a lot of time with lesson preparation. Since neither of us was a trained teacher—believe me, it would have been better if we had been, and many of the girls who followed us were—we had to work hard to be prepared for the next day's classes. One might think that we had a difficult time communicating with the children because of the language barrier, but they were like sponges, soaking up every drop of language and information we could pass on to them. They were so bright that I had the feeling that soon my teaching ability would be surpassed by their ability to learn.

"We also taught them the basics of arithmetic, and spent some time each day singing English songs. Tibetans are very musical, and that was their favorite part of the day. Their voices would echo across the hillside as they sang 'You are my sunshine' and 'Row, row, row your boat.' Their pleasure in music and dance inspired us to help the Tibetan teachers create a song and dance troupe.

"We set up a children's dance school. Two of the Tibetan teachers were excellent musicians and very interested in dance and drama, which provided the most wonderful form of expression for the children, most of whom had lost their families and friends. Those teachers had the kids dancing and singing songs day and night. I can still hear the noise coming out of the old, old building, where the wooden floors were falling to pieces, and the kids were dancing and stamping, while we were holding our breaths that the floor would hold up.

"I solicited contributions from everybody. I gave some of the money to the Tibetan teachers to go to the bazaar and purchase cloth, and we made costumes for all the dancers. If we'd been in Tibet, the costumes would have been silk and really gorgeous, but we would just buy brightly colored cotton and glitzy trim. I used the rest of the money for musical instruments. I was able to buy drums locally, I brought flutes in from Hong Kong, and I carried a long musical instrument in from my vacation, similar to a sitar, that you play with tongs. We had a full dance troupe and marching band. To hear those kids going through town—beautiful drums, beautiful flutes—Oh boy! It was incredible.

"After we had been working in the school for a month, the lama held a special ceremony outside to erect a flagpole and to give us our new Tibetan names. Margie was called YANG-CHEN-LA (Goddess of Learning) and I became known as GEY-LHAMOO-LA (Angel Teacher). The lama held a kata, the traditional white gauze-like scarf, in both hands and then passed it over our heads and laid it on our shoulders. From that time on, we were known by those names and are still called by them today by our Tibetan friends.

The Dance Troupe

"At the end of two months, Margie experienced some illness and was ready to go home, but I was in a state of near panic at the thought of leaving the children. I wrote an urgent letter to Mr. Pryor, asking for an extra month's leave. The reply came in a terse telegram: 'Permission granted to extend 30 days.' I raced to the school and rejoiced with the children. By this time I had learned one of their Tibetan songs and the dance that went with it, so we celebrated with that, over and over again.

"While staying in the hotel in Darjeeling, I became acquainted with Hope Cooke, the young American woman who later became the Queen of Sikkim. She asked me to accompany her and the Prince of Sikkim to Gangtok to welcome the New Year, where I spent three days as a guest of the Palace. A few weeks later, they announced their engagement.

"When I returned to Darjeeling from Sikkim, Dr. Chaney and Carl Weidermann (also a doctor with the Dooley Foundation) arrived to check up on their newest program. I took them into the school; they were amazed to find their 'experiment' working so well and at my rapport with the children. They were delighted that we had been able to establish a dispensary on a local standard that still met the requirements of good public health, and they felt that we had been resourceful in acquiring materials and information to propel us through the day. Dr. Chaney turned to me and said 'Well, Marleane, you two did it, didn't you? You really did it.' And I said 'Of course, we did.' It had never occurred to me for a moment that it would not work.

"Early one morning, the school received a letter from the Indian Government informing us to expect another 200 children coming in by train from the camps on the northeast frontier. We knew this would strain the living and teaching capacity beyond reason, but there was no alternative; the children were on their way.

"I immediately wired Pan Am in New York for another extension of my leave. It was granted, but I knew it would have to be the last. My airline had extended its courtesies as far as anyone could expect. All through February, I talked with the Tibetan teachers about what Margie and I could do from the States to help make living conditions better for 'our' children. We decided to concentrate on raising funds for clothes, shoes, wool for knitting sweaters, and also to support Tibetan cultural activities. We were particularly interested in continuing to fund the the dance troupe and band."

When the time came for Marleane to leave Darjeeling, the teachers gave her a dinner in the school and presented her with a Tibetan chuba (the traditional woman's dress), a blouse, and a fur-trimmed hat. She donned the outfit and walked into the assembly hall. The children cheered to see their American teacher in Tibetan dress, and put on a program of songs, dances, and speeches for her. She said her farewells with tears in her eyes, and promises to return. The children started to cry too, but soon their crying turned into loud wailing. They surrounded her and clung on to her as she left the hall and sadly climbed the trail back to the little hotel. As she lay down on her bed that night, her heart ached, but she knew she had fulfilled her promise to teach English and to keep the children alive. No one had died that winter.

On her return to the United States, Marleane had another meeting with Dr. Chaney. They both agreed that the experiment had been a success and wanted to expand the program. Marleane immediately set to work fundraising and spreading the word about the Dooley Foundation. She went on countless public relations assignments and appeared on 'To Tell the Truth' and on various children's programs on television. The idea of stewardess volunteers began to take hold. However, the Indian Government's unwillingness to grant work visas to the stewardesses (who were never paid for their work) became a stumbling block, and Dr. Chaney turned instead to the huge refugee population in Nepal. He had already initiated a public health survey in Kathmandu with a Johns Hopkins-trained Nepalese doctor. Dr. Shah could provide an anchor for a new stewardess program.

Pan American was less than enthusiastic about the idea of a permanent program. Marleane insisted that it had to be ongoing and overlapping, otherwise it would be cruel to the children. She suggested that, in the beginning, one person should go for four months, another for three, and then when the first person left there would be a replacement, and so on.

"It was a struggle to convince them, and I had a hard time trying to put this together from San Francisco. That's when I transferred to New York, to be close to corporate headquarters and to the Dooley Foundation office. If the program came into being, it would happen in New York. I finally made some progress, and that's where Sam Pryor came into the picture again. He was Pan Am's Washington liaison; he opened negotiations with various countries for the company, so his thinking was global. He worked closely with Dr. Chaney, and sure enough, we got it in writing. Stewardesses could take a three-month leave of absence without pay to work for the Dooley Foundation. They would lose some seniority, but Pan American would pay their fares to and from their destinations. The Dooley Foundation would provide food and housing. Any other expenses would come out of their own pockets.

"My friend, Beth Wilkins, was interested in the program, and became the volunteer to go into Nepal with me in November 1965. She was a qualified teacher and an astute evaluator. When we started, we took our lead from Dr. Shah. He felt strongly that we should work with Nepali children as well as Tibetan refugees. At that time, everybody was crazy about the Tibetans, and he felt there needed to be a balance.

"We started our investigation and our background work by meeting with local government officials and doctors, and organizations such as the Nepal Red Cross, the American Women's Committee of Nepal, the Tibetan Affairs office, and St. Xavier's School. We also met with the Swiss Aid and Technical Association which ran the Tibetan refugee camp. All these organizations gave us helpful advice and suggestions as to where our services were needed.

"We chose to work on a two-part program, shared between Nepalese and Tibetans. In the morning, we worked in the Tripureshwore Orphanage, located right on the bank of the Bagmati River. The river was like the main highway, huge and dirty. Everybody did everything in the river. They swam in the river, they played in the river, they washed their clothes and pots and pans in the river, people were cremated on the river, they drove their animals back and forth through the river. It was a huge public health problem—and the orphanage sat right beside it.

"Tripureshwore Orphanage was sponsored by the Nepalese Government, under the direction of Mr. Silwal. We were totally occupied with 38 Nepalese children, and this was undoubtedly the more difficult part of our day, because of the severity of their problems. All of them were wards of the government—some were without families, others had been abandoned or had parents in prison. Their general health was poor. Their diet consisted of rice and dal (lentils) twice a day. Eggs, meat, and fruit were totally lacking. The only water supply was the Bagmati River or a water pump a great distance away. The children were plagued with parasites acquired while playing, drinking, and washing in the river.

"Mr. Silwal asked us to start our day by teaching English, to which we happily agreed. However, many of the children were too sick to attend classes. Beth and I took turns escorting them to Bir General Hospital for Treatment. It was a never-ending task, first with one seriously sick child and then another. Five of our children had active tuberculosis and were on daily medication. Each day, we dispensed vitamin tablets along with other medicines prescribed by the doctors, and we were able to supplement their diet with Meals for Millions, supplied by the Dooley Foundation. We were also greatly assisted by financial and moral support from the American Women's Committee, who paid for all hospital expenses, medicines, transportation, and school supplies. In December, we were joined by Ingrid Rautenberg, of the German Peace

Corps, and she assisted with the medical problems while we concentrated on teaching English.

"We had four classes with eight to 12 children in a group. Each session was 45 minutes long, and we taught the lessons with the aid of flashcards, blackboards, illustrations, songs, and games. In the beginning, the children were lethargic and showed little enthusiasm for class or games. This changed as their health improved, and it was a delight to see sparks of energy and eagerness appear.

"We managed to teach a lot of public health along with the English, and we used as many of the local facilities as we could. We'd go to the health departments and get posters, some very beautiful posters, and pin them up on the walls. They didn't last more than a month or two, but they encouraged simple things like washing hands, all the things that a mother would ordinarily teach her children.

"Even so, the living and sanitary conditions were beyond recall. The orphanage had been neglected for too long, and there were rumors that it would be moved to Sita Bhawan, where suitable standards could be maintained. I believe that our role in the orphanage focused the attention of the proper officials on the needs of the children. In the summer of 1967, the move was accomplished, under the direction of the Second Princess and Mrs. Pandy. The stewardesses were asked to continue working in the new location, which was a sign of our acceptance.

In the afternoon, Marleane and Beth moved their skills and their compassion from the Nepalese orphanage to the Tibetan refugee camp. They made the journey by bicycle, and the road climbed past a Hindu temple, across the Bagmati bridge, and rose toward Jawalakhel. Each day, they stopped at a public well to wash and to gaze at the view. Not only was the water pure, but the view of the Himalayas with Langtang as the snow-capped crowning jewel was spectacular. By this point in the day, they were always ravenously hungry, and made their way to the quiet of the St. Xavier School compound for lunch. They had a favorite sunny corner where they unpacked their picnics, usually hot bouillon in thermoses, peanut butter sandwiches, and a 'dessert' of tomatoes and onions. After that brief, quiet moment, they would climb back on their bicycles, and resume their journey.

Marleane continues: "We formed the first nursery that the Tibetan camp ever had. We took children, infants up to five years old. Older children went to a regular school provided by the Nepalese government. There was a need for us because the mothers were working in factories, making carpets, and they would sit in a huge long room with all these looms and yarn, with their babies in their laps or on their backs. It was an unhealthy place for babies because there was such a lot of dust and sickness. The air was terrible.

"Our idea was to set up a nursery very close by so the mothers could come there and nurse their babies—they nurse them until they are two or three years old—and we would look after them in the meantime. There were also five ayahs who helped us look after the babies. We started out with about twenty-one children and it went to fifty in no time. At first the mothers weren't sure they wanted to leave their babies, but once they saw how well it functioned, they were delighted.

"We made a sandpile and we canvassed the European community for toys they didn't want. We kept all these beautiful things in a large box to tempt the children into staying with us. The only time they could play with them was when they were at the nursery. We had a strict rule that at the end of the day, everyone had to pick them up and put them back in the box.

"It developed into a beautiful little nursery. We felt we were performing a function that was very useful. Everything that we did, we did with the idea of its being self-sustaining; we didn't bring in a lot of money and buy a lot of milk downtown. We were conservative, wanting to make sure that whatever was being done could be continued later on by the people themselves. And it worked. It was beautiful."

At the end of the day, Marleane and Beth climbed onto their bicycles again for the long ride back to the Dooley compound in Kathmandu. On arrival, they bathed in cold water and changed their clothes, before joining other Dooley members in the dining room. Rice was the basis of every meal, and meats consisted of water buffalo, goat, boar, and deer; vegetables included potatoes, greens, onions, cauliflower, and tomatoes, with the occasional addition of yak cheese or local peanut butter.

After the meal and some lesson preparation, Marleane and Beth would hurry off to bed in their unheated room, exhausted but happy to have local wool blankets to keep them warm and the prospect of another day working with children in the mountain kingdom of Nepal.

Marleane often reflects on her time as a volunteer: "I was very afraid that I would lose touch with that part of the world; I was so taken with it that I wondered how I could ever leave. Then I would think, it must just be a passing phase. It will all go away at some period. It never has. There were many flight attendants who have said exactly the same thing: the three-month period when they were so enveloped in a totally different way of life with a purpose and a need for communicating and living with those people was not a passing fancy at all. Many went back year after year, and some of them put children through school and would send clothes and other contributions out. At one point, our Tibetan refugee children were all in blue, wearing phased out Pan American stewardess uniforms, cut down to size and tailored in Tibetan style.

"I think we made a significant contribution to the children as a group and in many cases to the children individually. And I know for certain that they utterly and completely changed my life. I am still in contact with many of my students. One of them, Dawa Norbu, eventually got his Ph.D. at Berkeley, and is the author of *Red Star Over Tibet,* his analysis of the Chinese occupation.

"When I first arrived in Kathmandu, my mind was totally focused on working with the children; the last thing in the world that I wanted was anything to do with a man and romance. We had plenty of that while we were flying. It seemed that you were always running from that sort of thing. I thought 'Phew! Here's my four- or five-month break.' That's when I met my husband, Dick Mitchell. He was a biologist and was part of the Tom Dooley Foundation's medical health survey. Even when I first saw him, I thought 'Well, I certainly don't have to worry about that guy. He's not my kind of person at all.' And he felt the same way about me. He likes to say 'Oh, so that is what a Pan Am stewardess is like?' Our friendship developed first; then came the romance.

"I quit flying when we got married because we had the opportunity to live in Nepal for three years. Dick's purpose there was to collect material for his Ph.D. thesis on the mammals of Nepal. The ticket to do that was collecting lice, mites, ticks, and fleas throughout all of Nepal. We were married in February 1968 in Kathmandu. There were lots of Dooley girls out there by that time and they all came to my wedding. There were several other Dooley marriages out there. Ah, the mystique of the Kathmandu valley—magic!

"I married for love and adventure, and I've had my share of both. We trekked together throughout Nepal for three years, during which time I stayed in constant touch with the Dooley Foundation. They acquired some flight attendants who were nurses and worked in the hospitals, and there were some trained teachers too. By this time the children's English was getting much better, and lessons required more preparation. They would often pair a teacher with a non-teacher, so that they could make lesson plans together and a non-teacher could be really functional. By this time there were as many as six or eight volunteers at a time in Nepal, and the programs were going full steam and expanding."

Marleane's favorite motto comes from Abraham Lincoln: "Determine that the thing can and shall be done, and then we shall find the way." She has lived her life being true to it.

By June 1979, just before the Thomas A. Dooley Foundation/ Intermed Airline Volunteer Program was phased out because of the airlines' changing economic conditions, 289 airline volunteers from 36 U.S. and foreign airlines had participated. Sixteen volunteers had served two terms, six three terms, and two four terms, making a total of 316 volunteer assignments in Laos, Vietnam, Thailand, India, and Nepal. Pan American carried all the volunteers to their destinations.

Dooley-Intermed is still flourishing. If you are interested in finding out more about this organization, please make contact with them at: 420 Lexington Avenue, Suite 2428, New York, N.Y. 10170. Telephone: (212) 687-3620.

Love is in the Air

Love is in the air, quite clearly.
Love is going around.

Steven Sondheim

Anything seemed possible in the early 'sixties, and perhaps my memories of that decade are particularly golden because it was the period of my own flying career. I was in the wave of European flight attendants hired in the early years of the decade, and I flew for the statistically-predictable 19 months before leaving to get married. I had no opportunities for heroism, in spite of one aborted take-off, one aborted landing, and one flight in which we circled New York in a thunderstorm for three hours and every single passenger and the rest of the cabin crew threw up lunch. Actually, that *was* my most heroic moment. I am not troubled by motion sickness, and the lot fell to me of dealing with all the airsick bags. I stowed them in one of the lavatories, which was waist deep by the time we disembarked.

My most disturbing experience was on a night-time trans-Atlantic crossing. We had served a meal, the passengers had settled down to sleep, the lights were dimmed, and the rest of the crew had gone to the front of the aircraft to eat their dinner. I was alone in the galley when a drunken passenger put his hands round my neck and muttered, "Hey, bitch, I could strangle you if I wanted to." In my best British accent I responded, "Ah, but you are a gentleman, Sir, and you certainly won't do that," and he refrained.

What does distinguish my career, however, is its peculiarly Pan American love story.

In February 1963, Pan Am flew the members of the first American Mount Everest Expedition (A.M.E.E.) from San Francisco to Calcutta via Tokyo, Hong Kong, and Bangkok, on the first stage of their journey to the summit of the world's highest mountain. That same month, I took my first Hong Kong trip. Still very junior, I had bid again and again for Hong Kong but repeatedly received Frankfurt. In February, however, I was on 90-minute standby in New York, and when the call came from Scheduling that I was to report immediately to Idlewild for a 12-day Hong Kong trip, I shrieked with joy. My suitcase was already packed (one of the conditions of being on standby) but I double-checked on my swimsuit, fled out into the street, and grabbed a cab. Rush hour traffic meant a tedious journey, and I had to run for the 'plane when I arrived at the airport. Once on board, I started work immediately. Just as the A.M.E.E. members arrived in Kathmandu, I was taking off on Pan Am's Flight PA2, which flew daily around the world from west to east: London, Rome, Istanbul, Beirut, Tehran, Karachi, New Delhi, Bangkok, Hong Kong. Together with its reciprocal flight, PA1, PA2 will endure in airline history as the quintessential intercontinental air route.

When I look back on that first trip to Hong Kong, I see a series of brilliant images: the red soil of Lebanon and the bar at the Phoenicia Hotel in Beirut with its glass wall through which drinkers could gaze at the underwater antics of swimmers in the pool; scruffy camels and colorful fortune tellers in Karachi; dawn at New Delhi airport and the amazing psychic weight of the Sub-continent; the sight from the aircraft of the Himalayan range stretching out mile after mile, with Everest's cloud plume flying like a white flag in the blue sky; and finally, the approach into Hong Kong. The flight crew knew that it was my first trip to Asia, and invited me into the cockpit for landing. I put on a head set and listened as we flew over islands in the South China Sea. The runway at Kai Tak was very short in those days and landing was notoriously tricky. Depending on the weather, the aircraft could fly over the mountain and rush towards the sea at the end of the runway, or could land from the sea and hurtle toward the mountain on a 'bent' approach. That day, we landed from the sea, an instrument approach, as always, even though the day was sparklingly clear. Suddenly, a crisp British voice came on the air from the tower, giving us our height and calling us in: "You are now at 10,000 feet. You are now at 5,000 feet. You are at 1,000, 500, 100. You are on the ground." We were. We were hurtling towards the mountain. "Welcome to Hong Kong."

While I was gawking at the sights of Hong Kong, buying pearls, dancing the night away, and then returning to New York, A.M.E.E. was readying itself for the approach march. All the expedition's supplies had arrived in Kathmandu, and 900 porters were hired, as well as 32 Sherpas to climb with the Americans at high altitude. During March and April, every effort was made to put the strongest team members in position for a summit assault at the beginning of May, the most clement time of year in the Himalayas. During March and April, I found myself shuttling between London, Frankfurt (of course), and Chicago.

On 1 May, Jim Whittaker became the first American to climb to the summit of Mount Everest, accompanied by Sherpa Nawang Gombu. Their triumph was followed by two other successful summit attempts. In all, the Americans placed five of their men atop Chomolungma, Goddess Mother of the World. (You can read all about this in James Ramsey Ullman's book, *Americans on Everest* and Thomas Hornbein's *Everest, the West Ridge.*)

In June, I struck lucky with another Hong Kong trip. Just as A.M.E.E. was concluding its return march and getting ready to leave Kathmandu, I set out from New York again.

Jim Lester was a 35-year-old psychologist, a member of the expedition as a scientist charged with studying the climbers' reactions to stress. Until he started training for the climb, he had no previous mountaineering experience, but he was fit and courageous, and was able to reach the advance base camp at 21,500 feet without using oxygen. He lived there for a month (setting an altitude record for psychologists), experimenting, questioning, counselling, and collecting the dreams (usually about red-haired women) of the various summit members and their support teams. After A.M.E.E.'s success and the return to Kathmandu, he flew to New Delhi for the obligatory trip to the Taj Mahal, after which he boarded Pan Am's Flight PA1 westbound around the world, just as night was giving way to dawn.

By that time, I was returning from Hong Kong and working in the first-class cabin, where there were just two passengers. As soon as I had finished that service, I told the purser that I would lend a hand in the main cabin where there was a full load. He handed me the passenger list and said "Take a look at this. EXCOR." (EXCOR meant 'extend extra courtesy' to those passengers whose names were marked *.) I read: Nawang Gombu*, Ang Dawa*, Girmi Dorje*, Nima Tensing*, Ila Tsering*, Captain Noddy Rana*, James Ramsey Ullman*, James Lester*. I recognized the name Tensing immediately because Sherpa Tensing Norgay had made history with Sir Edmund Hillary on the British Expedition to Everest in1952. Tensing subsequently visited Britain and became the favorite hero of children of my generation. I excitedly questioned the purser about the EXCOR passengers and he explained that the State Department, in a gesture of thanks and goodwill, had invited the Sherpas to visit the U.S. I dashed off to help in the main cabin.

It was hot and crammed with passengers, and the cabin crew was working feverishly, serving breakfast. I joined in, and soon located the Sherpas. When we finished the service and calm was restored to the cabin, some of the passengers fell asleep, while others strolled up and down the aisle of the 707. I made my move, uttering gushy, courteous remarks like, "I hope you enjoyed your breakfast" to the mystified Sherpas. Gombu spoke a little English but none of the others did, so Captain Rana, the Nepalese Army officer who was accompanying them, interpreted for me. And then two American men with beards joined in the conversation, which came to a rude conclusion when the purser arrived to summon me to the forward cabin to prepare for landing. As I started to leave, one of the men with beards said "Can I see you again? I'm getting off in Istanbul." "I'm getting off in Beirut today, but we'll be passing through Istanbul airport on our way to London tomorrow," I responded carelessly. My mind was already focused on the exotic swimming pool at the Phoenicia.

After returning to New York and spending a few days off, I was back on another London/Frankfurt/Chicago shuttle. On arrival for our layover in London, I checked the Pan Am mail box at the Kensington Palace Hotel on the off chance there might be a letter for me. I did not expect anything because all my friends knew I stayed with my parents whenever I was in London. To my surprise, there was a letter, folded into one of the small brown envelopes in which we received our per diem allowances. It read:

June 27

Dear Valerie -

Sorry if I'm addressing this note to the wrong person, but I have no way of knowing for sure. Let me explain.

On my flight from New Delhi on June 19 there was a tall, blondish, British stewardess, very lovely, with whom I wanted to talk but put it off until she separated from the plane at Beirut. As she was leaving the plane there, I expressed my disappointment, and she laughingly said to come to the airport the next day when she would be back on a plane headed for London. As a matter of fact I did meet the plane in Istanbul the next day, but too late to see any of the crew.

My detective work suggests you are that girl. I wonder? As for me, I was with the Everest team, am tall and temporarily wearing a beard, and on the flight from New Delhi to Beirut I was sitting with an older, grey-haired and very slightly bearded man. How could you possibly remember? But I have to give you something to go on.

Well—I'm staying until July 5th with my sister, just around the corner, and would like to see you for lunch, dinner—whatever—if you come in before then. What can you lose? and whether you are the same girl or not, I'm sure we can enjoy some time together.

I'm Jim Lester, my sister's home phone is WES 5793 and her office phone (you could leave a message with her for me, such as when and where I might call you) is WEL 0351 (she's Jane Lester).

Hoping very much to hear from you before July 5—

Jim

Jim told me later that he had been disappointed but undaunted by his failure to find the crew in Istanbul. He stalked up and down the airport and finally made his way into the Pan Am office area. It was empty and Kafkaesque, but he discovered, face up on a desk, the cabin crew list for Flight PA1 that day—six names. He ruled out the male purser's name, the two Asian names, the German name, and was left with two Anglo-Saxon names: Sally Leckie and Valerie Browne. He wrote them down in his diary and set off to explore Istanbul. On arrival in London a few days later, he continued his detective work; he called Pan Am and found out where the crew stayed and went straight to the Kensington Palace Hotel. There he had to face his greatest obstacle: Guy, the mad Yugoslav, who supervised Pan Am accommodations at the hotel and operated like a fierce watchdog guarding the flight attendants from unwanted attention. At first he refused to deal with Jim.

"We don't give out no names," he said.

"But I already have the names," Jim countered, "I just need to know which one it is." And then he poured out the whole tale of Everest and the flight and his pursuit of the elusive stewardess. Guy started warming to the tale, his romantic Yugoslav heart was touched, violins began to lament, and suddenly his deep voice boomed out:

"Valerie Browne. She's the one for you."

✈ ✈ ✈ ✈ ✈

Jim Lester and Valerie Browne, July 1963.

When I arrived at my parents' apartment, I showed Jim's letter to my mother who said "Doesn't he sound interesting, dear? Why don't you invite him and his sister over for a drink?"

I reached Jane Lester who said "Jim's out of town but will be back on Thursday."

I said "I'm off to Chicago tomorrow but I'll be back in London on Thursday too. Come for drinks that evening at my parents' home."

I was in the kitchen holding a elegant cut-glass tumbler and talking to my mother when the doorbell rang. The tumbler flew out of my hand and smashed on the floor.

"Don't worry about it, dear. I'll clear it up," said Mum, reaching for a dustpan. "Go and let your friends in."

I ran to the door threw it open and said "Am I the one?"

And Jim said "Yes!"

White House Press Charter to Dallas

Hail to the Chief who in triumph advances!
   Sir Walter Scott, "The Lady of the Lake"

The White House Press charters became a well-established and somewhat notorious feature of Pan American, notorious because they responded not to Pan Am Scheduling but to the White House Travel Office. For security reasons, the White House insisted on the same crew members for each trip, and Scheduling was impotent when it came to making changes in White House demands. Scheduling fussed about this, the pilots' union (the Airline Pilots Association) and the flight attendants' union (at that time, the Transport Workers' Union) fussed about this, but nothing could change the system. The Press charters were a closed shop. You needed a personal invitation to join the team.

Kelly Tangen was a member of the hand-selected Press charter cabin crew in 1963. Originally from Minnesota, she had been a volunteer on the 'Kennedy for President' campaign while working as a stewardess for American Airlines. When she left American to join Pan Am so as to fly internationally, she says "I ran into people from the Press room, people like Pierre Salinger and others who worked with him, and they kept asking 'Why don't you do the Press charters? We're going here, we're going there.' So I tried one trip to see what it was like, and the purser in charge was somebody I couldn't stand. He goddamned me up and down the airplane, and I refused to work with him again. The next thing I heard was that he had been bounced off, and Laite Bowden and I were bounced on."

During the Kennedy era, two pursers and five flight attendants worked on board each Boeing 707 White House Press charter flight. Kelly soon became chief purser. She admits: "I was about 22 at the time, and it was a big job for a little girl. I wouldn't have lasted long without working well." The job required total commitment; the flight attendants could be called out at any time, and might be away from home for weeks at a time, sometimes working 18 hours a day. Not everyone was prepared for that kind of devotion and if they were not, Kelly would recommend replacements, looking for crew members from a variety of nationalities, always seeking hard workers with even dispositions, those who did not watch the clock, those who were blessed with a sense of humor. Most important, she needed to be absolutely confident about the cabin crew's discretion and commitment.

In addition to members of the press, the charters carried Secret Service men, who worked three shifts a day, around the clock, and they all had specific duties. Sometimes their eight hours off work was time on board the aircraft, so the cabin crew would make up beds to ensure them some sleep, and would serve them hot meals before they went back on duty. Kelly says about the Secret Service: "I adored them. Nice, nice men. They all wore button down shirts and wing tip shoes, and were clean cut, all-American, strong, dedicated, mannerly. That job takes a certain personality because they have to be ready to give up their lives—in the absolute sense of that term—for the President."

The White House press charter aircraft usually carried between 40 and 60 passengers and relatively little baggage. This left plenty of room for the President's rocking chair, spare tires, and extra parts for Air Force One (the call-sign of the President's 'plane, but only when he is on board), on which

Kelly Tangen, Joe Chapel, Laite Bowden, Col. Jim Cross, Capt. Doug Moody, and Angela Corser take a break beside Air Force One.

space was at a premium because the whole forward cargo compartment was taken up by an auxiliary power unit, communication equipment, and far more radios than a conventional 707. The President's airplane was always 'hot,' that is, it had the ability to communicate with anybody, anywhere, at any time. The radio operator was always listening or talking, even when the aircraft was home in Washington. Air Force One might also be accompanied by Lockheed C-141s, huge cargo airplanes which opened up to disgorge limousines, communication stations and, sometimes, a helicopter with its rotor blades folded.

On board the Press Charter 707, the cabin resembled the combination of a newsroom and a home. Sometimes the forward lounge housed photocopy machines, and sometimes a row of seats was removed for them. Space was cleared at the rear of the aircraft for photography equipment. The press and the Secret Service came on board with briefcases and typewriters, and Kelly describes how the Press would start typing immediately and the Secret Service would settle down and surreptitiously clean their guns.

In spite of the presence of the office equipment, the passengers were encouraged to feel at home as much as possible. A bar was set up at the entry way, and the cabin crew prepared the exact drink that each passenger wanted ahead of time, so that he or she could grab it on the way to the typewriter. Because they spent so much time typing, the journalists needed food they could eat with one hand, and the flight attendants were far more likely to prepare sandwiches or a cup of chicken noodle soup than *caneton à l'orange*. Kelly adds: "That's the way they wanted to eat. We'd serve the photographers first, while the journalists were writing. They always had a deadline, so they wouldn't want the bother of a first-class tray. At the end of the day, however, when all their work was done, they would enjoy a sit-down meal. We knew everybody by name, everybody's eating and drinking habits, their favorite cigarettes or cigars, but most important we knew their filing times and when they would be ready to eat. There were unscheduled stops sometimes, and if we had run out of food, we'd drive off to the grocery store with whatever Air Force major was in charge and buy provisions." (Advance teams were headed by military aides who carried considerable authority.)

The Pan Am flight attendants generally tried to avoid invitations to state functions. These were formal occasions which they did not enjoy, but they were always popular guests at after-hours parties with the press, the White House staff, or the Secret Service, none of whom partied with each other, but all of whom welcomed the flight attendants as guests at their individual get-togethers. The parties often continued on return to the U.S. "It was an easy hop on the shuttle down to Washington, and we were invited many times," Kelly says.

The cabin crew grew to know the idiosyncracies of each member of the press team. They celebrated their birthdays. They decorated the cabin if the flight occurred during a holiday (by far the favorite holiday was Hallowe'en). They learned the names of wives and children. They listened, they were supportive, they encouraged; they were a vital part of the team that accompanied the President when he was away from the White House.

During the Kennedy years, Kelly and her team flew overseas with the President to Berlin, Rome, Paris, and Shannon. Kelly remarks, "The Irish people went crazy about Kennedy; they went wild with enthusiasm, welcoming the prodigal son. De Valera was thrilled. For us, that was the happiest trip of all with Kennedy. We landed and stayed in Dublin. From there we visited Galway and Shannon. It was spring, it was beautiful."

Kelly continues, describing the trip to Berlin: "We had no idea what the reaction would be because the Wall had just gone up. Our arrival in Berlin was very, very eerie. We landed first (the press always landed before the President), and boarded buses to go into town. There were throngs of people, thousands and thousands of them held back by the police, lining the streets holding German and American flags. The people just stood there holding their flags, utterly silent, as we went by.

"But when they saw President Kennedy, they went mad. Gleefully mad. They exploded with glee. The Germans were jumping out of their skins in a most un-German manner. And then he made his '*Ich bin ein Berliner*' speech, and they went wild with joy. It was unforgettable."

(In addition to accompanying the President on overseas trips, the Press charters also operated nationally during presidential campaigns. Kelly and her crew had already followed candidate Kennedy to Boston, Palm Springs, Palm Beach, and Cape Canaveral.)

On 21 November 1963, Kelly and her team spent the night in Fort Worth, Texas. It was raining. Kelly recalls: "It was President Kennedy's campaign kick-off trip. You have to remember that Kennedy Administration popularity at that time was only 23%. Everybody seems to forget that. This was a fence-mending trip, and Johnson could bring in a lot of votes. It was a serious time and these jobs had to be taken care of if he wanted to be re-elected."

The following morning, the press 'plane accompanied Air Force One to Dallas. The rain had stopped, and they had a clear flight to Love Field. As was customary, the press 'plane landed first and then the two aircraft parked side by side. The Pan Am crew disembarked, becoming part of the crowd to welcome the President to Dallas, cheering and clapping as he and Mrs. Kennedy stepped out into the sunshine. Kelly says, "Had it continued to rain, Kennedy would be alive today. The bubble would have been put on the car. Although we were always given the opportunity to ride in the motorcade, we didn't go into Dallas, preferring to stay at the airport.

"In addition to the members of the Press whom we had on board that day, we also carried some White House staff, White House Press secretaries, and the White House transportation officer, 'Jiggs' Fauver. I remember how happy we all were because after lunch all we had to do was to fly to Austin. It wasn't going to be one of our gruelling 17 or 18 hour days. By four p.m. we'd be finished, and we had a good party planned in Austin. We teased the President that he couldn't go because he had to go to the L.B.J. ranch."

The cabin crew on Air Force One and Pan Am's cabin crew often invited each other to meals aboard the aircraft. That day, Kelly and her team had been invited to lunch on board the President's 'plane. Their meal was suddenly interrupted by the radio operator announcing that he had received the horrifying news that the President had been shot. He instructed them to return to the Press 'plane and to prepare for departure at a moment's notice.

As was customary, the Press 'plane had been refuelled to maximum landing gross weight the moment it had arrived in Dallas, giving it the capability of flying off instantly to almost anywhere in the U.S. The crew hurriedly went down the check list and then waited... and waited..., speculating on where they might be sent. They reckoned that the most likely place would be Boston, so that the President could be cared for in a Boston hospital. They had no idea of the severity of his injury. Finally, after half an hour, Carl Gray, Pan Am's navigator, set off for Air Force One across the tarmac in search of further information. As he walked up the ladder, Colonel Swindell, President Kennedy's pilot, met him at the door. His face told the story. The Secret Service had just called in on their radio: the President was dead. Carl returned to the Press plane bearing the terrible news.

The cabin crew had huddled together in the rear of the aircraft. Kelly looked up at Carl as he walked down the aisle, his face as white as a sheet. "He didn't have to say anything; I knew what the news was," she says. With tears streaming down their faces, the crew prepared as best they could for the return of the members of the Press. Ironically, the media had not rated the Dallas trip an important one, and had not sent their first-string journalists on the assignment. In addition, Pierre Salinger, the White House Press Secretary, was flying over the Pacific on his way to Asia to plan the President's next trip. His aircraft was immediately turned back.

The idea that the assassination could be part of a conspiracy suddenly surfaced, and several of the Secret Service men were dispatched to lookouts on the roof of the terminal building. Kelly continues: "The radios were busy, and people were coming on and off the airplane, very upset, not knowing what to do. The day wore on and on." Finally, the flight engineer aboard Air Force One hurriedly removed four rows of seats and stowed them in the aft cargo hatch so as to make room for the President's casket. Kelly and her team left their aircraft and watched as a hearse pulled up. Pan Am's captain, Doug Moody, stepped forward and helped to carry the casket up the awkward stairway. They watched in silence as Lyndon Johnson and the blood-stained Jackie Kennedy followed the casket on board.

Kelly continues, "Then we walked slowly back to our 'plane, as Air Force One took off for Andrews Air Force Base. At that point, we still had no idea of what had really happened. All we knew was that the 'Boss' was dead. I didn't have time to be sad or frightened. I didn't have time to think. There were so many things to do, people here, people there, suitcases all over the place. People desperately needing care. I vividly remember washing down Ron Kellerman, one of the Secret Service men, who was covered in the President's blood. He and Clint Hill (the agent who leaped onto the back of the Presidential limousine) were absolute basket cases. I remember Ron hitting his head against the wall, in agony, not knowing what to do with himself, because they had lost a president.

"We left Dallas quite a few hours after Air Force One. The whole east coast was blanketed in fog. New York had closed down, but we managed to squeeze in to Washington at around midnight. There was an eerie quiet on board. The wire service and T.V. people had already filed their reports in Dallas, but the Press who worked for newspapers and weekly publications came back on board and started typing furiously, tears streaming down their faces. The photographers had nothing to do but stare into space. But in spite of everything, the passengers were hungry. Sad and hungry. Of course, there had been no luncheon in Dallas that day and nobody had eaten anything, so we served them whatever they wanted.

"There were muffled conversations here and there on the 'plane, and at one point, the White House Press transportation officer said to me 'Well, we have a new boss,' and I went 'I guess so.' Then he said 'Let's try to keep this thing together.' My first reaction was 'NO. I don't want to. I really don't want to. I don't want a new boss.'"

But Kelly Tangen changed her mind. Her team and the cockpit crew all went to work for President Johnson. She continues: "At first I disliked Johnson

Kelly Tangen (3rd from right) and her crew greet President Johnson.

intensely. Then I felt sorry for him because everybody, the staff, the Press, everybody, was giving him such a really bad time. I felt sorry for the underdog, and now I miss him. He was a bigger-than-life character, who never got used to those teleprompters; he sounded like a dork making a speech. That's why I felt sorry for him, because one-on-one he was so personable. He was crazy, warm, incredibly funny, and so much better in person than in the media.

"A year after the assassination, there was another election, and we ended up flying to all 50 states. It was gruelling for us. President Johnson had the capacity to hop on his 'plane, take a ten-minute catnap, and be refreshed, but the rest of us didn't have that opportunity. We were always working and we were always late because the schedule was very tight, very close. We often had no idea where we were going because of the President's whim. It was brutal, but funnily enough we enjoyed it anyway. The boss set the tone, and it was very relaxed. There had been more formality with the Kennedy group, much more distance. Most of them were from Massachusetts, and right there you have the difference: Massachusetts vs. Texas. All of Johnson's White House staff were exceedingly capable, friendly people, and we ended up knowing them well because we were always campaigning. We were like a great big family."

When Nixon became president, Kelly Tangen decided to call it quits. She had worked for seven years on the Press charters, and she concludes: "I had no interest in working on them when Nixon came in. It was time for someone else to take my place."

Two African-American Experiences

Ex Africa semper aliquid novi.

Pliny the Elder, *Natural History*

In the 1940s, Pan American started hiring European stewardesses to add to its Euro-American cabin crew. In 1950, Pan Am recruited its first Hispanic stewardesses to fly to Latin America. In 1955, it hired Japanese-Hawaiian stewardesses. With the advent of jets in 1958, Pan American went on an enormous hiring binge in Europe, and hired hundreds more European stewardesses. In 1963 it hired six stewardesses in the Caribbean: two from Haiti, two from Guadaloupe, and two from Trinidad (with the intention of basing them in Jamaica; when the Tranport Workers' Union got wind of this, the six were located in Miami). As late as 1964, no African-American flight attendants were yet on board Pan American aircraft. When the N.A.A.C.P. accused Pan Am of discriminatory hiring practices, the company quickly pointed to its Caribbean flight attendants. Finally, in 1965, the company's first African-American went into training to become a stewardess; it was her idea, not the company's.

1. Doris Bulls (Scher)

Born in 1941 and raised in Florence, Alabama, a small, segregated town in the northwest corner of the state, **Doris Bulls** was one of eight children. She was academically gifted, and after moving with her family to Chattanooga, Tennessee, she soon perceived that her passport to a wider world was attainable through education. After graduating from high school, she attended Alabama A. & M., a segregated college, for a year, but the world was still not wide enough for her. She left the South and went to live with her aunt and uncle in New York City, where she learned to speak Spanish and completed her degree at Hunter College. After graduation, she applied to work for Pan American. The company offered her a job as a ticket agent, but she was determined to fly. She approached flight service, and refused to take no for

Doris Scher

an answer. At last, she had her way. On 18 January 1965, Doris Bulls went into training in Miami, along with 12 other young women: two French, two German, one Swedish, one Irish, and six white Americans. Immediately after training, Doris was based in San Francisco where she flew from 1965 until her death from breast cancer in 1989.

Alice Flynn (see page 203) remembers working with Doris on her first flight. She comments, "We were rolling the cart down the aisle. Doris was on one side and I was on the other. When Doris asked, 'Would you care for a drink?', people were flabbergasted. They could hardly answer her. As she'd go by them, their heads would swivel round, and they would stare after her. I was looking directly at the ones who were turning around, and I was awed by how difficult it must have been for Doris. I don't think that any of us realized what it must have been like to live in a black skin at that time. She was the only black person at an all-white base working with an all-white audience. I said to myself, 'This woman has guts.'"

Arnie Scher, Doris's husband, explains: "Doris was a universalist, a woman of the world, and she realized this as soon as she got to New York. Flying gave her the opportunity to see herself beyond her community, beyond her little southern town. She adored travelling. It was always a joy for her; she was one of the few flight attendants I knew who always had something good to say about flying, although she could be vocal about the treatment of black flight attendants. I remember one time, when Najeeb Halaby was president, she was incensed about something that happened regarding black flight attendants and the company. She was vulnerable, her job was at risk, but she had the courage to write him a letter, and he responded. The company knew that Doris was vocal, and wanted to help her. She had an excellent performance record."

Doris was one of the seven founding members of the International Union of Flight Attendants. She is remembered by all who flew with her for her integrity, her enthusiasm, her dedication, and her captivating elegance.

✈ ✈ ✈ ✈ ✈

2. Sheila Nutt, Ph.D.

"My father used to tell me that I had to do extraordinary things," says **Sheila Nutt.** "He marketed information the way they do in commercials, in short sound bites and loudly. He would say again and again, 'You come from exceptional stock. Your grandfather was a man who went to college. He went when black people didn't know how to spell college. He went when many whites did not go to college. Your grandfather finished Morehouse College. Your grandfather attended Harvard Law School at a time when Harvard Law School did not allow blacks to sweep the floor there. Your grandfather served in World War I and was an exceptional soldier. Your grandfather came out of the Army, finished law school, became a lawyer of significance and a community activist, and died of tuberculosis before he was 40. Your grandmother was a registered nurse when black women were not allowed to change bedpans in many hospitals.' He would keep telling me this, and sometimes I would tune him out. But his words sank in indelibly.

"I grew up in a white neighborhood in Philadelphia, knowing white people. I went to an all-girls prep school. When I look back, I recognize that the black girls in the school had racist experiences—for instance, we were counselled to do non-college things like vocational training or secretarial school—but I learned how to cope.

"I started college to please my parents even though I wanted to run off to New York, to be a dancer or a model. It was the 'sixties and a turbulent time for many people, blacks in particular, because we were trying to redefine ourselves. I was restless in college; I wanted to be part of all the excitement, Woodstock, flower power, and I wanted to make a difference in the black community.

"I entered the Miss America beauty contest in 1967—I was the first black in Pennsylvania to do so—because I thought it would help my career as a dancer or a model. I was first runner-up and I was told by one of the judges that if I had been white I would have won. It was at that point that the person who won the Miss Congeniality award said 'Listen, why don't you become a flight attendant?'

Sheila Nutt

"When I went for my interview with Pan American in 1970, I glanced around the waiting room at all the beautiful, blonde women in their little white gloves and pill box hats, and I said to myself, 'I'll never get this job.' But I read Pan Am's brochure as I was waiting, and the words Rome, Istanbul, Paris jumped out at me, and I said, 'Dear God, get me this job.'

"I didn't tell my family or my fiancé about the interview, but two weeks later a telegram arrived for me as we were all sitting in the house. My mother was convinced it was a telegram kicking me out of college, but it said 'You have been accepted by Pan American.' My fiancé demanded, 'What do you mean, you're going to be a flight attendant?' My parents demanded, 'What do you mean you're going to leave college?' And I said calmly, 'This is what I want to do.' One of the fears that my dad had was that flight attendants were nothing but prostitutes. I know his anxiety influenced my behavior because I made sure that I didn't have a succession of relationships while I was flying; that would have played right into his hand. But I did notice that a few women were working 'overtime.'

"As soon as I started training, I knew I was in the right place at the right time, and I realized that the airline offered me the opportunity to do exactly what I wanted. I was the only black in my class, and I was put in a room with a girl from California and a girl from Oregon, neither of whom had seen a black person in their entire lives. And these were Americans! But everybody in the class was great to everybody, regardless of her value system, because they all wanted that job too. I was chosen to give the valedictory speech at the end of training.

"Miami was my first base, because of my Spanish language qualification, and my two roommates from training and I decided to rent an apartment together. It was difficult for us to find an apartment because I was a double-whammy for the landlords. Some of them did not want to rent to blacks and some did not want to rent to Hispanics, those landlords who decided I was Puerto Rican. That was when I found out that one of my roommates couldn't stand black folks. She told me 'We'd have an apartment by now if it were not for you.'

"We ended up finding a really nice place, although my mom was scared out of her wits about my being in the South. She's from Virginia and she grew up in the 'twenties and 'thirties when Jim Crow and racism were acceptable. She said 'You be careful down there. Those people can tar and feather you.'

"Shortly after my probation, I transferred to New York and worked in management as a supervisor, not flying at all for a while. Then Pan American started a program where you could go to school during the week and fly at weekends, and I decided to complete my degree. I took courses in education because I figured that at some point I'd be living in Africa and I would open a school. By that time I was married and my husband was African. I had realized that I was an educator at heart, and liked to influence the way people think.

"I continued to fly and study. I liked the travel and the freedom that I didn't see in other professions. I took advantage of everything that Pan American offered me. I had organized my life so that I could finish my education, get a month's paid vacation, go around the world for free, take my family with me, meet exciting new people on the airplane, read about Rome and Paris and the Pyramids, and then go and see them.

"I started a Master's program, and shortly afterwards became pregnant. At that time, when you were pregnant, you had to stop flying and would receive workman's compensation. I said 'Hey, you can't beat this with a stick!' I did the whole nine months in school, had my last final December 14, gave birth December 19, and was in class again January 19. After I gave birth, I could take a year off to nurse my baby, and get my job back when I was ready. In 1977, where else could you do that?"

"The years went by and, for the most part, I was treated well on board the aircraft. However, I remember one unpleasant incident on the way from New York to Johannesburg. We were about to land in Liberia after flying all night, and I was doing the coffee service. I put the tray out and offered this gentleman coffee. He said 'Do you have Sweet and Low?' I looked on my tray, but I didn't have any. We were about to land, so he said 'That's O.K.' and took regular sugar. Shortly after I moved on, a male flight attendant with Sweet and Low on his tray walked past the passenger, who grabbed the sweetener and yelled at me 'YOU. COME HERE. LOOK AT THIS. WHEN I ASK YOU FOR SOMETHING, YOU'D BETTER GET IT FOR ME, YOU UNDERSTAND?' He woke everybody up with his voice, with his ugliness. At that time, I was in the middle of a divorce, I had a mortgage and two kids to take care of, and I was not going to allow him to intimidate me into saying something that would make me lose my job, but my body language and my eyes told him exactly what I was feeling. I turned my back and walked away from him. I was not going to allow a man like that to determine the value of my being. I determine. I empower myself.

"I remember another incident, in the Caribbean, when the mother in an American family said to me 'Oh, you're so pretty! My goodness, your English is so nice! My husband thinks you're from Jamaica, but I bet you're from Trinidad. Where are you from?' I said 'I'm from Philadelphia.' Their faces dropped, and you could tell I was only attractive as long as I was exotic. As an American, I was no longer of interest."

Sheila never forgot her grandfather's words and his insistence on higher education. She continued to take advantage of the flexibility that her Pan Am job offered her.

"During the winter months, the company would often ask flight attendants to take unpaid leaves of absence because business was slow. So I would take a leave and make money teaching in the Boston Public Schools. Then I obtained a fellowship with free tuition and a monthly stipend to do my doctorate in education, with the focus on administration and curriculum. Flight attendants were the subject for my dissertation. (*Occupational Stress: Sources and Amount Found Among Flight Attendants*, Sheila Nutt-Birigwa, Boston University, May 1986.) One of my conclusions was that certain behaviors and characteristics were common among flight attendants and their families. When a flight attendant would take out her uniform and luggage to leave on a trip, her household pets would behave strangely, her kids would become hyper, and her spouse would get up-tight. Family members would argue with each other, and that was their way of saying 'We don't want you to go.' They could not say it out loud because they knew it was her job and she had to do it, but they showed it with their behavior.

"While I was going to school and flying, if the crews invited me to go sightseeing or out for dinner, I would say 'No. I'm not going to join you.' And they'd say 'What are you going to do?' And I'd reply 'Study. I have a paper to write.' When we arrived back in New York, they would say 'Gee, how do you do it all?' I responded 'You have to cut out shopping at Bloomie's, you have to cut out luncheons. You won't be able to sleep till noon. You'll come in from a flight and go to school instead of discoing. Something has to give. I don't have a social life. I don't have the most up-to-date wardrobe. I don't have a whole set of Louis Vuitton or Gucci. I don't have all the jewelry. But I feel real good having my education.

"If flight attendants don't get an education or don't have a driving interest other than flying, something happens to them after about seven years and by ten years they're stuck. They can't change the lifestyle. I know that some of my colleagues disagree with me and would like to string me up by my fingernails for saying this, but I say it for the record because I believe it: being a flight attendant is not a lifetime career. It is not a real lifestyle. It envelops you; you don't envelop it. Scheduling has control over your life.

"A lot of my friends would say 'Ah, but I can manipulate Scheduling. I can trip-trade,' and I would say 'But you're not doing anything of substance; you don't use your brain. Go to any cocktail party and nobody gives you respect. The airline industry doesn't respect you. The public has no respect for you; your employer has no respect for you. It's a female industry, dominated by men who have no respect for you.'

"But it's hard to tear yourself away. I would hear people say 'I have to stay with the airlines because I want free travel.' I used to say that too, because my husband was from Africa and we enjoyed going there for free. But I suddenly said to myself on the aircraft one day: 'Wait. Why am I putting up with a job that is not a career, just for free travel? Look at all these passengers, these full loads. If these people can afford to pay full fare, why can't I?'

"But flying was hooked into me. I was a flying junkie. I knew that, and I had to go cold turkey, but it took me a long time to make the decision to leave. It was like a difficult divorce, but in the end, Pan American offered me an early out. I was blessed. I had that settlement and my education. Many women were not so fortunate."

Bigger and Bigger Jets

[The Boeing 747] is so big that it has been said that it does not fly, the earth just drops out from under it.

Ned Wilson, *For Pilots' Eyes Only*

The 'sixties were the boom years in the aviation industry, particularly for Pan American. The company purchased a total of 137 Boeing 707s and 19 DC-8s, and in 1962 the company completed its 100,000th flight across the Atlantic. Pan American also became the owner of Intercontinental Hotels, a rapidly expanding chain. The Pan Am Building, at that time the largest commercial office building ever completed, rose plumb out of the center of New York, sitting astride the train tracks that terminated at Grand Central Station, arrogantly flaunting aviation's triumph over the railroads, and blocking the view up and down Park Avenue. The building was crowned with a helicopter pad to provide the quickest possible access to Idlewild/Kennedy. Juan Trippe wanted the words PAN AM at the top of the building to be 30 feet high and illuminated at night, a beacon to travellers, a brilliant advertisement. The architects resisted the size and a compromise was reached at 15 feet.

With business booming at an unprecedented rate, the time appeared ripe for Pan Am's next step. The British and French were cooperating in building a supersonic airliner, the Concorde, which would be capable of a three-and-a-half-hour trans-Atlantic crossing, but it was years away from completion, and there was resistance to the idea of supersonic transport within the U.S. Government and environmental groups. In the meantime, however, there had been a major development in the design of the jet engine, resulting in the fan-jet. It was the fan-jet that opened the door to the manufacture of wide-bodied jets.

After lengthy negotiations, Juan Trippe rejected offers of stretch-jets and double-decker jets of existing generations from Boeing, Douglas, and Lockheed. He was adamant; he wanted an airliner that flew just under the speed of sound, that could cruise above 35,000 feet (a largely traffic-free zone), an airplane with a 5,100-mile range that could carry 400 people, and which could take off and land at already existing airports. Finally, Boeing agreed to produce the behemoth so long as Trippe agreed to buy 25. On 22 December 1965, the deal was struck.

Many rumors were running around Flight Service about the Boeing 747 before Pan Am actually received delivery in 1969. One of the most persistent (and most accurate) of these was that the huge airliner would require a special super-purser to run the show. The rumor became fact, and guesses abounded as to who would be the first to assume the newly-created position of In-Flight Director. It came as no surprise when **Jay Koren** was chosen. The company knew it could rely on him to solve the inevitable problems of cabin service on a new aircraft with grace and equanimity.

Jay Koren was born in Chicago in 1930, but moved to California with his family during the Depression. At the ripe old age of 19, after graduating from Beverly Hills High School, he persuaded the Flying Tiger Line, an all-freight airline, to employ him, and between classes at U.C. Berkeley, he went to work on the Korean airlift. At that time he shared an apartment with a Pan American employee who told him that he ought to "go to work for a real airline." Jay applied to Pan American and was interviewed by a panel of seven. He was turned down but, after the interview, the lone woman on the panel sidled up to him and whispered "Try Seattle." That was all he needed. He flew up to Seattle and was interviewed by a panel of one, Harry LaPorte, who recognized his potential immediately, even going so far as to waive the issues of age (too young) and height (too tall).

From the moment he was hired, Jay showed exceptional ability. His intelligence, charm, good looks, and easy manner delighted the passengers. Perhaps it was his time at Beverly Hills High that made Jay so aware of the need for showmanship on the aircraft and of the importance of meal services being 'class acts.' In any case, it was not long before the company realized that they had an invaluable asset, a flight attendant on whom they could call to perform elegantly and reliably on their most important flights. For this reason, Jay was regularly chosen to be a crew member on many special flights, including the 707 and 747 inaugurals. Perhaps for this reason also, Jay's uniform represents Pan American in the display case of such attire at the Smithsonian's National Air and Space Museum.

Before his first working flight on the 747, Jay went on a press flight from New York to Seattle. He was amazed, and says: "It was thrilling. I couldn't believe this enormous, enormous aircraft. As we approached Seattle, the captain dramatically announced that the airplane would be landed strictly by computer. Usually the captain wouldn't tell you about that sort of thing until the 'plane was on the ground, but these weren't revenue passengers so he could say what he wanted when he wanted."

Early in December 1969, the 747 inaugural was finally announced. The aircraft would fly from New York to London on 20 January 1970. In-Flight

Director Koren would head up a crew of 18 flight attendants. He was the only cabin crew member to have actually flown on the aircraft before working on it.

After all the fanfare that surrounds an inaugural, the 747 and its crew had to suffer the ignominy of a delay. Jay explains: "I believe it was simply a matter of not having the engine rotating fast enough right after start-up. Winds were gusting heavily that evening as we backed off the gate, and caused a flame-out in one of the engines. We ended up having a long wait while they switched aircraft." The passengers disembarked and were entertained in the Clipper Club by Madeline Cuniff (see page 69), while the second of the two 747s that Pan American had received was brought out and made ready. The flight finally took off after midnight, following a five-hour delay, and arrived in London the following afternoon, where the British newspapers had a heyday at Pan American's expense, dubbing the aircraft 'the Dumbo Jumbo.' They would continue in this vein until British Airways acquired their own 747s, at which time, miraculously, the 'Dumbo Jumbo' became the 'Super Jet.'

Jay continues: "From that date forward for months, I flew every fifth day to London or Paris. One day over, one day back, two or three days off. Within a week the company appointed a dozen more flight directors, mainly the guys who had been flying on the President's Special. The intention was that they all be men, but Dottie Bohanna (see page 63), the most senior flight attendant at the base, objected and became the first woman flight director."

Jay admits that the flight director's job was the greatest challenge of his life: "I was the pioneer, the guinea pig. As soon as I returned from a flight, people in management and also other crew members would call me and demand, 'What can we tell the others? What is the best way to do this or that?' It was a terrible learning process because good old Pan Am middle management gave us no ground training to prepare for an aircraft that was, just to begin with, more than twice as big as anything we had set foot in before." The flight attendants were all extremely nervous about working on the 747 because of the lack of ground training, and as a result the flight service briefings before each departure became longer and longer. The flight directors found that blackboards were a useful tool in explaining 'the flow.' With so many flight attendants on board to deal with the unprecedented number of passengers, it was of vital importance to establish zones and flows. (The 747 was divided into zones from A to E, with A being the front and E the back.)

Jay continues: "In the early days of the 747, the flow might go well for two thirds of the cabin, but then the flight attendants in, say, the E zone would be doing it absolutely the wrong way, and there would be four rows of people who would finally start ringing their bells and saying 'We never got fed.' The last four rows in that zone might never have seen the cart."

The intention, at first, was that the flight directors should not participate in meal services at all. Rather, they would delegate, supervise, make all the announcements, and do the documentation. "Even with all the problems, it was a wonderful job," Jay says, "because you could make of it what you wanted. Of course, some saw it as an invitation not to work at all, the ones who would pass an hour or two doing *The New York Times* crossword puzzle. But most of us jumped in wherever we were needed, and there was always a need. It was absolute chaos for quite some time following the inaugural."

Jay had never experienced such stress in his life. "I lost ten pounds in the first few weeks of working as a flight director, and Dottie Bohanna told me it would sometimes get so bad for her that she would lock herself in a john and try to pull herself back together. The passengers and flight attendants came at you from all quarters with demands: 'That won't work. This won't work. The man in seat so-and-so is incensed and insists on seeing 'the boss.' ' So you'd set off to deal with the angry man, who was 25 rows back and on your way there, your uniform was practically ripped off you by people saying 'It's 9:30 and we haven't had a bag of peanuts yet. What's going on?' And you kept trying to apologize, saying 'We're working on it.'"

Jay continues: "Although another of the original flight directors, Joe Kapel, and I have been best friends for over 40 years, he claims he'll never forgive me for suggesting to the company that he be made a flight director." Joe recounts: "I actually passed out one time from turning round and round in response to certain questions. You were torn in so many directions. We just couldn't make the 'plane work for us."

The cabin crew was required to make a major adjustment in terms of meal service. While other airlines had introduced the cart to deliver meals long before, Pan Am cabin crew continued running trays out to passengers from the galley. Jay comments: "We were certainly not prepared for it when the company suddenly sprang meals-on-wheels on the 747. We had a lot of problems with those new carts: brakes not working, brakes working so well that you couldn't get the cart moving again. On top of that, for the economy entrées the company gave us a *bain-marie* service [where casseroles of hot food were placed over pans of scalding water in order to keep the food from cooling]. The bain-marie would be placed on a cart and pushed down the aisle, with the flight attendants dishing up the entrées from the bain-marie. It was a nightmare and the cause of many messy accidents. In the end, many of the crews would elect to run meals out in the old way.

"Things would take forever. We were suddenly dealing in hundreds instead of dozens. With a 7 p.m. departure, it would be 10 p.m. by the time we finished the cocktail service and had dinner going. Then we'd turn the movie

Jay Koren (second from right) and friends on his last working flight.

on and the sun would start coming up before it ended and we were into a fast half-breakfast service. The lavatories were always malfunctioning, and we had constant electrical problems."

Like its predecessor, the 707, the Boeing 747 was an immediate hit with the flying public, and it flew at full capacity for months after the inaugural. Jay points out an interesting fact: "Whether it was because it was a new aircraft and they were scared, all the passengers drank like crazy, far more than in recent years when I've even had flights where I would not have to open the liquor kits because nobody ordered a drink. But in the early days of the 747, the pursers would dump hundreds and hundreds of dollars and pounds and marks and francs on the flight director for movies and bar service. I'd sit in my hotel room for hours, counting up money and filling out forms to deposit at the airport before we left."

The company kept reassuring the flight directors, insisting that everything was going smoothly. Everything was not going smoothly. There were still very few trained flight attendants for Jay and the other flight directors to count on. Each trip became a training flight: "There were always new people on the aircraft who didn't know the ropes. And, of course, there were spies—representatives from other airlines about to take delivery of their own jumbos who came on board to profit from our mistakes. There they'd be, giggling and smirking because of the chaos."

But Pan Am cabin crew learned quickly. Jay and his flight director colleagues were experienced flight attendants with years of training and all the right instincts behind them. They soon learned how to streamline service on the 747 and trained legions of other flight attendants to follow their lead. After a couple of years, the position of in-flight service director was eliminated. There was no further need for it in Pan Am's second jet era.

Open Letter

With the advent of the 747 fleet in 1970, it seemed as though there could be no limit to Pan American's dominion in the world of international aviation. However, the 1970s was the decade which saw the empire begin to crumble for a variety of reasons: the oil crisis, terrorism, deregulation, poor management, overspending on the fleet, and, most important, intransigence on the part of the U.S. Government. Hopes that the Government might mete out fair treatment to the airline, and thus boost its income, were dashed time and time again. This lack of support from a government to whose aid the airline had frequently come was extraordinarily painful. The pain, however, acted as a catalyst which banded the employees together. They never doubted the worth of their airline. They united in a common cause—the survival of Pan American—and they took up a collection in order to publish the 'Open Letter' which appeared in *The New York Times* on 23 September 1974, the contents of which are shown on the following page.

THE NEW YORK TIMES, MONDAY, SEPTEMBER 23, 1974

An open letter to the American People from the employees of the World's Most Experienced Airline.

After a decade of dangling in a storm of outrageous discrimination, both at home and abroad, and writhing, every time the International Oil Cartel raised their prices, the 32,500 men and women of Pan American World Airways have a few confessions we would like to get off our chests.

We plead guilty, first of all, of having worked our tails off for nearly fifty years, carrying the spirit of American private enterprise to the rest of the world. We admit also, pioneering every significant overseas air route.

We plead guilty, of actively having prevented the outflow of more than four hundred million dollars a year from the American balance of payments, and of kicking them directly into the nation's economy.

We plead guilty, of having flown two-million American servicemen out of Viet Nam on five day combat leaves, on a cost-plus one dollar contract. We admit also, providing the Defense Department a fleet of perfectly maintained, fully crewed airplanes that were used extensively in World War II, Berlin, Korea and Indo China.

We plead guilty, of overtly supporting the American aerospace industry. Pan Am® was the first to operate the flying boats, the Intercontinental 707s and the Jumbo 747s. We cannot say, at this point in time, how many billions of dollars have been generated by foreign airlines following our leadership in the purchase of these new airplanes.

We plead guilty, for having had the lowest operating expense per revenue ton mile in 1973, among all U.S. trunkline carriers.

We plead guilty, of having once been an enormously successful private enterprise. We admit also, failing to report a crime, *as it was taking place.* The men and women of Pan Am have watched their great airline being reduced, over the last decade, from a healthy, contributing, national resource, to a poor, paralyzed, potential welfare patient. Finally, we've been bled white by this recent oil crisis business . . . NOW WE'RE IN TROUBLE, and we think that the American people can see why, merely by asking a few simple questions of *our own government.*

Ask our own government, first of all, why the Postal Department pays the foreign airlines as much as five times what it pays Pan Am for hauling the same U.S. mail. Not receiving the same pay for the same work costs Pan Am forty million dollars a year.

Ask our government, why nothing is ever done about overseas airports that charge Americans exorbitant landing fees. Qantas Airlines, for example, pays one hundred seventy-eight dollars to land their jumbo 747 in Los Angeles. Pan Am pays forty-two hundred dollars to land in Sydney, Australia. Not paying foreign governments the same user fees that their airlines pay in America costs Pan Am twelve million dollars a year.

Ask our own government, why the U.S. Export-Import Bank loans money to airlines of "underdeveloped" nations, like France, Japan and Saudi Arabia, at six percent interest while Pan Am pays twelve per-cent. Their low interest loans are used to buy airplanes that they use to compete against Pan Am. Not allowing Pan American access to these same interest rates means that we pay seven million dollars more than the foreign airlines for the same Jumbo jet.

Ask our own government, why it is opposed to letting Pan Am fly passengers within our own country . . . it just doesn't make sense. The domestic airlines now have rights to the international routes that we pioneered, and the foreign airlines now serve more cities in the United States than we do. The right to compete freely at home, the most elemental privilege of a free enterprise society, has always been denied Pan Am.

You see, when it comes right down to it, Pan Am does a lot more than compete with other airlines. We compete with whole countries, sometimes even our own.

The men and women of Pan Am are just not the type who enjoy asking for a handout. The only subsidy that we have ever needed was fair treatment . . . *From our own government.*

IF PAN AM WERE ALLOWED DOMESTIC ROUTES WITHIN THE UNITED STATES . . . OR TO BORROW FROM THE EXPORT-IMPORT BANK . . . OR TO PAY REASONABLE LANDING FEES OVERSEAS . . . OR TO RECEIVE EQUAL POSTAL RATES FROM OUR OWN GOVERNMENT, WE WOULDN'T NEED ANY SUBSIDY AT ALL!

In fact we wouldn't need to have taken up a collection to run this ad.

The 32,500 Employees of Pan Am

Grace Schereci
Secretary of the Pan Am Employee's Ad Fund
Pan Am Building, 200 Park Avenue, New York, N.Y. 10017

The opinions expressed herein are strictly those of the employees and do not necessarily represent the official position of the management of Pan American World Airways, Inc.

Eight Minutes to Cairo

*...but they, following
their own impulse, and giving way to marauding violence,
suddenly began plundering the Egyptians' beautiful fields
... and soon the outcry came to the city.*
                    Homer, *Odyssey, XIV, 262-265*

Sailing ships have always been easy prey for pirates, and horse-drawn carriages were the prey of highwaymen. In the Old West, travellers by covered wagon lived in dread of bandits. It should come as no surprise that aircraft, too, would sooner or later fall prey to some kind of marauder. After a slow start, the menace spread throughout the industry like an epidemic, and the travelling public was held hostage in the sky by individuals who were desperate for escape, seriously deranged, or politically suicidal.

The first recorded skyjacking occurred in February 1931 in Peru, and each subsequent decade brought an escalation of incidents. By the late 1950s, the two-way flow of hijacked aircraft between Cuba and the U.S. mainland or Mexico gave rise to the term 'Cuban shuttle.' Pan Am aircraft were certainly not immune, and its flight attendants were often the first to be accosted in a given incident.

For instance, on 9 August 1961, a Pan American DC-8 was skyjacked to Havana. In the takeover struggle, the perpetrator held a gun to purser Andres de Leon, who resisted him and was struck to the ground. On 3 August 1970, in the first skyjacking of a 747 (in this, as in so many aviation firsts, Pan American was once again the leader), the hijacker pulled a gun on purser Esther de la Fuente, saying, "Take me to the pilot. I want to go to Cuba." Esther thought he was joking and brightly replied, "No. Let's go to Rio. It's a lot more fun at this time of year." The hijacker's response was to produce a bottle containing explosives and to demand that both Esther and stewardess Regina de Silva accompany him to the cockpit, which they did. Recognizing that the man was deranged and potentially dangerous, the captain changed course from San Juan to Havana. Because the incident occurred in the first-class cabin, few of the 360 sleeping passengers were aware of the detour. Not until the airliner arrived in Havana in the early hours of the morning and they looked out the windows to see Fidel Castro inspecting the 747 did they realize that they were not in San Juan. The Cuban leader had made a special trip to the airport at dawn to inspect the giant 747, the first of its kind to land in Cuba.

Unfortunately the skyjacking disease knew no boundaries, and soon a deadly mutation of the virus threatened the skies in the form of political fanatics, determined to attack a nation at a particularly vulnerable place: on board its airborne flag-carrier. The oozing sore of the Palestinian refugee camps became the breeding ground for the most virulent form of the disease.

Members of the Popular Front for the Liberation of Palestine (P.F.L.P.) soon emerged as the professionals of aviation blackmail. After years of escalating terrorism and extortion in the late 1960s, they began planning an elaborate campaign, a move intended to precipitate the release of fellow guerrillas. Their intention was to commandeer three aircraft, one each from El Al, T.W.A., and Swissair, and intimidate the flight crew into flying the aircraft to Dawson's Field, an obscure, sandy airstrip in the Jordanian desert, where they would blow up the 'planes.

On 6 September 1970, the plans for the T.W.A. 707 and the Swissair DC-8 skyjackings were executed with precision. T.W.A. was commandeered shortly after take-off from Frankfurt and, at almost the same moment, Swissair was hijacked as it left Zürich. Both captains were instructed to fly east, and both captains managed to land their jets safely in the dark, without navigational aids, and on a tiny airstrip that was never intended to bear even a fraction of the crushing weight of a passenger jetliner.

Meanwhile, in Amsterdam, two 'Senegalese' passengers, who had purchased their first-class tickets with cash, attracted the attention of El Al security officers, and at the last moment they were bumped from the flight. The security officers' hunch was right, but they had missed two other terrorists. Already on board El Al's Flight 219 were 24-year old Leila Khaled and a male companion, the other half of the hijacking team. After take-off from Amsterdam, they were determined to carry out their mission, even without their two cohorts. Leila Khaled removed the grenades she had been carrying in her brassière and her companion pulled out his gun. Together they raced towards the first-class cabin, but never gained access to the cockpit. They were overwhelmed by the El Al steward and an Israeli security agent, who shot the man; quick-thinking passengers tore off their neckties and used them to tie up Leila Khaled. The aircraft made an emergency landing in London where Khaled was taken into custody.

The two 'Senegalese,' maddened that their plans had been foiled, also took matters into their own hands. They discovered that Pan American's Flight 93 would shortly be taking off from Amsterdam. They quickly purchased first-class tickets and hurried aboard the giant 747. Whether or not the two terrorists had any idea, as they made their purchase, that they would be dealing with a wide-bodied jet is a matter of speculation.

Nelida Perez (Beckhans) was born in Cuba and came to the United States in 1961, during her second year of high school. Like so many young women of her generation, her mind was set on becoming a flight attendant, and like most adventurers, she applied to Pan American because she wanted to fly internationally. She was interviewed in 1967 but, because she did not yet possess a U.S. passport and her Cuban passport would present problems for passage into certain countries, she was offered a job on the ground in New York as a special service representative. Once she became a U.S. citizen in 1970, however, Nelida applied again to fly, and this time she was accepted into training. Her class graduated on 4 May 1970 and she entered her six-month probationary period, enjoying her flights to Europe out of the New York base.

The crew members on board *Clipper Fortune*, Pan Am's Flight 93 from Amsterdam to New York, had just started a month of flying together. They had spent a pleasant layover in Brussels and the flight to Amsterdam had been uneventful. Apart from veteran pursers John Ferrugio and Augusta Schneider, the 12 other cabin crew members were 'new hires,' probationers, or trainees. However, it promised to be an easy trip for the predominantly unseasoned flight attendants because only 187 passengers were on board the brand-new 747, far from a full load.

After the passengers had boarded and the doors were secured, the 747 taxied out to the runway. Nelida continues: "I remember I was sitting in R3, by the door over the wing exit, ready for take-off. After we started to taxi, something happened and the airplane made a sudden stop. I was very curious to find out what it was, and I kept looking toward the front of the aircraft. A doctor from the Netherlands was sitting in front of me and he could see all the way forward. He said to me, 'Something's going on. The captain just came down from the cockpit.' I said, 'WHAT?' and he replied, 'Yes, there is a commotion going on.'

Captain Priddy had just received a warning from ground control that he was carrying two passengers who had been bumped from El Al. He had halted the aircraft and sought out the pair. On finding them seated in the first-class cabin, he asked their permission to frisk them. They consented. Captain Priddy admitted to *Time* magazine, "I'm no professional, but I went over their bodies and hand luggage fairly closely."

Nelida Perez

Nelida continues, "Then we took off, and everything seemed normal. We started the meal service, but suddenly John Ferrugio made an announcement that the plane had been hijacked to a 'friendly country.' That's what they usually said when they were not exactly sure where we were going. The two men had entered the cockpit bearing hand grenades and guns that they had hidden under their seats. My first reaction was to turn to another flight attendant and say jokingly, 'We're going to Cairo.' A friend of mine had been on the 747 hijacking to Havana and he had said to me afterwards, 'Nellie, if you fly in the Caribbean nowadays, you get hijacked to Cuba. If you fly in Europe, you go to Cairo.' He was right.

"Then we were very worried, flying and flying and flying, not knowing where we were going. The hijackers wanted the plane to go to Jordan where the others were, but the captain told them it was out of the question. The 747 was far too big for Dawson's Field. It seemed as though we flew forever. We tried to keep the service normal and avoided serving alcohol as much as possible. The hijackers made no objection to our serving the meal. They were not aggressive at that time, although they were carrying guns, and they mingled around the plane, talking to the flight attendants and the passengers. One of them asked me questions about the door on the brand new 747, how you arm and disarm it. I looked him in the eyes and told him how the doors were prepared. He understood some English; he asked me where I was from and I told him I was born in Cuba. They kept asking if all the passengers were U.S. citizens. I believe they were looking for Israelis.

"I kept thinking we were going to run out of fuel because we kept on flying. Finally, the purser announced that we were going to land in Beirut although no 747 had ever landed there before. Going to Beirut made us very happy because we thought the crew would be able to disembark and have a nice layover there, go to the Phoenicia Hotel, buy our gold, and forget about the hijack. No way.

"When we landed, we remained in the middle of the runway. I was very curious to see what might happen next. I walked to the front of the airplane, to the L1 door, and saw some people approaching with a ladder. Terrorists had taken over the airport, and another hijacker was boarding the 'plane. I heard somebody say, 'That's dynamite.' That's when I became really, really worried and started shaking. I didn't want to see any more, and I returned to the back of the airplane.

"We took off from Beirut with an expert in dynamite and a supply of explosives on board. One of the original hijackers stayed in the cockpit with his gun at the captain's head, the other wandered around, and now we had a third with the dynamite, who began placing the charges. All of a sudden, I realized with a feeling of horror that they intended to blow up the 747 in the air and we were going to die."

The chief purser, John Ferrugio, gathered the flight attendants together, telling them that they were proceeding to Cairo and to prepare themselves for the fastest evacuation the world had ever known. Calmly and deliberately, he gave each cabin attendant explicit instructions and responsibilities, leaving nothing to chance, and changing some of their positions. He moved Nelida to the R4 exit. She adds, "John Ferrugio did an excellent job. He kept us together and boosted our morale. The hijackers would not allow the captain to talk to the cabin, so John had all the responsibility for the arrangements and announcements. He kept the passengers calm, reminded them to remove their shoes and eyeglasses and any sharp objects, and gave us all very clear directions for the evacuation. He was able to communicate the importance of evacuation discipline."

After the evacuation briefing, Nelida made her way to one of the rear restrooms, and just as she was about to enter it, one of the hijackers barred her way. "Don't go in there!" he said. "Why?" asked Nelida. "It has a bomb and dynamite in it." Nelida hurriedly made her way to one of the restrooms in the center of the aircraft.

Strange little details assume importance in moments of stress. Nelida figured out that if she stowed her handbag in the galley, she would be able to retrieve it with ease later on. She removed her passport and a medal of St. Jude and put them in a pocket in her uniform before hiding her purse in one of the galley storage compartments.

As the aircraft made its final approach to Cairo, purser Augusta Schneider was approached by one of the terrorists who requested a match. "We are about to land," she admonished. "No smoking now." Forcing her to hand over a pack, he strode off with it into the cabin and lit the fuse to the explosives, warning the passengers as he did so that they had eight minutes before the 747 would explode.

Captain Priddy had never landed in Cairo; no 747 had ever touched down there. Unaware that the fuse had been lit, he might have taken extra time or made an extra circle before landing at the unknown airport. He chose not to, and brought the huge airliner safely down onto the landing strip. Even before it came to a halt, the flight attendants had the doors open and chutes deployed for the 360 passengers to make their desperate bid for safety into the black Egyptian night. By this time, there were two minutes left before the bombs would explode.

The tower advised Captain Priddy to move the aircraft. Unaware that the evacuation was already in progress, he gently eased the 747 forwards. The last of the passengers, still sliding down the chutes, were jolted to the ground. Like greased lightning, John Ferrugio bolted into the cockpit screaming at the captain to stop and insisting that the hijacker and the captain follow him out if they wanted to escape with their lives.

Nelida continues: "One of the trainees, Lisa Hanson, was at my door, R4, the door right behind the engines where you get more of a blow from the exhaust. When all our passengers were out, I told Lisa to go next and I would follow. It was pitch black, truly black, dark, dark out there. You could see nothing. As I was going down, I felt the jolt as the airplane moved and I rolled down the slide, and hit the ground. I knew I was hurt. I felt as though something had struck me on my left side, and I couldn't get up. I screamed for Lisa, saying, 'Help me, Lisa. I can't get up!' She came back; she pulled me up; she grabbed my hand around her neck; she ordered me to run even though I was hurt; she yelled that the 'plane was going to explode. We had run less than a block when all of a sudden that airplane erupted in a fireball and disintegrated. It was not like an explosion where pieces fly around. That airplane went straight up in the air in a ball of flame, lit up the sky, and came right down; everything was utterly destroyed except for the tail with the Pan Am logo on it.

"We heard voices ahead of us, and people kept running farther away from the airplane. It was so dark that we didn't know if people had been hurt, but when the rescue buses arrived we could see everyone, and very few were injured." In fact, everyone had evacuated safely in just 90 seconds, including the hijackers, who boarded the buses with the rest of the passengers and then surrendered to authorities in the terminal.

"I didn't look too good. The left side of my uniform was ripped, and I had cuts and bruises on my hands and knees as well as the huge wound on my hip. I still had my passport, but I had lost my little St. Jude," says Nelida. After the cabin crew was reassured that everyone was accounted for, Augusta accompanied Nelida to the hospital, where her injured hip was X-rayed and treated. When they returned to the airport, they were overjoyed to learn that a

707 was on its way to take them back home that afternoon, with a stop in Rome before going on to New York.

"In Rome, a doctor came on board and gave me a pill to ease the pain and the tension. I took that pill and had just begun to relax when I thought I saw something that looked like my medal on the floor of that 707. One of the flight attendants picked it up and said, 'Hey, Nellie. Isn't this yours?' I couldn't believe it. It *was* my little medal. It was my St. Jude. Isn't that something? What a miracle!"

Skeptics had always doubted that a 747 could be evacuated in a hurry. The cabin crew of Pan American's Flight 93 proved quite definitively that it could.

Terror at Rome

Let the reader observe how succeeding generations have declined more and more until we have plunged downward headlong into the dilemma of our own times.

Livy, *History of Rome*

On 16 December 1973, at the Metropole Hotel in Rome, the Pan Am cabin crew was in a state of delicious anticipation. They had lined up an elegant evening for themselves: a trip to the ballet to see Natalia Makarova perform in *Giselle*. (Makarova had recently defected from the U.S.S.R., and was displaying her perfect blend of passion and technique to the West.) First they readied themselves for the occasion. The women fixed their hair and their nails and made sure that their evening dresses were perfectly pressed. The one man in the group, purser Dominic Franco, put an extra shine on his brand new Bally shoes. He was, after all, the sole escort for five beautiful women. Then they all met for a pre-theatre snack of caviar and champagne before boarding taxis and setting off for the ballet and an evening of blissful enchantment.

In the bus on the way to the airport the following day, 17 December 1973, they read rapturous reviews in the Rome *Daily American* of Makarova's performance. They arrived at Fiumicino and went through their routine briefing before picking up the continuation of Pan Am's Flight 110 to Beirut and Tehran. The aircraft was due to leave at 1 p.m.

Most of the passengers were already on board when the new crew arrived, but a few more stragglers were still expected from an incoming flight. The flight attendants went about their tasks. Purser Diana Perez and Barbara Marnock were working in the first-class cabin, and Lari Hamel was in the galley. Dominic Franco was in the rear cabin with stewardesses Linda Jacobson and Sharon Dyer. They expected 59 passengers, far from a full load on a Boeing 707; it promised to be an easy flight, and the crew was still under the spell of the previous evening.

To pass the time while they were waiting for the remaining passengers, the flight attendants moved about the cabin, chatting to the passengers. Lari struck up a conversation with a young brother and sister, high school students, who were travelling to Beirut to spend Christmas with their parents. They reminded her so much of her own experience of travelling to Italy to be with her parents for the holidays. In a mood of happy reminiscence, Lari returned to the first-class galley.

Suddenly, all hell broke loose.

Laurette Ruth Hamel (known as 'Lari') is an international American. Born in Rhode Island, she moved to Puerto Rico as a child. Often flying on Pan American between the U.S. and San Juan, she became acquainted with the flight attendants, many of whom were only too glad to let the charming little unaccompanied minor make the announcements in Spanish for them. Lari has a perfect ear for languages, and after her father was transferred to Naples, she added Italian and French to her growing collection. Travelling to and from Italy, she also notched up many more Pan American miles, and it came as no surprise that, as soon as she graduated from college in Boston, she applied to Pan American, and was accepted as a flight attendant. She flew out of Miami for a year, then New York for a year, and Honolulu for a year (where she added Japanese to her arsenal of languages) before returning to New York. Because there was a shortage of Italian-speaking flight attendants out of New York, Lari flew to Rome on a regular basis.

"There's trouble in the terminal. Everybody get on the floor. Stay away from the windows." It was the captain's voice coming from the cockpit over the public address system. Lari grabbed her microphone, threw herself down beside the galley, and gave the captain's directions to the passengers in Italian. Diana lifted her head, looked out the window, and screamed, "My God, Lari, they're coming on the airplane."

"The only thing I could imagine," Lari continues, "the worst possible scenario that I could think of was that it was part of a bank robbery, that these people had robbed the currency exchange bank. I had no idea who 'they' were, but I could tell from her voice that it was bad." In fact, three terrorists were running up the steps to the first-class cabin and another three were approaching the rear.

Lari scrambled into her station in the galley and remembered, to her horror, that the emergency slide was not hooked up because Commissary might still return with further supplies. Ken Pfrang, the engineer, burst into the galley and started to open the door, and Lari yelled "My slide's not hooked, my slide's not hooked." She continues: "He opened the door anyway, and the slide pack was just hanging uselessly on the door. I yelled, 'I'll get the slide.' Ken said, 'I'm going to the back,' and dashed out of the galley. To close the door, a pin had to be pushed on the door hinge, and I had to lean three feet out the airplane to grab hold of the door handle. I seriously considered jumping to safety. I closed the door. Now I had to hook the door slide to the galley floor. My hands were shaking uncontrollably as I tried to fit the hook into the floor D-ring. As I struggled, the terrorists threw the first hand grenade, and it exploded, killing Diana, who was lying in the aisle next to the galley. I was crouched over, trying to hook up the slide, and the concussion was so great that it propelled me through the air and I landed on passengers in the aisle by Row 1, clutching my stomach. Bob Davison, our First Officer, later told me that as I flew through the air I was screaming, 'I've been hit, I've been hit.'

"I landed in the middle of the flames that were rapidly spreading throughout the first-class cabin. Then I stood up, and the terrorists threw another grenade. Remember, we were in an aluminum tube, and the concussion was so great that the whole airplane was just rocking uncontrollably. With the second explosion I fell down again and several passengers fell on top of me. Next, they threw a bomb on top of us, a white phosphorous one, which cannot be extinguished with water, blankets, or dry chemical. It just burns to the bone. Then they started shooting everyone on top of me. Everything was on fire: the passengers, the hand luggage, the seats. All I could hear was shooting. I couldn't breathe because of all the smoke, everyone on top of me was crushing me, and I passed out."

Three more terrorists ran up the rear steps, pushed past the flight attendants, burst into the tourist cabin and started shooting and tossing hand grenades and white phosphorous bombs. The ringleader took a look at a panic-stricken 80-year old woman, hanging on to her granddaughter's arm, and started laughing. He pointed the gun at her head and pulled the trigger and shot her dead. Sharon, in the galley, opened the door, but realized that her slide was also unhooked. Instead of jumping out to safety, she, too, quickly closed the door, hooked the slide, and with Linda holding on to her so that she wouldn't fall, reopened the door so that others might leave.

Because all three terrorists were facing forward into the cabin, several passengers were able to stuff themselves into the restrooms for safety. Dominic started inching his way towards the rear stairs, but the old woman's killer caught sight of him, swung around, put his gun to Dominic's head, and pulled the trigger. There were no more bullets. (At the investigation following this incident, Dominic was asked how big the gun was. Opening his arms as wide as they could go, he said, "This big!")

The aircraft was full of black smoke and noxious fumes from the burning interior, but Barbara and Ken Pfrang managed to open the wing exit and hurried some passengers to safety by that route. Then suddenly, the terrorists left as swiftly as they had arrived, running down the stairs and racing over to a Lufthansa 737 which had already been commandeered by a second group of guerrillas. That hijacked 'plane took off for Athens with the terrorists demanding the release of two jailed Palestinians.

When Lari regained consciousness, the cabin was filled with black smoke and utterly silent. She then set about the gruesome task of extricating herself from a heap of dead bodies. "It was horrible. I just can't tell you how horrible it was. It was like dismembering people. I kept yelling 'MOVE! MOVE!' No one was moving. I began to get frustrated; my head was pinned against the floor and I couldn't move. I reached up to the first person on top of me, yelling 'MOVE!' and tried to shift him, and while I was trying to pull him off me, I realized that I was holding a burning arm. I was repulsed, and reached up again and came back with a foot in a shoe, also still burning. Everyone was in pieces smoldering. But by this time, at least I had freed my head. No one on top of me in that pile was alive; no one in first-class was alive. I was alone and I was terrified."

Lari started to crawl towards the back of the aircraft. "You'd crawl a foot, and you were coughing, coughing, coughing, and the airplane was silent, not a word. You'd be crawling and all of a sudden you would pass out because of the heat

*Lari Hamel after her
miraculous escape.*

and because you couldn't breathe, and then you'd come to momentarily. I kept going and going and finally I said to myself 'I've been going for so long. Where am I?' So I stood up to feel for the bump on the hat rack where the emergency exits were, and just as I did that, an oxygen bottle exploded. I thought it was another bomb, and I dove for the floor. When I started crawling again, I was facing the other direction. I thought I was crawling aft, but I ended up in first-class again."

The first-class exits were completely blocked by the life rafts, which had come down from the ceiling and were on fire. "I was screwed, I was so screwed. I didn't know what to do. I noticed dimly that two seats in first-class weren't burning, 4A and B, so I just crawled onto those seats and lay there. I thought I had been on the airplane for hours; it seemed like an eternity." (Lari's horrendous experience lasted, in fact, 22 minutes.)

"It was pitch dark, I couldn't breathe, and I passed out again from the smoke. The next thing I knew, it was all light and wonderful and from about nine feet up I could see my body on the seat in the middle of all the flames. I knew it was me and I wondered why I wasn't moving, why I wasn't being harmed in the middle of the fire. I had such a feeling of love and joy. Right through the smoke, I saw the emergency exit, and then I heard a woman's voice screaming 'Open the window, open the window!' I thought, 'I have to help her,' and the next thing I knew, there I was again in the middle of the fire, but the difference was that I knew how to find my way out. I still had my shoes on, and I started kicking the window. (I learned later that it was one of only three or four left intact.) I never heard another word after that.

"I couldn't see anything. My contacts had just fried on my eyes. I went down on all fours again in the aisle and started crawling towards the left wing exit. All the briefcases had caught on fire, they were all in the middle of the aisle, and the aisle was loaded with burning bodies. There was complete silence, interrupted occasionally by the crackling of flames and explosions. I crawled and crawled and crawled through the cabin. It was black, black, black, and then I saw a lighter shade of black, and then I could see light gray, and I knew it was the exit. I was so weak. As I lay on the floor with both hands on the bottom of the open wing exit, I whispered, 'Somebody help me. Somebody, please help me.' There were more explosions in the cabin behind me, and I suddenly realized that the only person who could help me was myself. I gathered all my energy and dragged myself through the wing exit. I stood up on the wing and began vomiting black stuff. The air outside the flaming cabin was cold, and I then became aware that there were large burn holes in the back of my uniform and the hair on the back of my head was singed. I just stood there on the wing, out of it.

"Then I saw my friends. It seemed as if the whole crew was on the tarmac yelling at me, 'Jump! Jump! The airplane's going to explode,' and I thought 'Holy Shit, they're right!' and I did one of these double ups like at the start of a race, and I ran and jumped off the wing up into the air."

Dominic caught Lari as she came down, and held her in his arms, saying, "Lari dear, what beautiful Pucci underwear you have!" to which Lari, without dropping a beat, responded, "Why, thank you, Dominic!" Then he became serious again and yelled "Let's get the hell out of here!"

Lari was the last person to leave the aircraft alive. Twenty-eight passengers and purser Diana Perez had been murdered inside the 707.

"It was chaos, chaos, on the tarmac," Lari continues. "I saw a policeman trying to hide behind a large barrel, and I yelled at him 'Help us. You've got to get those guys.' And he responded '*Sono pazzi. Non mi uscideranno!*' ['They're crazy. I'm not going to get killed.'] Then I saw this little girl running around, crying 'Mommy, Mommy, Mommy!' and I grabbed her and said 'We'll find your mom.'"

When Lari tried to enter the terminal with the child, the official refused to let them in without their passports. Lari said, "I'm from Pan Am 110. Look at me. I have no passport. Everything's gone." The official was adamant. Finally, Lari took the little girl by the hand and walked firmly through the barrier saying 'So shoot me, shoot me.' She hurried with the child to the safety of the Alitalia V.I.P. lounge, told her she was going to find her parents, and started to leave. The other occupants of the Alitalia lounge grabbed hold of Lari and the little girl, hugging and kissing them, begging Lari to stay, insisting that it was not safe for her to return outside. But Lari extricated herself from their arms, and ran back to help the surviving passengers.

She continues: "Operations had fallen apart. One of its mechanics had been shot as the terrorists stormed our airplane. People were hysterical, all sitting around crying. So it was up to us to load the ambulances. Dominic and I were doing the translating, asking who needed to go to the hospital and who didn't. We were just piling them in. We had 30 survivors, but many of them died at the hospital. The ambulance driver was ready to leave, but I could still see people wandering around. I recognized the young girl from the pair I had talked to before the flight. The ambulance driver asked 'Her, too?' From a distance, she looked fine, so I said 'No.' I ran up to her and went to put my arm around her shoulder, but there was nothing there. A bomb had caught her. I don't know how she was moving. She was a face but no head. The bomb had sliced her right in half. I couldn't believe she was running. I grabbed her and threw her in. Her brother had survived." (Two years later the crew received a letter of thanks from him.)

"Then I rushed back to Operations where I found the parents of the little girl, crying and frantic, running up to everyone asking, 'Where's my baby? Has anyone seen my baby?' I immediately told them where she was, and they tore off down the corridor to find her. Then we just started pulling things together, writing down people's names and where they were sitting, trying to..." Lari's voice drops and then it rises again in anguish and indignation. "The crew is doing this! The surviving crew are doing the ground staff's job. Everyone else has fallen apart, and we're running the show! We stayed there for hours. We stayed there until dusk. We remained coolly professional at the airport, but when we finally boarded the taxis to go to the hotel, we all began sobbing hysterically. Even the taxi driver was crying.

"We were not taken to the Metropole where we usually stayed, but to another beautiful hotel where the press couldn't find us. The manager gave us adjoining rooms because we couldn't bear to be separated from each other. We couldn't be alone. We all sat together in one room, comforting the captain, whose wife had been in first-class and had died along with Diana. We sat huddled together, sobbing and recounting our stories, over and over. But every now and then, we would begin laughing uncontrollably over something as trivial as one of us cutting the gold sleeve off a champagne bottle incorrectly. Removing the entire gold sleeve top could send us into gales of laughter, and we all fell off the bed, giggling like maniacs. The room service waiters couldn't get out of there fast enough."

Lari wanted to return home immediately after the debriefing. She was still unable to see well because of the loss of her contact lenses. When she and Barbara landed at Kennedy Airport, they were met by the base manager, who took them out through a special exit so as to avoid the press. As they were leaving the terminal, he sidled up to Lari and said, "Listen, Lari, by the way, we've looked at your line, and we see you're scheduled to fly Romes for the rest of the month. We're really short of Italian-qualifieds right now. Do you think you can fly 'em?"

Lari continues: "There was no way. I was a wreck. I just fell apart after that. I was angry. I was so angry about the lack of safety precautions. I was angry that we weren't allowed to hook up our slides as soon as Commissary had loaded the galley. I was angry that people had died because they did not know how to unfasten their seat belts and couldn't see where the emergency exits were. I was angry that the hand luggage was not secure. Most of all, I was angry that God let me live but made Diana die. She was just about to get married and was madly in love. She was 40 and at the pinnacle of her life, and I was at the worst point in mine."

Lari immediately began channelling her anger by working zealously for safety in the cabin. She made a list of recommendations, and came up with eight major suggestions, deciding to focus at first on the three most important. She took them to the base manager and was told, "We'll take care of it, Lari. We'll take care of it."

On 25 January 1974, a little more than a month after the Rome incident, Lari went back on the line. In her purse she carried a letter from the company which said that under no circumstances should she be sent to Rome. As the weeks went by and she recognized that none of her suggestions for cabin safety had been acted upon, she became more and more frustrated. Everywhere she went, she tried to influence Pan Am management and crews about the importance of cabin safety. "I considered it my role to educate people," she says "so that all those passengers should not have died for naught. I kept saying 'If we had had a clear aisle, if all the passengers had known how to unfasten their seat belts, if they had known exactly where the exits were, if there were strobe lights to indicate the exits.' No one listened."

Finally, in March, just as her aircraft was coming in to land at Kennedy Airport, Lari learned that a Pan Am base director was on board. All the passengers were buckled in, and the 'plane was in its final approach, but Lari found out where he was sitting and ran to his seat, blurting, "I only just learned you were on board. I'm Lari Hamel, and I was in the Rome incident. I keep asking for three safety items, but no one is listening to me." As she spoke, Lari kept glancing out the window to see how close they were to to the ground so that she would be able to return to her seat in time for the touchdown. "He thought I was a fruitcake because I kept looking away. He didn't realize I was checking our altitude."

As soon as she arrived home, Lari received a telephone call from her supervisor, cancelling her next flight and asking her to report to Medical the following Monday. The company had grounded her because she was 'depressed,' and wanted her to see a psychiatrist because of her behavior on the airplane. Lari visited the psychiatrist twice, after which he wrote to Pan Am praising her mental competence, remarking how valid her safety points were, and asking the company why they had not followed through with her suggestions since the modifications she recommended made good sense to him. Based on the psychiatrist's report, Pan Am's corporate physician, Dr. Constantino, un-grounded Lari, and both he and the psychiatrist gave her some advice for the future: "Be a little less Italian. Work quietly through the system." Lari remarks, "I had lived in Italy. I use my hands a lot. I talk with my hands, and I was too expressive in dealing with that base director. I should have been much more subdued. I needed to be calmer, more direct." She took the two doctors' suggestions and began a writing campaign.

"I had found my mission, and my mission was safety and health. I became director of Health and Safety for the organization called Stewardesses for Women's Rights in New York, representing all airlines. I felt strongly that the Transport Workers' Union, which was representing Pan Am at the time, was not addressing our concerns and that we needed to put more pressure on the company and the F.A.A. Neither the union nor the company would listen to us, to our valid concerns regarding the ozone issue, for instance. When you have flight attendants coughing blood on Tokyo flights, there is definitely a problem.

"Seven San Francisco flight attendants took steps to start a new union. They succeeded, and I became the Chairperson of Health and Safety in New York. I began working with the Los Angeles and San Francisco Health and Safety people, and we took our concerns to Washington where there were Senate sub-committee hearings.

"Just about all the safety points I made have become law. Now there are hundreds of people who will survive those accidents that are survivable because there are luggage guards on the aisles, because there are lights by the wing exits, because people know how to put their seat belts on and off, and because the flight attendants take time to point out the exits very carefully. It took me a long time, it probably took ten years to resolve everything, but I did it, a little bit at a time, obstinately, quietly, working through channels."

Here is one of life's strange para-doxes, a paradox that aviation terrorists probably never reflect on: the murderers on board Pan Am 110 on 17 December 1973 may have ultimately saved more lives than they destroyed because they sparked off Lari Hamel's anger which led to the legisla-tion that resulted from her mission.

Lari Hamel
recovering, one
month after the
terrorist attack.

Last Flight From Saigon

And there to my astonishment I found
New refugees in a great crowd: men and women
Gathered for exile, young—pitiful people
Coming from every quarter, minds made up.
Virgil, Aeneid, II, 796-799

The Vietnam War officially ended for the United States on 3 February 1973, and the last U.S. troops left in June of that year. However, the war was not over for the Vietnamese people, nor did business with the U.S. come to a grinding halt; Pan Am, I.B.M., and many other corporations remained in Saigon.

The situation for the South Vietnamese people started seriously unravelling in February 1975, when the U.S. Government cut back on aid. The Army cried out desperately that it could not contain the advancing North Vietnamese forces without U.S. help, but Congress refused to budge. Immediately, the South Vietnamese troops, demoralized and unpaid, started giving up territory that had already been secured, insisting they could not hold it. As they pulled back, the North Vietnamese poured into the South like water through a hole in a dyke. But they, too, had been caught off guard. They were in disarray because they were rapidly achieving goals that they had not imagined they could achieve for another five years. Saigon was the plum that was just within their grasp.

This is the point at which Pan Am's station manager in Saigon, Al Topping, recognized that the end was near. His problem was to figure out when exactly it was going to happen. "You don't want to be the last one out," he says, "but you don't want to leave too early. Flying Tigers shut down its operation a month earlier than we did, Citibank left six weeks earlier, I.B.M. and Esso left about two months earlier. And New York kept asking me 'When do you plan to leave?' And I said 'I don't know yet.' And they said 'We think you ought to leave now.'"

Al felt he had a little time left and wanted to hang on because so many people were still desperate to get out. He argued: "We're operating a 747 with a lot of seats on it and people are still buying tickets, so let's keep flying." "Until when?" asked New York. "I don't know. Just trust me," he replied.

One night early in March, Al found himself pacing the floor, still trying to figure out when Saigon would collapse. He glanced at the calendar hanging on the wall, and the date of 1 May leaped out at him. "It suddenly dawned on me that 1 May would be the day, May Day, the communist equivalent of the Fourth of July. Then I looked at our schedule and saw that Thursday, 24 April, was just seven days before that, which would give us a cushion of one week."

Al continues: "I sent coded telex messages about the date back to New York. What was really hard for me was keeping it a secret from our employees, who would all be leaving on the last flight, except for those we had already managed to sneak out. The most dramatic unauthorized departure was that of my secretary's three-month-old baby. My secretary wanted to leave with him, but I decided that would not be good for morale. We gave the baby to a volunteer who went out on a scheduled flight, then my secretary called her husband in Boston and told him to fly to L.A. right away so that he would be there when the baby arrived. It worked out, and she herself did leave on the last flight."

But Al's biggest worry was whether the company would be able to find a crew that was willing to come into Saigon's Tan Son Nhut Airport. "I was putting myself in the shoes of a flight attendant or a pilot back in the States, reading about what was happening in Saigon, and asking myself 'Would I want to fly there?' No way! When that airplane came in on 24 April, it was like AHHH! That was the most beautiful sight that I have ever seen—that blue ball descending from the sky. That's the proudest looking bird you ever want to see."

Pamela Borgfeldt (Taylor) was born in Hollywood, California. She passed her first screen test at the age of five and was selected for Shirley Temple's part in a remake of *Little Miss Marker*. However, this was not to be the beginning of a film career; her childhood was spent moving from place to place with her military family. She grew to love travelling and determined that when she grew up, her career would involve travel. Cornered by a Pan Am recruiter at the Miss Universe pageant in Miami in 1964, where she was representing the state of Alabama, she jumped at the opportunity to become a flight attendant.

Pamela's beauty was matched by her courage, and she never refused assignments into dangerous places at dangerous times, places such as Beirut, Tehran and, during the Biafran War, Lagos. In addition, much of her career was spent flying troops into and out of Vietnam on Rest and Rehabilitation (R & R) missions. (Flight attendants who worked on R & R flights were given

2nd Lieutenant status, which meant that under Geneva Convention rules they should be treated as officers in the event of capture. During the Vietnam War, Pacific-based cabin crew flew thousands of R & R flights, and many of the flight attendants made a point of visiting the injured during their stays in South Vietnam. A hospital visit from a Pan Am stewardess could do wonders for an injured soldier's morale.)

Pamela's greatest challenge came when she volunteered to be one of two pursers on the crew of Pan Am's last scheduled flight out of Vietnam on 24 April 1975. She was at her home in Berkeley when the call came. She felt a chill of excitement run up her spine but no hesitation at all about flying to Saigon to evacuate the Pan Am employees. Her scheduling supervisor was unable to give her any idea how long she would be away or what demands would be made of her, but experience warned her that there would be long periods of waiting. An enthusiastic tennis player, she packed her racquet before she flew off.

Pamela was the first of the volunteers to arrive in Guam, which was the staging point for the evacuation and also one of the stops on Pan Am's regular Pacific schedule. She occupied her time during the ten days of waiting for the other crew members by playing tennis, working off the frustration of having to sit around in a state of anxious anticipation.

One by one, the other cabin crew members showed up. They comprised Pan Am's usual individualistic assortment, some U.S.-born, some foreign, various ages: Laura Lee Gillespie as senior purser; Tra Duong, Gudrun Meisner, Susan Matson, Valerie Chaulk, Sissel Donnelly, Jean Stewart Kelly, and Sally Pearl as flight attendants; and Pamela herself as junior purser. The one thing they had in common was that they had volunteered to evacuate their fellow employees when Pan Am ceased operations in Saigon. They had no idea who their cockpit crew would be, and Pamela says that they just hoped for an easy-going captain, one who did not think he was God Almighty. They agreed that flexibility in their cockpit crew would be a paramount requirement, in the form of willingness to bend rules for humanitarian reasons.

Throughout the Vietnam War, in addition to military charters, Pan Am had maintained regularly scheduled flights in and out of Saigon's Tan Son Nhut Airport on Tuesdays and Thursdays, except for times such as the 1968 Tet Offensive when the airport was closed because of nearby combat. The newly-assembled cabin crew finally learned that they would be going into Saigon on Tuesday, 22 April, but it was unclear to them at that time as to whether or not that would be the evacuation flight itself. On 21 April, they discovered that Captain Chuck Kimes would be in charge of the aircraft—and decided that he was just the kind of captain they had hoped for.

Boeing 747 Flight 841 to Saigon via Manila left Guam early in the morning of 22 April, but it was not destined to be the last flight. As soon as this was made clear to them, the cabin crew decided to use it as a reconnaissance mission to learn everything they could about evacuating as many people as possible on the last flight.

Going into Saigon that day, there were a mere 19 passengers on board the Boeing 747, whose full load was usually 350. Even so, Pamela was at a loss to understand why anyone at all would want to go to Saigon when everyone there wanted to leave. She questioned the passengers about their motives and listened to their desperate stories. Several of them were American servicemen going to try to find their Vietnamese sweethearts. A colonel in the Army of the Republic of Viet Nam (ARVN) was returning to Vietnam to try and evacuate his young son. He had a wife and four daughters as well, but was resigned to the fact that they would all die; the son was the designated survivor. This was Pamela's first chance to contribute actively to an escape, and she and the colonel started making plans.

Tra Duong, the Vietnamese-American flight attendant, had volunteered to be on the last flight for urgent reasons of her own. When Pamela told her about her plan to help the colonel, Tra immediately grasped the opportunity. She approached the colonel and offered to help him with his son if he would assist her in getting her five sisters to the airport. A deal was struck. The next time they flew in, Tra would escort his son past the emigration desk; in return, the colonel would spirit her sisters through the heavily guarded airport entry and into the cargo hangar, where she could pick them up.

On 22 April, the North Vietnamese army was only nine miles from the airport. To avoid anti-aircraft fire along the flight path down to Tan Son Nhut, the 747 flew high until it approached the airport and then descended in a tight spiral. As they landed, Pamela watched South Vietnamese fighter planes taking off, heavily loaded with bombs and rockets, and she could hear crumps and booms as the bombs exploded close by. The 747 made its way to its regular place in front of the terminal, and the flight attendants disembarked.

Pamela was horrified by the utter chaos. Hundreds of South Vietnamese soldiers were everywhere, toting machine guns, and far more than the usual number of laborers were at work on Tan Son Nhut's interminable construction projects. Pamela recalls: "There was always construction of some sort at the airport in Saigon. But how incongruous: at a time when everyone was clamoring to get out, here were the laborers picking up stones and digging ditches. I wondered if they were North Vietnamese, watching our movements. There was always that fear in Vietnam. Who was who?"

But worst of all were the huge crowds that had gathered behind the chain link fence surrounding the terminal, women weeping and screaming, reaching their arms out, begging the flight attendants to take their children. Pamela was overwhelmed by the sheer numbers of frantic people, by the massive military presence, and by a feeling of despair. But Tra was filled with purpose. She went straight to Pan Am Operations to make contact with a friend who could take a message on foot to her sisters, alerting them that the colonel would collect and deliver them to the airport in time for Thursday's flight.

Suddenly Pamela was shaken out of her despair by the sight of Valerie Chaulk, waving at her from deep in a crowd in a corner of the terminal. A Vietnamese woman was clinging to her, weeping, pleading with her to take her little girl. "Take her, take her," she begged Valerie, shoving the child at her again and again. Pamela and Gudrun converged on the scene and, with Valerie, gathered around the woman as she bade her grief-stricken farewell; then they parted to allow her to vanish into the crowd. They formed a block around the four-year-old, concealing her with their skirts, their legs, their handbags, and marched past the single emigration desk for the flight to Manila. The desk was taller than the child and the official behind it did not see her as they swept quickly by. As soon as they were safely on board, Valerie folded the little girl in her arms and hid with her in one of the restrooms.

When Pamela returned to the terminal, she was approached by a Vietnamese woman who, with her American husband and their children, had witnessed the little girl's escape. They were all about to depart, except for the 14-year-old son, who did not have an exit visa. (These exit 'visas' could cost as much as $20,000 per person.) They had brought him to the airport on the off chance that somebody could help. He was an unattractive child, and Pamela felt as though she were being offered some kind of mongrel that no one wanted, the family reject. Tears well up in her eyes and her gentle voice breaks as she recounts: "The boy was in shock from the time I met him. He was numb and expressionless because his family was abandoning him at the airport. As an Amerasian—a very tall, heavy, and ugly one—he had little hope, and it showed. He was a boy without a country, an outcast. It was clear that his parents really didn't care what happened to him, and they didn't even try to hide their feelings. I took the boy."

Pamela's bluff with a boarding pass at the emigration desk failed. The official refused to listen as she insisted that his family was already on board. Undaunted, she turned back into the terminal, walked with the boy out of the building, and circumnavigated several large hangars. They were approaching the 747 when suddenly, "A lone guard appeared as the boy and I rounded a

Susan Matson, Gudrun Meisner, the rescued child, and Pamela Taylor.

corner. He pushed us back with his gun and grunted in Vietnamese, motioning to us to get back—in other words to return to the area we had just left, the entry where one would file into line for emigration." That, of course, was the same route that Pamela had already tried.

Inside the building, she spoke firmly to the stricken boy, hoping he would understand. "English? You speak English?" she asked. He nodded. "Thursday," she insisted, "You be at the airport on Thursday. I will come for you. We will get you on the 'plane then. Do you understand?" He nodded again, his face blank with sorrow, and she turned away. She felt his stare following her as she made her way past the emigration desk without him.

"After all the passengers had boarded," Pamela continues, "emigration officials with machine guns came on board the aircraft and checked each passport, visa, and ticket. They banged on all the restroom doors, and Valerie opened hers a crack, so that they could see her Western face, then she slammed it shut again. After the emigration officials departed, the ground agent came up the ramp, carrying two children. It was her job to make a short announcement, leave the aircraft, and close the door from the outside. She got it half-way shut, but then suddenly thrust one of the children into Pamela's arms, swiftly slipped on board with the other child, and drew the door shut behind her." She was utterly distraught. The children she had brought on board were her own, but she had not been able to inform her husband and the rest of her family about her precipitous departure.

As soon as the door was secure, Captain Kimes started the engines and made for the runway. Just 91 passengers were aboard Pan Am's next-to-last flight out of Saigon, a number that Pamela found obscenely small in light of how many people the 747 could carry and all the panic-stricken people who had been left behind.

The flight attendants were required to remain in Manila that night. Valerie, however, flew on to Honolulu, going AWOL because she refused to be separated from the little girl she had rescued. Captain Kimes and the cockpit crew flew to Guam, along with most of the passengers.

Once again, the flight attendants raised the question: who would be flying the aircraft to Saigon on Thursday, the 24th? With the North Vietnamese army so close to the airport, Pan Am's departure was dramatically critical. As soon as the cabin crew disembarked in Manila, Pamela hurried to check the cockpit crew list for Thursday. She discovered that Captain Bob Berg, who had just come in on a regularly scheduled flight, would be in charge. One of the other flight attendants knew him and gave the seal of approval. "Yes, he's flexible too," she said. Pamela said later: " We trusted him immediately. He was just as nice as he was good-looking—warm, friendly, and cooperative. " There were still no names for the co-pilot and engineer.

What remained a vivid memory to the cabin crew after their 'reconnaissance mission' was the desperation of the women they saw at the airport and their willingness to hand over their children to total strangers in the hope that they might survive. Also evident was that a person wearing a Pan Am uniform could pass the emigration desk without being stopped. The flight attendants made their plans accordingly. As soon as they reached the hotel, they set about collecting as many uniforms as they could from other flight attendants who were in Manila on layovers, acquiring a skirt here, a jacket there, some slacks, a scarf or two, some shoes, adding them to their own extra outfits. They also collected wigs and dark glasses.

Still in Manila on Wednesday, 23 April, they all tried to relax in individual ways. Pamela, of course, reached for her tennis racquet, and when she found Bob Berg on the courts in the late afternoon, she joined him in a game. As they played, they discussed the probability that the next day's flight might be the last. Suddenly they were interrupted by a breathless Pan Am employee, who rushed up to warn them that Saigon was falling. Pamela's stomach gave a sickening lurch of disappointment when she realized that Thursday's flight might not be able to get into Tan Son Nhut.

Undaunted, Captain Berg and the cabin crew rose before dawn on Thursday, 24 April, and when they arrived at Manila airport, a co-pilot and engineer appeared for the flight, as if by magic. The flight attendants were whisked into the small, windowless back room belonging to Pan Am Operations. Very solemnly, the operations manager informed them that Tan Son Nhut was closed. "We all looked at Tra," Pamela says, "and there was a chill because it sounded as though we would be unable to go in. We waited anxiously while Ops negotiated with U.S. officials on the telephone, and finally the approval came—from President Ford himself. We were to go in as a military charter, and the operations head stressed again and again 'On a voluntary basis only.'" He explained that the Clipper would fly to Saigon according to its regular schedule so as to evacuate the Pan Am employees, even though the F.A.A. had announced that Tan Son Nhut was too dangerous for commercial aircraft. As a result of negotiations with the Air Force and the State Department, PAA Flight 841 became an Air Force mercy flight, to be known as Special Air Mission 1965/31 Evacuation Charter MNL/SGN/MNL.

Pamela describes her feelings at that moment: "I felt a wave of fear and a quickened awareness of responsibility. We all knew what we wanted to accomplish, and at the same time we knew it could be dangerous, involving hazards that we tried not to imagine. As a U.S. passport holder and with Pan Am behind us, however, I felt safe. Pan Am had always taken care of its employees, and the flight attendants knew that this was a mission to save their own people." Pamela recalls that none of the women expressed any fear or ambivalence. She herself had awakened that morning with a strong intuition that all would be well, and she was confident of the absolute rightness of their mission. It was one of those rare moments in life when a path appears straight and clear.

The operations head explained what a mercy flight involved and showed the crew the astonishing wire he had received from the F.A.A., lifting seat restrictions and certain emergency procedures. It was astonishing because it displayed such a lack of bureaucratic rigidity and broke rules in the greater interest of humanity.

REFERENCE MT 231330 HEREWITH APPROVED PROCEDURES FOR PASSENGER CARRIAGE ON EVACUATION MISSIONS NOTE ALL NORMAL FAA/FAR PASSENGER CARRIAGE REQUIREMENTS ARE WAIVED

ONE/FICL SEATS 2 PASSENGERS PER DOUBLE SEAT 1 PASSENGER ON FLOOR BETWEEN EACH ROW /BACK TO WALL FEET TO AISLE/REMAINING PASSENGERS ON FLOOR WHERE SPACE AVAILABLE STOP

TWO/ECONOMY AREA 10 ABREAST CONFIGURATION INCREASE EY PAX BY 10 PER CENT 3 PAX PER TRIPLE SEAT 3 PAX PER DOUBLE SEAT/RETRACT ARM RESTS 5 PAX ABREAST IN CENTER SECTION OF SEATS/RETRACT ARM RESTS

THREE/LOAD 28 PAX IN UPPER LOUNGE CMA AFTER ALL SEATS OCCUPIED REMAINDER OF PAX ON FLOOR

FOUR/MAXIMUM NUMBER OF PASSENGERS BASED ON ABOVE PROCEDURES AND USING CONFIG 30/370 IS TOTAL 495 PASSENGERS STOP

FIVE/BASIC LIMITATIONS OBSERVE NORMAL WEIGHT AND BALANCE LIMITS SEAT BELT REQUIREMENTS ARE WAIVED EMERGENCY REQUIREMENTS ARE WAIVED EMERGENCY EQUIP-MENT REQUIREMENTS ARE WAIVED DO NOT ADD LIFE VESTS/LIFT RAFTS/OXYGEN FOR ADDITIONAL PAX NO LIMITATIONS FOR INFANTS IN ARMS OR SMALL CHILDREN IN LAPS

SIX/ALL ABOVE WITH CONCURRENCE OF CREW AND EVAC-UEES STOP

Meanwhile, in Saigon, eleventh-hour preparations were under way because even Pan Am's Vietnamese employees were not allowed to depart without exit visas which, even with costly payoffs, could take as long as two or three years to acquire. Al Topping explains: "The U.S. government put a lot of pressure on the South Vietnamese government to come up with some alternative options on how to get people out, rapid fire. One of the ways was for Americans to sponsor the Vietnamese. The way I got all of our people out was by officially and legally adopting them all. My staff worked on a huge pile of forms and papers and finally got it all together just in time. I signed all these papers—I had no idea what I was signing; it was all in Vietnamese." But those papers made it official: Al had just become father to an enormous Vietnamese family that had the right to emigrate.

Most of the Pan Am employees and their relatives spent their last night in Vietnam in the back rooms of the downtown Saigon ticket office. Al continues: "Two or three hundred people slept in the back rooms. This was necessary because we had arranged for the buses to pick them up at the ticket office early the next morning. The last two weeks or so, I actually slept at the airport. I didn't go downtown any more because I wanted to be able to help people at the airport at any time. Saigon itself was boiling and you could very easily get trapped there if panic broke out. It was a scary time, but I didn't seem to have any real concern about myself because I knew I would get out on something or other, but I was very concerned about our employees; there was no back-up plan for them."

Pamela remembers little about the two-hour flight from Manila to Saigon on Thursday, 24 April, except that it was empty. The usual bustle of flight service was completely missing and they seemed to be floating through the quiet eye of a hurricane. The aircraft descended in the same tight spiral as it had on Tuesday's flight, but after it touched down the tower refused permission for it to park in its usual place in front of the terminal. Instead, it was ordered to remain at the end of the runway, starkly visible, totally unprotected, and a long, perilous, and disconcerting, hike from the airport terminal and cargo buildings.

The cabin crew and the captain discussed the F.A.A.'s revised passenger limit and agreed that they would simply stuff as many people into the 747 as they could. When Al Topping came on board, he told the captain that they would be carrying a large number of Pan Am employees and their families plus a few regular, ticket-holding passengers but admitted "I don't know how many people are going on this thing today. What's the maximum?", and Bob Berg replied "As many as you want." Concerning cargo, Al decided that the aircraft would carry the regular passengers' baggage, but Pan Am employees would leave the country with just their carry-on flight bags, in order to convert cargo weight to passenger weight. (Later, when two C.I.A. agents came up the moveable stairs, carrying three enormous duffel bags, Pamela refused to let the bags into the cabin. "It's four million, in green, from the Embassy" the agents argued. "Not in here," said Pamela, turning them away. They trailed down the stairs and managed to stash the bags in the belly themselves.)

Before the flight attendants set off for the terminal, Bob Berg gave Pamela his solemn word that he would not leave Tan Son Nhut until they were all back on board. The red anti-collision lights flashing on top and bottom of the 747 would be his signal to them to return immediately to the aircraft.

When Pamela opened the cabin door, a member of Pan Am's ground personnel was right there to whisper in her ear that Tra Duong's five sisters and her little nephew were hiding in the cargo area. Tra and Gudrun Meisner joined Pamela, and together they scurried to the hangar, carrying the bags filled with Pan Am clothes that they had collected in Manila. At first they could not find Tra's sisters, and their hearts sank, but the colonel had kept his promise; they were in a small back room, sitting silently on top of a packing crate. The colonel had taken Tra's sisters to his home on the base the previous night and had then delivered them to the cargo hangar. They had a message for Pamela from the colonel: his family, including his little boy, had already escaped on a Navy boat.

The flight attendants wasted no time. They yanked the clothes out of the bags and told the girls: "Put these on, and when you walk onto that aircraft, hold your heads up proudly. Act as though you know your way around, as if you are a part of Pan Am." As soon as Tra's sisters were dressed, they boarded a cargo van with the little boy tucked securely in their midst and rode across the tarmac to the aircraft. Once they were on board, they were handed other children to care for and did, in effect, function as the flight attendants they were dressed up to represent.

Again and again, the cabin crew ran the half-mile in and out of the terminal, bringing passengers out to the aircraft. In Pamela's words: "People had begun to feel panicky. They couldn't wait to get onto the aircraft. At that point, South Vietnamese cities were falling every hour, and the soldiers had thrown down their guns and started to flee. Heads were hanging from poles in the country and in the small cities, heads of those who worked for the Americans." She continues: "We were working so hard getting the passengers on board, running back and forth, back and forth, or hitching rides on three-wheel scooters. We were exhausted, and it was an overwhelmingly sad situation."

Suddenly a South Vietnamese soldier with a machine gun appeared at the foot of the stairs to the aircraft, and refused to allow anyone else to board. He gathered a crowd there, most of whom were immobilized by the machine gun, but a few people managed to flee up the ramp. Just as suddenly as he appeared, the cabin crew realized what it would take to get the crowd on board. Cash. They started to bribe the guard who immediately smiled, became amenable, and let the first person through. Then the next. Inside the cabin, two of the flight attendants passed pillow cases around the aircraft, collecting Vietnamese piasters (which no longer had any worth for the passengers). As the pillow cases stuffed with money were handed to the guard, his smile became broader, and a steady flow of passengers boarded the aircraft. As more and more people came on board, it became easier and easier to collect the money.

Inside the terminal, Gudrun Meisner took over the Pan Am ticket counter and dealt with passengers so that the ticket agents could hurry out and board the aircraft (she herself would be the last person up the stairs). Meanwhile, Pamela searched the terminal frantically for the boy to whom she had given her promise. She found herself in the same position as a Vietnamese mother, desperate to get her child out, begging strangers for help in finding him. "Everyone in the chaos of the airport was running in different directions. There was no one keeping order, no one to help, and no one who remembered a strange-looking boy from two days past, just another bit of flotsam in the flood. I tried not to feel frantic when I couldn't find him. I told myself he could have escaped some other way. So many other tragedies were occurring right before my eyes that I didn't have time to feel sad for him in particular. That came later when I realized that he represented for me, in one Vietnamese child, the sorrows of thousands of hopelessly abandoned family members. But at that moment, there were hundreds of others whom I could help." Pamela felt the minutes ebbing away, and she glanced out of the terminal windows. The lights were flashing on the 747. It was time to flee.

Once Gudrun had hustled the last passenger on board and the 747's doors were closed and the engines started, Al Topping bade farewell to the ramp operations manager, Nguyen Van Luc, Pan Am's last employee in Saigon. He had decided to remain behind because of his nine children and sick mother. Then Al sprang up into the nose wheel well and climbed from up there into the cabin. Nguyen Van Luc, wearing noise suppressors to protect his ears from the piercing whine of the 747's engines, waved the wands to direct the aircraft from its parking place towards the one runway that remained open; 463 people, of whom 315 were Pan Am employees and their families, were on board.

Captain Berg increased power and taxied to the take-off area. As they taxied, both the crew and the passengers recognized the sound of artillery fire and were aware of just how vulnerable the 747 was. In fact, an ARVN fighter 'plane had just been hit by crossfire, and debris was all over the runway, blocking their escape. Al Topping describes the situation: "We were told by the tower to wait, and the wait dragged on for 50 minutes. It was really difficult. You're on this 'plane with almost 500 people. You're sitting there and you're sweating. I was getting worried that they were going to call us back to the gate because we had people on there that weren't supposed to be on there."

Bob Berg was keenly aware how valuable a 747 would be to the North Vietnamese. He knew it was absolutely crucial to take off immediately. With his engines still running, he negotiated calmly and deliberately with the tower, insisting that the wreckage of the the fighter plane be bulldozed from the runway. Finally, the tower acquiesced. As soon as the bulldozer had completed its dismal task, *Clipper Unity* started to roll. On and on it rolled, wallowing along the entire runway before it heaved up, free of the ground. "Vietnam's terrain in the Saigon area is very flat and the North Vietnamese could have just blown that 747 out of the beautiful blue sky," Al says. "I'll tell you, when we took off, I was in the cockpit, and as we finally crossed the coastline of South Vietnam, and I looked down and saw all these American ships out there, that's when I knew that we had made it out."

At this point in the Hollywood version of these events, the movie *Last Flight Out,* the passengers begin to clap and cheer. This is a flagrant misrepresentation. Pamela says that the reality aboard the evacuation charter was utter silence. "It was absolutely quiet and there was an enormous amount of sadness, not joy. Again and again as I walked down the aisle during the journey, hands would stretch out and grab mine in a beautiful squeeze of thanks. My heart was breaking for our employees who were all leaving their homeland. Their country was being overrun, and they were desolated. Remember that for many years the people of South Vietnam had thought that the Americans would defeat the North. This sudden, ignoble fleeing was shocking. Nothing we said could help, but sometimes when something awfully sad happens a hug or a squeeze can do wonders. It was almost reverent on the flight; it was so quiet. We only set to work passing out the few trays we had because that was what always happened after take-off. No one really cared, no one was hungry—we only did it to give the illusion of normality. There was nothing we could really do for them. It was a death—of a country and its people."

But almost imperceptibly the atmosphere shifted a fraction and despair began to give way to a glimmer of hope as the aircraft rose above the cloud cover, the sky became an open blue, and sunlight filled the cabin. "Then some of the passengers wanted to help, and started handing out trays too, acting like crew," Pamela says. "It was so sweet the way they acted. We had helped them and now they wanted to help us. They were like members of our family—the entire family of Pan Am—and we felt close to them without ever having met them before. Such a feeling of kinship, born of a life-or-death situation, is unforgettable and irreplaceable."

A reunion was held in Washington on 24 April 1990, to celebrate the 15th anniversary of Pan Am's last mission into Saigon and the première of the movie *Last Flight Out.* Five of the eight flight attendants attended, as did Captain Berg and many, many Saigon ground personnel and their families. The first officer and engineer, who had so mysteriously appeared in time for the flight and then disappeared again, did not attend, but "they were on hand when we needed them," Pamela says.

Last Flight Out has been seen on television by millions and is the only way that most people know about these events. Although the film is moving and full of suspense, it is nonetheless a Hollywood production, and it is the nature of a dramatic production to exaggerate and to distort reality. Pamela likes the film, likes the fact that it was made, but is only too aware of the distortions. Instead of a Boeing 747, she points out that the makers of the film used a Lockheed L-1011, a significantly smaller aircraft with far less presence than the 747. "It was the sheer size of the 'plane and the number of people that we were carrying that made it so significant," she says. There were other minor distortions, which were included to heighten the drama, but again and again, Pamela insists that the biggest distortion was the clapping and the cheering as the aircraft took off. For her the reality was far more poignant— the absolute silence on Pan Am's last flight out of Saigon.

✈ ✈ ✈ ✈ ✈

Excerpt from a speech given at the reunion by Pan Am employee Lang T. Nguyen:

"Fifteen years have gone. We left Vietnam on Panam's 'last flight out' only few days before the country fell into the communists' hands. The falling of my country is forever lasting in my memory. Sometimes I wish that I can become a bird flying back to my homeland to hug my parents' graves, to touch the earth where I grew up and to weep openly so that all the pains I have kept deeply in my heart would be relieved.

Gudrun Meisner, Pamela Taylor, and Tra Duong reunite 15 years after the last flight from Saigon.

Thanks to God, after the long years of suffering, we have been successfully settled in the United States. Fortunately, I have been continuing to work for Pan Am, my husband also has a good job, and all my three children have been graduated from universities and have gotten good positions. I am proud of them; at least they are useful to the country that has generously taken them in. Furthermore, most of my fellow employees from Vietnam have also well settled in the United States."

Text of flight attendant Tra Duong's speech, which she prepared for the reunion but was not given the opportunity to deliver:

"Tonight's occasion brings back some vivid memories of my time with Pan Am, in particular, the last Pan Am flight out of Saigon. I remember well the courage and dedication that my friends, many of whom are here tonight, showed in the face of adversity. We were professionals then and still carry that trait with us today. I am glad to see all of my dear friends who volunteered to make that last flight out possible. Without your personal efforts and sacrifice, we could not have saved the lives of the Pan Am Saigon staff and my sisters.

Tonight, however, we are gathered here to see old friends and renew acquaintances from that bygone era. I want to express my deep appreciation and personal thanks to Captain Berg and my flying partners who volunteered to undertake that mission of mercy as we all watched the news reports of the communists marching down South Vietnam towards Saigon. Those were times of chaos, uncertainty, and especially grave personal danger for each of us. In Manila, when word went out for volunteers, there were very few, but we were able to gather enough to fly into that inferno.

I am sure that many of you have wondered what happened to some of the people we took out on that last flight. For myself, I want you to know that all of my sisters are doing well and are all married. I want to thank you again for the opportunity that you gave to each of them to pursue a life of freedom and liberty. Thanks from the bottom of my heart."

An Independent Union

*At the end of the 1970s, the Transport Workers Union, AFA's larg-
est rival union competitor, underwent enormous upheaval.
Charging male domination, more than sixteen thousand flight attendants voted to disaffiliate with TWU. Within one year, flight attendants on Trans World Airlines, Pan American Airways, and
American Airlines disaffiliated and formed their own independent and unaffiliated unions.*
Georgia Panter Nielsen, *From Sky Girl to Flight Attendant*

S ince 1942 Pan Am flight attendants had been members of the Transport
Workers Union (T.W.U). The Union membership consisted of railroad
workers, transit workers, and certain airline personnel: mechanics,
baggage handlers, port stewards, commissary, cleaners, ground staff, and
flight attendants. It was a large, male-dominated union, and Pan Am's T.W.U.
representatives were mostly older pursers whose main interest was money.

Most of the flight attendants meekly paid their dues, and kept quiet
about the lack of progress towards the improvement of working conditions
that employees with other airlines were experiencing. By 1976, working
conditions for Pan Am flight attendants were the worst in the nation, even
though women's roles in society had radically changed since the 1960s.
Instead of being an entertaining two-year diversion, flying had become a
career for women, many of whom were raising families.

Pan American flight attendants suffered particular hardships on board
the Boeing 747s, where flight service bunks were not provided, in spite of
their being part of Boeing's design. (Bunks were provided in the cockpit for
the flight crew.) On the long trans-Pacific flights, cabin crew might be awake
for 24 hours before having a chance to sleep. Also, on their long flights from
Tokyo to New York, attentive stewardesses began to notice problems with the
air on board the high-flying 747SPs. They tried to focus attention on the
ozone issue, but no-one listened to them at first, even though they would
cough blood at times. (In the 28 March 1978 edition of *The Wall Street
Journal* William Carley writes: *"But at first no one realized ozone was the
villain. Stewardesses were the first to complain; unbelieving pilots attributed
the complaints to 'hysterical women.' Pan Am officials suspected dry air.*

202

F.A.A. officials yawned. "When I first worked on this, I figured it was a fluke,"
one F.A.A. man says.")

Enter **Alice Flynn.**

Alice was born and grew up in South Berwick, Maine. After first working in Washington, D.C., she and her roommates moved to San Francisco, where Alice soon found a job she enjoyed. However, two pursers who lived in the the same apartment building said to her one day, "Hey, Alice, Pan Am is hiring flight attendants. Why don't you give it a try?" Alice tried and Alice succeeded, as she did in so many other challenges in her life.

Alice remembers going to one of her first union meetings and hearing someone tell a stewardess: "Sit down. Shut up. We'll get to you later," but her question was never addressed.

"I knew we were not being represented. In a way it was our fault because we were not real active and the company knew this, so they took advantage of us. Even the flight attendants who were active took advantage too. They had positions in the union and most of them had full time off flying to fulfil their union obligations. They would negotiate only what they were interested in: wages. You have to understand that when a company negotiates with unions, they have a certain amount of money. It's like a pie, and they really don't care how that pie is split up so long as they don't get asked for more pie. When you go in to negotiate, everybody's there, vying for the biggest piece. Flight attendants were getting the crumbs. Not even a sliver of pie, just the crumbs," says Alice.

Alice Flynn.

"I kept looking at the contracts that other unions had negotiated for their flight attendants. United Airlines had just negotiated a tremendous contract. I could not believe how extensive it was in comparison with ours and what attention it paid to working conditions. United had all kinds of work rules. Our contract was about 25 pages thick; theirs was about 340 pages! We had a lot of work to do if we were to keep abreast of the industry."

Alice was tired of going to meetings with the T.W.U. at which only five or six flight attendants would appear. She felt that if she could mobilize interest and increase the number of attendees, they could work within the TWU to effect changes in working conditions. She asked the union if she might circulate a letter through their system, written on their stationery. They turned her down. In August 1976, at her own expense, she wrote to all the flight attendants at the San Francisco base asking them to attend the next union meeting at which their contract would be discussed. Here are extracts from her vigorous call to arms:

> Now is the time to get down to business on our new contract...A few people cannot do this alone. We need your help. *ALL OF YOU!*....Only in strength do we have power.

> I know how all of you can work. I have seen some of the impossible feats you've been asked to perform by our company. Most of you excel in stamina and drive. Now is the time to channel this tremendous effort into something for ourselves and our future. Remember, with our power as a group, nothing is insurmountable. WE CAN DO....

> Our job has been belittled in times past, sometimes by our own company. It is rare that we are ever given the opportunity to climb the executive ladder; there seems to be no crossing over for Flight Service. It isn't that we lack the education or the know-how. We have the highest average of education of any group in this company. Higher than the executive group and higher than the pilots.....Well, let's show them where our place is in our next contract....

> GET TO YOUR UNION MEETINGS—GET ACTIVE—STOP COMPLAINING AND DO SOMETHING ABOUT IT.... If all of us could attend at least three union meetings a year, then we should never have less than 50 in attendance at any meeting, and more likely 100. Can you imagine our strength? *PICTURE IT.*

Because Alice could picture the strength of mobilized flight service, she was able to endure the T.W.U.'s response. She was accused of treason, of undermining the union in spite of the fact that she was trying to work within it, and she was vilified. But her rallying cry was heard by the audience she wanted to reach. At the next union meeting, instead of five flight attendants showing up, more than 200 were in attendance. More important, Alice had attracted several women who threw in their lot with her. Together they became known as the San Francisco Seven, and together they would move mountains. The group included Mary Ellen King, Doris Scher (see page 157), Pamela Taylor (see page 188), Carol Rankin, and Linda Fister. Other interested women soon joined in the effort and among them were Brigitte Smith, Ute Harriss, and **Sharon E. Madigan.**

Sharon was born in Buffalo and raised in an upper-middle class community on Long Island. Both her parents worked, her father for the F.B.I. where he was one of J. Edgar Hoover's early speech writers, and her mother was a fashion coordinator for Bonwit Teller. Unions were not a big item in their household. When Sharon started flying with Pan American, she soon learned what it was like to be part of a muffled labor force, and recognized how much an active union could improve working conditions for flight attendants.

She picks up the story "We started meeting at Alice's house, and the first question we had to address was, 'Do we have the right to form our own union?' Alice brought in a friend from the Postal Workers' union who talked to us about how one goes about it. But there were still several people who thought that, as we were coming close to contract negotiations, we should try to work a little harder within the existing T.W.U. structure. They went to the meetings, brought up the issue of the contract negotiations, but came away feeling that the doors were closed. The union was not responsive; they were doing nothing at all for us."

In February 1977, the San Francisco Seven sent out a letter to the flight attendants listing their grievances against the T.W.U. and their reasons for organizing another union. They insisted it could be done. The letter included a list of over 200 flight attendants who committed themselves and their energies to forming the new union. They were encouraged by Art Teolis, president of the Independent Federation of Flight Attendants (I.F.F.A.) representing T.W.A.'s cabin crew, which had recently broken away from the T.W.U. In addition, Sandy Lenz, Professor of Labor Relations at Cornell University, adopted the fledgling Pan Am union, and watched as it grew to maturity, generously sharing his wisdom and encouragement.

With these waves of approval from the outside, Pan American's flight attendants began to take themselves seriously. They examined their own behavior and recognized the importance of self-respect and motivation and the debilitating nature of fear. They underwent consciousness-raising sessions. They also recognized any new organization's basic operational needs: a name, an address, a Post Office box, a logo, and funds with which to operate, funds for mailings and publicity.

Sharon continues: "We formed telephone committees, and developed a whole base of operation. Alice's husband had a business in downtown San Francisco, south of Market Street, which is now quite chi-chi but wasn't at all fashionable then. You had to be very, very careful. He gave us some space. Then we started the business of passing cards. We needed signatures on the cards from 51% of the flight attendants to be eligible for a representational election. The blue cards became I.U.F.A.'s most valuable possessions, and my job was to go to the post office box and pick up them up. I am not the type that normally worries about security, but I thought that someone from the T.W.U. might just hit me over the head. But it was no problem at all. We thought that at least they would work harder to hold on to us, a large number of people on whom they spent no money, just took their dues.

"Katherine Koelsch designed a great logo for us, and as far as raising funds went, we had Cheri McElliott, who was dynamite at creating events that were extremely successful and which supported our activities and expenses during the whole campaign. Dynamite. Jazz parties, beer and popcorn parties, garage sales, auctions. And flight attendants know people—everyone from those who own Caribbean resorts to those who own beauty salons: you name it. We made over $100,000 that summer. The most successful fund raisers were the auctions.

"In April 1977 we instituted interim officers: Mary Ellen King as president, Alice Flynn as vice president, and myself as secretary/treasurer. Here's how I got into this: we were having an organizational meeting to make a business plan, a budget, and some cash flow projections, and we were parcelling out committees. We had no problem with the president and vice president positions. Then it came to secretary/treasurer, and everybody was totally silent. Lots of people were in the room. Utter silence. I am a very impulsive speaker sometimes, and I blurted out, 'Damn it all, somebody has to do this job.' All of a sudden, every head in the room turned towards me and all the eyes looked at me, and I said to myself, 'Sharon, you just did it.' I had no business experience before, none whatsoever, so I turned to my friends in the financial community for their assistance. I felt I achieved the equivalent of an M.B.A., working as secretary/treasurer of the I.U.F.A."

"Then the T.W.U. brought charges against us, accusing us of treasonous activities. There was a hearing and I acted as our group's counsel, arguing our

Doris Scher, Sharon Madigan, Ann Miltimore, Diane Milner, Alice Flynn, and Ute Harriss raise a toast to the I.U.F.A.

case. I told them that if they placed us in a separate local council, just flight attendants, we might consider remaining. They did not consider doing that. They did nothing during this entire campaign to appease us or to make realistic or practical plans to change anything. It was unfortunate for them; it was very poor strategy. If they had done that, they might have pulled off the election. As it was, we ended up winning by the largest margin the National Mediation Board (N.M.B.) had ever seen.

"The movement had been spreading in the spring of 1977. In addition to San Francisco, we held meetings at all the other major bases. Alice and I were placed in charge of organizing at New York's international airport, JFK. We held our meetings there every week during our layovers at the Berkshire Hotel. Alice would talk the people at the front desk into giving her a big corner room. They were very cooperative and would bring up folding chairs, turning the large sleeping room into a large meeting room. After Alice and I had these initial meetings and a core group of people in New York was developing, I took two months leave of absence from flying to canvas the base thoroughly. It was a horrible job. I had to stay with friends, on a couch in their living room. My hours were very strange. I would go to the airport at midday, and I would stay in the crew rooms until midnight. Each day, I had three or four T.W.U. supporters to debate, people who were taken off the line fully during this period of challenge. It was very psychologically demeaning each time they said, 'We're going to open the bottles of champagne soon.' I'd be there all by myself with nobody to back me up, but I kept debating the issues."

In September, the group spent a great deal of its hard-earned funds publishing a pamphlet to be sent to all 4,500 Pan Am flight attendants. "We made the decision to put a lot of bucks into this," Sharon recalls. "We set it up with questions and answers, and blue and red print. The moment the pamphlet went out—it looked very professional for that time—it made all the difference. I suddenly knew we were going to win. And suddenly we did.

Alice adds: "On 29 October 1977, we were recognized by the N.M.B, and started negotiating a contract with Pan Am on 1 November, three days later. I was the chief spokesperson for our union and chief negotiator on the contract. I was always negotiating. I negotiated continuously during late 1977, all of 1978, and we finally settled our contract in March 1979." Alice was almost always in New York during that time, hardly ever seeing her husband for 18 months. After the interim period, she became president of I.U.F.A.

Sharon continues: "Pan Am immediately gave us problems. With T.W.U. we had dues check-off cards that were signed by every flight attendant so that our dues were automatically removed from our paychecks. These cards can be transferred over to a new union, but Pan Am refused to transfer them, so we had to pass out all the cards again. We had received a start-up loan from a bank, money to keep us solvent until we started to receive the dues. Suddenly the bank backed away. We had to go out hat in hand to other banks.

"We held meetings into the wee hours. We worked all hours of the day and night. We wrote our constitution. We had battles over it for every single point. We talked people at all the different bases into taking on positions. Even overseas, the London-based flight attendants finally got to vote. We were very militant. It was a wonderful period, full of enthusiasm—everybody's enthusiasm."

Under the terms of the new 126-page contract, working conditions for Pan American's flight attendants were significantly improved. Even before the contract was signed, Alice Flynn had been able to negotiate rest areas on the long 747 flights.

The courage and dedication of the San Francisco Seven and their early supporters in forming an independent union should act as inspiration to those who need to follow their example. In Alice Flynn's words, "CAN DO!"

Holocaust at Tenerife

They shall mount up with wings as eagles;
they shall run and not be weary;
and they shall walk, and not faint.

Isaiah, XL, 31

D orothy Dawson (Kelly) was born in Newark and raised in New Jersey. Educated in Catholic schools, she wanted to be an attorney when she grew up. However, aptitude tests during the first week of college declared that she was best suited for animal husbandry. Her own inclinations led her into the art world, an environment to which she has returned since the demise of Pan Am. After studying and then working in Geneva for a year, she realized that she had a strong desire to travel further afield. She applied to various European airlines, who thanked her for her interest but made it clear that they hired their own nationals. On return to the United States, Dorothy applied to Pan American. At the time of her interview, she was the only American in a field of European applicants, and was not hired. Her Spanish and her French were fluent and useful, and Dorothy believed that she had been rejected merely because she was not European. She sent a carefully worded letter to the Pan Am management and on the strength of this she was called back, re-interviewed, and received her telegram of acceptance the following day, in October 1966.

Until 27 March 1977, Dorothy's flying career was fairly predictable. Because of her Spanish, she flew at first to South America and the Caribbean. Then she transferred to the International Division and flew east out of New York to Europe and Africa, after which she flew for several years out of San Francisco, working mostly on Rest & Rehabilitation flights between Vietnam and Southeast Asia, Australia, and New Zealand. On her return to the East Coast in 1974, she resumed flying eastward around the world. With her (then) husband, a flight engineer with Pan Am, she bought property in New Hampshire, and during the time they lived there, Dorothy gained her pilot's license, and they started their own charter airline in and out of Keene.

In 1977, times were hard for Pan Am, and Dorothy's husband expected to be furloughed. Because they had serious financial commitments, Dorothy decided to work as much overtime as she could; she was delighted to pick up a charter flight going to Las Palmas, in the Canary Islands, and then on to Paris because it meant many flying hours.

There had been no clue that Pan American Charter Flight B150, leaving New York on the evening of 26 March 1977, would be anything other than a routine charter flight. When she entered the crew briefing lounge at Kennedy Airport before departure, Dorothy Kelly learned that the Boeing 747 would have a full load of vacationers, and that she would be the junior purser. However, just before boarding, the senior purser, Françoise Colbert de Beaulieu approached her, saying, "Would you mind working first-class today? I'm so self-conscious about my French accent in front of all these people. I hate doing the announcements in front of such a crowd." Dorothy responded, "Sure. I don't mind making the announcements. I'll work up front."

Once on board, Carla Johnson joined Dorothy in the first-class cabin. Carla's height, her blonde hair, fair skin, and blue eyes were a vivid contrast to Dorothy's shorter stature, dark brown eyes, pink and white complexion, and long brown hair, which she wore tied back from her face. Their personalities were complementary, however, and Carla knew they would work well together because Dorothy was respected for her common sense, the high standards she set for herself and her crew, her practical streak, and her obvious enjoyment of her work.

Most of the 380 passengers were from California, some were from Chicago, and they were all going to the Canary Islands to join a cruise of the Mediterranean on board the *Golden Odyssey*. Also on board were an experienced, three-man cockpit crew, 13 flight attendants, and two Pan Am station representatives, one from Madrid and one from London.

Dorothy Kelly.

Graduation day (Dorothy is third from right in the front row).

Clipper Victor, a Boeing 747, took off from Kennedy Airport bound for Las Palmas as night was falling in New York. The flight across the Atlantic was busy but uneventful until about 30 minutes before arrival when Captain Victor Grubbs received word to divert to Los Rodeos airport on the island of Tenerife because of terrorist activity in Las Palmas. The Movement for the Self-Determination and Independence of the Canary Archipelago had detonated a bomb in the terminal buildings, the airport had been closed, and all aircraft were being diverted to the single runway at Los Rodeos. Captain Grubbs followed instructions and landed *Clipper Victor* without incident, and parked in front of the terminal next to another 747, K.L.M.'s *The Rhine*.

Dorothy recalls: "We were so busy during the whole time on the ground. There were a million demands: why, what, update, I need a glass of water, I want a drink, I'm hungry. The ground staff did not allow the passengers to disembark because there were so many aircraft at this tiny airport and the terminal was packed. They could not fit any more people in. After a while, passengers become restless and hungry and thirsty, and most of these people had already come all the way from California. It is always a very busy time on board when there's a situation like this on the ground.

"I had had nothing to eat or drink and I remember another flight attendant, Miguel Torrech, coming over and saying: 'I've just made some fresh coffee. At least you must have some coffee. You have had absolutely nothing in all this time.' So he poured the coffee, and I said, 'Black,' and he said, 'No. You're going to have it with milk because you need some energy. This is good for you,' and he poured a slug of milk into it. I was getting ready to close the doors and he disappeared to give some coffee to Mari Asai, who was working in the upstairs lounge. Then we started to move.

"This is how it happened. I was standing at R1—the forward right door—drinking the coffee Miguel had given me, and Carla was standing a few feet away. The K.L.M. 'plane had gone ahead of us, turned around, and was waiting for permission to begin the take-off roll. In the meantime, we had been given permission to taxi and were moving down the runway towards the Dutch aircraft, as the only runway was also the taxiway. For whatever reason, the K.L.M. pilot misinterpreted a radio transmission and thought he had been told to take off. I would like to believe, with all the people who are supposed to be monitoring these transmissions, that mistakes could not be made. But the final decision is still a human one and there are many factors to consider: fatigue, weather, foreign accents, health, time limitations, even personal problems and personality conflicts. On that particular day, we had all been working through the night, and after hours of being cramped up in a confined space with hundreds of people, we were running way behind schedule and certainly none of us was at our best. It was also very foggy and the K.L.M. crew was running out of duty time.

"They prepared their jet for take-off and started the fatal run. When our pilots saw the speeding hulk coming at them, they tried to veer the 'plane off the runway into the grass, but a 747 doesn't turn very far very fast. The Dutch captain made a desperate effort to avoid the inevitable collision and rotated his aircraft, hoping he had gained enough speed for it to achieve lift. It had not, and in its short-lived death throes rose only enough off the runway to peel off the top of *Clipper Victor*, just like opening a sardine can. Then it crashed behind us, blew up, and burned. Our flight crew ducked when they saw it coming, which is the only reason they survived. No one in the lounge directly behind them lived.

"At that point I was still standing with Carla at the right forward door area. I don't remember an explosion, but things flying around and everything in slow motion. Nothing was like it had been moments before. I thought we had been bombed, because that was what was in all our minds, and I started to look for the oxygen bottle so that I could get around in smoke. Then I thought, 'No, that's the worst thing because if there are bombs, there'll be

"... rose only enough off the runway to peel off the top of Clipper Victor,
just like opening a sardine can."

more explosions and fire, and you don't want a lethal weapon hung around
your neck.' These were split second impressions. 'Yes, this is a good idea. No,
this is not a good idea if there are explosions.' There was this furious conversation going round in my head. Because things were flying around, I
wondered how I could find anything. And then I was aware of everything
settling, and it was quiet, except for the reverberating explosions. I was
conscious of fire, but not great fire all around."

   Then Dorothy was struck on the head by a piece of superstructure,
which drove her through the cabin floor, and she crashed through, unconscious, into the cargo compartment. But she regained consciousness quickly
and found herself muttering, "This thing is going to blow up and how the hell
am I going to get out of here with no obvious exit?" She could see no way out
of the cell-like cargo hold—no door, no window, nothing that made sense.
Finally she pulled herself up and started climbing towards a jagged patch of
sky. "I continued climbing and climbing. I lost my shoes. Everything was
unrecognizable; distorted, disturbed, confused. I felt as though I had just
awakened in the middle of a Fellini film."

   When she reached the top of what was left of the upper deck, she saw a
few people there, staggering around, dazed. No way was visible for them to
walk down to a lower level. At this point, all Dorothy's training surged to the

fore, and she started giving directions. She yelled, "WE'VE GOT TO GET OUT OF HERE. WE'VE GOT TO JUMP. WE HAVE GOT TO GO." Her normally soft, lilting voice, rang out sharply and forcefully.

"I remember people jumping. I looked over; it was like looking out of a second floor window, about 25 feet down, and I was really scared because my feet were bare and you saw nothing but jagged metal down there, and I said to myself, 'Oh, my God, we've survived this and we are going to kill ourselves jumping down on that stuff.' In the split second it took me to look down, someone wandered off, so when the last man up there started walking away too, I pulled him back and shouted 'YOU'VE GOT TO JUMP. Right after you jump, we've got to get out of here. JUMP. JUMP. JUMP. JUMP.' And we jumped, and I think that's when I hurt my arm.

"Once we hit the ground—luckily we didn't land on the metal debris— I thought, 'That's a miracle. I've made it now.' I no longer felt confused. I only felt disoriented when it first started and everything was flying around. I shouted at the man, 'RUN AWAY.' By this time, major fire had broken out in different places in the back of the 'plane and other people were milling around and I shouted, 'RUN, RUN, OUT THAT WAY, RUN THIS WAY, GET AWAY FROM THE 'PLANE.'"

Once she had directed the people away from the aircraft, Dorothy herself began to run, but as she ran she had more and more trouble seeing. She concluded that she had been hit on the head and that it was probably affecting her vision. She ran up to the other flight attendants who had survived, and asked them desperately, "Tell me, what does this look like? What does my head look like?" They reassured her that the wound was not serious and that she was having trouble seeing because blood was running into her eyes. She wiped her face clean and said, "Fine," and started back towards the aircraft. They yelled at her, "Dorothy, don't go back. You're getting too close. Don't go back!"

"I ignored them. I knew what I had to do. I went back and started pulling people away from the airplane. Those who could get out were jumping off the wing or out of openings in the fuselage. There was fire all over and frequent explosions continued to shower the field with debris. I guess it was about that time I saw something white underneath the airplane— this white thing on the ground attracted my attention in the brush. Then I noticed that the inboard engine had started to spin out of control, like a children's top that blows in the wind. I said to myself, 'That engine is going any second now.' And then I suddenly realized that the white thing on the ground was moving and it was one of the pilots, really dazed. I shouted, 'CAN YOU WALK?' and he just said, 'No.' Then I recognized Captain Grubbs. I yelled,

'Do you think your leg is broken?' He was really bewildered and he didn't know. Just then the airplane started making crunching noises above us, and I thought, 'Oh my God, this thing is going to fall on us. Even if the engine doesn't blow up, we've got to get out from underneath it.' (We were underneath the forward section, the area where the double deck is located.) I shouted, 'WE'VE GOT TO GET OUT OF HERE RIGHT NOW. I'M GOING TO PULL YOU.' I turned him over, grabbed him under the arms and started running backwards with him, dragging him, hauling him. We were about half way back from the airplane when the inboard engine did blow up, and white-hot metal started shooting all over and I thought, 'Here we go again. This stuff is going to kill us, not the explosion itself.' But we were able to dodge the flying debris and soon were safely out of range. A few seconds later, that front section heaved a moan and settled down onto one side, quiet and still, like a great beached whale finally succumbing to the exhaustion of battle."

A witness who saw Dorothy hauling the captain away from the engine said that she "looked like the Road Runner dashing backwards at 50 miles per hour." She left Captain Grubbs on the grass at a safe distance from the aircraft, and ran back to help the remaining surviving passengers. Dorothy found that she could not climb back onto the aircraft herself, but kept running back to a point where she could motion to people to jump out safely or assist the injured away from danger. "Now that the engine had gone, it was just a matter of trying to avoid fire or the wing blowing up. The problem was that we had just refuelled. The aircraft was full of fuel and they couldn't shut the engines down, because the control cables had been severed by the 'plane coming over us, taking the roof off."

A few passengers were able to escape from the remains of the front section by walking along the burning windows and then jumping off. "Two girls burned their feet, but they survived. Their mother was on board with them, and she was quite a heavy woman and they were trying to pull her—she needed to step up and over something, jump over something to get out. They kept trying to pull her from the other side, and she kept saying, 'No, no, I can't. I'm too heavy, I'm too heavy. I can't get over that.' Their last memory of her was of letting go their gripped hands and slipping down on opposite sides of the obstacle that determined their life and her death."

Most of the remaining survivors were stunned and directionless, and Dorothy was keenly aware that motivating them to run from the aircraft was vital. She learned from people who had escaped that, incredibly, others inside the aircraft were still sitting in their seats waiting to be told what to do, and, equally incredibly, those who had been able to jump down were standing around near the aircraft, chatting. Dorothy continued to run back and forth, yelling at them, making them run from the aircraft. She was amazed to see one survivor sauntering around in high heels.

At one point, Dorothy came across a woman lying under the wing, covered in blood. She had jumped off the aircraft and others had jumped on top of her. A local man had tried to pull her clear but failed to move her out of danger. Clearly in searing pain, unable to lift herself up, she was inching her way along the ground on her back. Dorothy leaned over her saying, "We have to get you out of here. I'm just going to pull you away from under the wing. I've got to get you safely away." As carefully as possible, speaking quiet, comforting words, Dorothy dragged the woman away from the aircraft. Once they were at a safe distance, Dorothy said gently to her, "You have to stay here now. I'll find somebody to come and help you."

By this time, ambulances had arrived, along with some vans which appeared in response to a radio appeal for help. They began to take people to the closest hospital, and when that was full they went in search of beds at other hospitals. Dorothy, meanwhile, aware of increasing explosions in the cabin, continued to shriek at people, guiding them down and away from the burning fuselage, wondering as she did so how much time was left before the remains of the 747 blew up. She was not aware of the passage of time itself, although she does remember looking at her watch and thinking, "Look at this! I've been through this whole thing, and my watch is still running."

As Dorothy continued to cajole and to drag people back to safety, she heard a man's voice yelling from a parked van. "This guy kept shouting at me and I went over and said 'What?' and he said 'Come on; get in. I'm taking them.' Dorothy noticed the three other surviving cabin crew and the captain sitting on benches in the back of a van. The man tried to push her in, and the crew kept calling her. But she ran away, shouting "NO, NO, NO," and as the van pulled off, she started back to work. She caught sight of Bob Bragg, the co-pilot, and he, too, was running back and forth directing people away from the aircraft. She ran and joined him and together they continued cajoling, persuading, and bullying.

They worked until quite suddenly, it seemed, no more passengers were escaping from the corpse of the 747. Dorothy recalls, "That was the really hard part, because the remaining people simply could not escape and we couldn't reach them. Obviously they were being burned. You could just see them at the windows. It was the most awful, awful part of the whole thing, remembering those screams and seeing those people at the windows, and you couldn't do anything. You couldn't get back in. Once the thing started to disintegrate, everything became compartmentalized and isolated. There was nothing like an aisle that went all the way down to provide entry and escape routes. They couldn't get out, and we couldn't get back to them. THERE WAS NO FIRE CONTROL. I never did see a fire department, and yet you would think there would be one at the airport. Why weren't they shooting water on this thing? I NEVER SAW A FIRE TRUCK. Nothing. I never found out why."

When they fully realized that no more people could escape from the left side, Bob Bragg said "Let's take a walk around the airplane to make sure there isn't anyone on the other side." They circled the remains of the huge 747, but found no one. When they returned to the safe grassy area, they started to assist the injured and to help them into the ambulances and vans.

After most of the injured had been removed to hospital, just a few people were left. Dorothy recalls: "Bob was there and myself and the badly-injured lady, a few stragglers, and this guy who was wandering around, bewildered. His clothes had been completely torn off, and he was in a daze, just wandering around in circles. Some people helped me to manipulate the injured woman into a van. By then she was really in excruciating pain. Although she had broken her hip and her leg, and her foot was completely smashed, she never really screamed but would utter brief cries of pain when she was moved or the van jolted her.

"I kept trying to tell the van driver and his helpers to be careful as they lifted her. There was no stretcher, so I said, 'Lay her across the seat.' Then I grabbed the guy who was wandering around, and put him in the front seat. I tried to talk to him but he didn't respond at all. I climbed in the back, and Bob said, 'O.K. Fine. I'll come with the other few people in the next van.'

The driver let out the clutch and set off at a furious pace for the nearest hospital. Using the left side of her body as an anchor, Dorothy pinned the injured woman to the back seat, meanwhile trying to reassure the silent man in the front seat, gripping him with her right hand to keep him from flying into the windshield each time the driver braked. The van screeched to a stop at one hospital, only to be sent to another which was ready to receive them. The silent, tattered man got out and wandered into the hospital, just as an attendant rushed out with a stretcher for the injured woman, who cried out to Dorothy, "Don't leave me! Don't leave me!" And Dorothy, who quickly realized that her work with the passengers was still unfinished, responded, "I won't leave you. I'm going to be here with you. Don't worry. I have to try to help a few more people, but I will be here, and I will come back to you." And then she ran into the hospital.

"People were all over the floors and in all the little rooms—this was the emergency section—all over. Medical staff were running around frantically. I remember walking into one room and stating firmly that I was a stewardess and I could help, but they kept trying to treat me, make me sit down, give me a shot, inspect me, telling me, 'You sit here, wait, we'll get to you. Wait.' And I said, 'No, no, no. I am a stewardess and I can help you.' So they put me to work helping people get settled, and then this doctor said, 'Come in here and assist me.' I went into a room where there were, maybe, four people and he said, 'Just start tearing the clothes off their bodies.' They were mostly burn victims but they did have other injuries. The hospital staff had given these people very, very little medication because they needed to find out who they were and what was wrong with them. If they were knocked out, there would be no way to obtain information about medication or allergies and it would reduce their ability to isolate injuries. So I just started ripping the clothes off or cutting them away.

"Then the doctor said, 'Now, start pulling the skin off.' By this point, the skin was just draping. Festoons of skin draped from some of these people. Like thick, charred cobwebs. I never knew much about burns before, but removing the skin is a terribly critical thing because burns quickly become infected, plus the victims are in shock. There were so many burns, people were just horribly burned, but I can remember doing what he said, pulling the skin and getting as much of it off as possible. I was worried—I kept thinking about sanitation, but the staff was furiously dealing with the most life-threatening problems in order of priority. Then they wash the victims down with a solution, put something on the skin, bandage them very quickly, and treat them for shock."

As the doctor worked on a woman's arm, blood suddenly started spurting from her head. "Help," he called to Dorothy, thrusting a roll of bandage into her hands, "Keep pressure on the wound." She pushed down on it as hard as she could and watched helplessly as the bandage absorbed the flow and the blood began to seep through her fingers. "This isn't working," she said to the doctor. "Just hold her," he replied, reaching for a pair of scissors, jabbing it into the wound, saying, "Twist it and hold it," before rushing off to aid another victim. Dorothy reflected, "This is absolutely absurd," but she did as she was told, realizing that he had no other instruments and this was a primitive tourniquet which was actually working. All the time, she kept talking to the woman, who remained calm. "She had no idea what we were doing or what the situation was with her head. This woman had a husband there who died, but she didn't know it then. She was amazingly calm. I was truly impressed with how calm the people were, the lack of hysteria.

"I kept talking to these people. I never stopped trying to appear composed and slow so that they could understand, so that they knew there was somebody who spoke English, somebody taking care of them, the American accent. Many were very concerned about their companions. You couldn't help with that because you didn't know the facts. You just had to say, 'We'll find out. There are a lot of people here. There's more than one hospital. We'll find out, but we have to take care of you first.'"

After the flow of blood was staunched and the woman was comfortable, the doctor instructed Dorothy to continue pulling skin off other burn victims. "I was fine until I got down to the nails. I couldn't pull the skin off over the nails. It wouldn't come off, and we had to cut it. For me it was gross, but for him it was just the correct procedure. When it got to the nails, I almost lost it." But Dorothy gritted her teeth, forgot about her own beautiful, small, carefully manicured hands and continued following the doctor's directions.

When they had finished taking care of the burn victims, Dorothy moved around, going wherever help was needed. She remembers seeing the other crew members sitting in a waiting room, and calling out to them, "Can somebody help me?" Carla stood up and joined her.

At another point, Dorothy remembers walking down the main corridor, seeing an old man enter the hospital, stumbling, with blood pouring from his mouth. Dorothy guessed that he was an airport worker because he did not look like an American passenger, but she assumed that as he was in the hospital, he was another victim of the collision. She started speaking to him, but he did not respond, so she made him sit down in a wheelchair and kept talking to him as she tried to attract help. There was nobody around. Finally, he opened his mouth and his tongue was hanging off. Dorothy leaped up and ran for a nurse who, when she saw the situation, wheeled him away in search of immediate attention. "Apparently, this was a local guy who had had a fight or an accident. Somebody cut his tongue or something. I remember that was so gross. Black humor stuck in the middle of all this."

One of the nurses requisitioned Dorothy, saying, "What's really important is to start labelling people. Some of them are dying and we don't know how to identify them." She thrust a roll of tape, scissors, and a pen at Dorothy and continued, "Please identify as many as you can and put names on them. If they're dead, see if they have any possessions which might identify them. If you can talk to them, find out anything you can about their health condition, medication, or allergies." Dorothy took the tape, hooked it on her arm, and started back to work.

"That's when my arm started to hurt. I was taping and identifying when I noticed—I'm left-handed—that I was having trouble cutting the tape. I thought, 'This is awful. I must have sprained my arm or something.' I was finally tearing the tape with my teeth because as time went on I couldn't function with my left hand. I did that until one of the nurses called me into the waiting room, where I found the rest of the crew. She said, 'We have to give you tetanus innoculations now.' A nun came in (it was a Catholic hospital) and made us all lower our drawers and gave us a shot in the hip. Then I went back to work for a while, and finally things quieted down. I must have worked for about three hours in the hospital, and I started wondering how long it had been between the time of the collision and when we got to the hospital. It couldn't have been more than 45 minutes or an hour."

Suddenly someone insisted that Dorothy be treated, and she was made to sit down in a wheelchair. "My arm hurts," she said, pulling her sleeve up. That was when she saw the bone sticking out and exclaimed, "Oh! That's why it hurts," as a nurse wheeled her off to radiology.

"That was the first time I really felt, not panicked, but frightened, because I didn't know what else was wrong with me. They knew there was something wrong with my head, but it didn't seem to be badly hurt; I hadn't yet bruised. I was cut and I had a few stitches, but these were minor scratches. You know, you had cuts all over you, little cuts. I still have little scars, but certainly nothing serious. But the doctors kept mumbling about the head and I thought, 'Oh, my God, what if I need brain surgery or something? Here I am in this hospital in the middle of nowhere and they're going to cut my head open.'

"The badly injured woman went up to radiology at the same time I did, and they put her in a room next to mine. I remember hearing these shrieks when they reset her hip. It must have been agonizing. I was desperate to run in and comfort her, but when I tried to leave, they wouldn't let me. I said, 'I just want to talk to her,' but they wouldn't let me go in. That was the only time I heard her really scream.

After Dorothy's arm was X-rayed, it was bound in plaster of Paris and strung up in a sling, with her left hand on a level with her right shoulder, a position that was both painful and uncomfortable. She said to herself, "Why is this thing like this? If I have to spend a whole day like this, I'll go nuts." The nurse returned her to the wheelchair and wheeled her downstairs. The uninjured crewmembers were just leaving the hospital for the hotel, and when Dorothy saw them, she rose to join them. Her doctor demanded, "Where are you going? You have to stay here for observation."

"NO. NO. I'm not hurt. I'm O.K," Dorothy responded.

"You have to remain here," the doctor insisted.

"I'll stay with you, Dorothy. Don't worry," said Carla.

"I'll tell you what," said Dorothy to the doctor, "I'll stay if you let me make a phone call."

"You're driving a hard bargain," replied the doctor, smiling.

"We have to put the word out as to what has happened, who has survived, who has not that we know of, and a first-hand report of the details," Dorothy continued. She knew that the captain, who was still suffering from shock and covered in serious burns, was not in a position to make telephone calls.

Dorothy remembered that her husband was visiting friends that day, and she was able to reach him at the friends' house on her first try. She told him that there had been an accident and where she was. She listed the surviving crew members' names, told him that she didn't know how many passengers were alive, explained that they were in several hospitals, and reassured him that she had not been seriously injured and would try to call again soon. She instructed him to call Pan Am right away, especially Flight Service, so that they would have the names when family members started calling in.

That first night in hospital, Carla and Dorothy were assigned separate rooms, but a thoughtful nurse said,"Why don't I put another bed in here?" and wheeled Carla's bed into Dorothy's room. Then she said, "You haven't eaten in a long time. I'll find you something," and reappeared with cocoa, biscuits, and fresh fruit. For the first time in many, many hours, life began to feel almost normal. Things stayed in place.

"By now it was ten or eleven o'clock at night. I had been up for a long, long time, but the adrenalin was still pumping. In times like this you don't even notice that you're fatigued, but you begin to slow down because there is nothing else you can do and you're starting to feel the mental effects as well as the physical ones. By now my face was swelling, my eyes were swelling, my scalp was tightening.

"Carla is a very sensitive person, so we were actually able to go over what had happened. We stayed up for hours, just talking and talking. We kept going to the bathroom, and then we started laughing. We couldn't stop, and I can remember her saying, 'I guess that's what's called scaring the shit out of you.' All of a sudden we were able to let go a little bit, release the tension, but we didn't shake and we couldn't cry. Not at all.

"Two or three times during the night, the medical staff comes in, switches all the lights on, shines flashlights in your eyes, takes your temperature, your blood pressure, gets you up every two or three hours. By the time morning comes, you are absolutely exhausted. But they keep to their schedule, feed you breakfast, keep you going, rounds for the doctors, you do this, you do that. However, for an institution, the food was wonderful and there was plenty of it."

When Dorothy got up and looked at herself in the mirror, she thought she was looking at a stranger. Gone was the smooth skin, the familiar pink and white complexion. In their place she saw a face that bore the blues and purples of severe bruising, a face that looked as though it had been rearranged, the face of a prize fighter after a particularly brutal fight. At that moment Dorothy had a glimmer of what she had been through and said to herself, "What a mess this is." Her thoughts immediately turned to the captain, and she said to Carla, "We must talk to Captain Grubbs and make him realize it's not his fault. We ourselves are probably alive because he was able to veer the airplane that little bit." They set off in search of the captain and the first officer, both of whom had been detained at the hospital because of their injuries—the captain's severe burns and Bob Bragg's broken ankle.

"The captain is like God on the airplane, the supreme commander, the general, the admiral, and you follow him without question. Captain Grubbs was a dedicated person. He took his responsibilities seriously. And I kept saying to myself, 'My God, this man is now probably alert and has been awake for hours thinking about all these people he probably thinks he killed or could have saved.' By now the reality of what had happened was filtering through and we now knew that many, many passengers and crew members were dead.

"We went in and talked with him and he was coherent. In fact, he was never incoherent, just dazed. I asked him what he felt, what he knew. It wasn't easy for him to talk because he had not realized the full extent of what had happened, and a lot of people, especially men, can't talk about emotional things, when you or I might let something out or cry. I can remember his lips were so dry that they were parched and peeling. The doctors had given him all this treatment and nobody had thought to put something on his lips. I went back to my room and found my Chapstik and put some on his lips.

"So we started our hospital life. Carla and I and Bob Bragg made rounds, Bob in a wheelchair or on crutches. We visited the passengers and talked to them. The job carried on; it didn't stop in the hospital, but it wasn't something you thought about. You just said to yourself, 'O.K. We've taken care of the captain. He's all right. Now we have to talk to the passengers, take care of them.' They were still our passengers.

"You got to know people very quickly on a first-name basis. I was amazed at the end of that first day how calm the people were, even though some of them had found out that their mates or loved ones had perished. Most people wanted to talk, and I think that was very good for them. We never gave people false hopes but reminded them that some people were still unconscious and we had no names for them. We had no information for the badly-injured woman, but I visited her all the time. She became a life-long friend. Her glasses had been broken and she couldn't see to read, but she remained calm.

"Her bravery and patient demeanor was, and is, awe-inspiring. Never did I hear a complaint or sense a feeling of self-pity, even though she lost the treasure of her heart, her husband of only a few years. She has been my anchor so many times through the years, and I've often called on her strength vicariously. As life has continued to challenge her, she remains steadfastly her own best friend—an uncommon spirit who will leave behind her a legacy of tenacious love and faith."

The hospital staff were the ones who broke the news of a relative or friend's death to the patients, and the chaplain visited them immediately afterwards to offer solace. A particularly thoughtful man, he offered the crew comfort of a more practical nature. He arrived bearing toothbrushes, toothpaste, and soap because supplies of everyday items had run short owing to the deluge of patients into the hospital.

After they had visited all the passengers in the open wards, Dorothy and Carla made their way to the isolation unit. The nurse on duty had no objection to their going in, but required that they wash and put on sterile clothing— gowns, bootees, and masks—before entering the unit. The rooms were dimly lit, very cool, and no one spoke above a murmur. The patients lived in a highly protected, sterile environment.

"We would give them a beverage, help them drink through a straw, talk to them. Some were coherent, others weren't. Sometimes they could only respond by motioning with their eyes or a hand. But I remember entering one of the dimly lit rooms and hearing a voice say, 'Do you have my rings?' It was the badly-burned woman with the head wound. I was amazed how alert she was and by the fact that she had recognized me. When I returned with the rings, I noticed her body was completely covered in bandages and that her head had been shaved. I told her she should look for a new hairdresser, and without missing a beat she quipped, "And you'd better look for a new plastic surgeon!" Her husband had been killed, and she would spend almost a year at the burn center in Texas undergoing gruelling treatment day after day.

"I remember one man in particular, a Native American, a first-class passenger, a large man who was on his honeymoon. On the flight, he and his wife were covered in the most beautiful Indian silver and turquoise. Incredible jewelry. She had the most exquisite squash blossom necklace—(I had always wanted one). She did not survive; he was terribly, terribly burned, and of course devastated by his loss. He kept talking about the fact that they were on their honeymoon and that he didn't want to live without her. His eyes were shut tight by the swelling, and we had to lean over him to hear the heartrending account of their courtship, and their marriage of two weeks. He just wanted to know that she was alive. We told him the lists weren't complete yet, but her name was not on the list we were trying to put together. Then he told us he wanted us to contact his family, and at that moment a nurse called to say that his brother was on the telephone in the hall. Carla was able to describe the circumstances to his brother and then to pass on messages of comfort to the suffering man. I believe he died later.

"You see, as time went on, people died of their injuries, especially the burn victims. I learned at that time just how devastating fire can be. It had never bothered me before, but after that it became a major cause of concern. I'm not afraid of dying or of physical injury, but I now fear fire or even surviving a fire. I still feel that way because I spent months and months writing to passengers in Texas at the burn center to which they had been transferred. I learned about how they treat the victims, and I cannot imagine having to go through this every day. They put you into tubs and they scrub the skin off, and they have to keep doing that otherwise the scar tissue forms and the skin never grows smoothly over it.

"After we did our rounds, the nurses brought all our meals into one room so that we could eat together, and Bob Bragg would cut up my food for me because I couldn't move my arm."

Then the media circus began. The European reporters arrived first along with Americans from the various agencies. They would wander through the hospitals, even into the patients' rooms. This created another major problem for the hospital staff—protecting the victims from the media—and they tried to intercept them before they could get upstairs.

"The crew was particularly harrassed because the reporters would dress up and pretend to be doctors. They knew all the tricks. The hospital staff finally put quarantine signs on the crew rooms so we would have some peace. But it didn't help. They learned the names of patients and called indiscriminately, night and day.

"The second night we were in the hospital, one of the nuns called me in the middle of the night and said, 'Get up, Dorothy. Your father is on the 'phone.' She wrapped me up—she wouldn't let me go out in the hallway without my bathrobe. I picked up the 'phone. The man's voice was not one I recognized, and he said, 'Look, I'm really sorry I had to do what I did. There was no other way I could get in touch with you. I knew they wouldn't let me talk with you unless I said I was a family member. I'm from the *Boston Globe,* and your family and husband are very worried, and I can get information to them.' (I was, in fact, in daily communication with my husband). I said, '*Boston Globe!*' Then he went right into his little routine: 'How are you hurt? What's wrong with you? We've got rumors. How many people? How many this, how many that?'

"I was appalled. I yelled, 'FIRST OF ALL, YOU ARE TALKING TO ME IN A HOSPITAL. WHY DO YOU THINK I AM IN A HOSPITAL? I'M HERE BECAUSE I AM INJURED. THIS IS DISGRACEFUL. YOU HAVE

NOT ONLY GOT ME UP IN THE MIDDLE OF THE NIGHT, AND YOU
CERTAINLY KNOW THERE'S A TIME CHANGE AND WHAT IT IS,
YOU HAVE LIED. WHY WOULD YOU TRY TO POSE AS A FAMILY
MEMBER WHEN YOU DON'T EVEN KNOW ANYTHING ABOUT MY
FAMILY? WHAT IF MY FATHER WAS DEAD? I THINK THIS IS
DISGRACEFUL, AND I WILL CERTAINLY MAKE SURE THAT NO
MORE 'PHONE CALLS GET THROUGH HERE.' And I hung up on him. I
was just so angry.

"Nobody from Pan Am contacted us at first, but on the third day, the
Tuesday, Fran Wood arrived from the States as the representative for Flight
Service, along with our union representative, and they came to us in the
hospital. It was the first touch with Pan Am, the first real contact, and Fran
wanted to know what she could get for us, how she could help."

Jeff Kriendler, Pan Am's Vice President for Public Relations, arrived
next, along with Dr. Constantino, the head of medical staff at Kennedy, and
they made arrangements to take the passengers out on a MEDEVAC flight—
a military flying hospital; they particularly wanted to transfer the burn victims
to a burn center. But there was a glitch because nobody had a passport and the
authorities would not allow anybody out of the country without one. Jeff
Kriendler went to work with the State Department, and convinced the bureau-
crats to expedite matters because the burn victims simply could not wait.

"Suddenly, on the Wednesday afternoon we got word that all was in order
and the evacuation would start immediately. It was time-consuming as most
patients were removed in their beds or wheelchairs, but no-one seemed to mind
and there was a sense of excitement and relief. But, of course, everyone who left
the building was at the mercy of the ubiquitous press vultures closing in for yet
another offensive violation of privacy. As Carla and I watched from a fourth
floor window, our last sight of Captain Grubbs was of his being surrounded by
reporters jostling for space. When they found they couldn't get close enough,
an extension to the microphone assured their final victory.

"We knew we weren't going on that flight because we still had not had
the National Transportation Safety Board hearing, required of all crew
members before they could go home. Carla and I were eager to leave the
hospital for the hotel, but I needed a doctor's release. Finally, Dr. Constantino
informed me that I was to be kept under observation for a few more days
because he was concerned about my head injuries. I pleaded with him to let me
go, but he was adamant; I was to remain quiet, preferably in bed. If moving my
facial muscles hadn't been so excruciating, I would have broken into tears.
Once again, sensing my disappointment and apprehension, Carla came to my
aid. 'Don't worry, Dorothy. I'm not going to leave you here alone.'

"All of a sudden, Carla and I were the only two left on the whole floor, the entire wing of the hospital—there wasn't even a nurse. It was eerie because a wind picked up and howled around the windows. It was really lonely up there and I began to be concerned, asking myself: 'Why are they keeping me here? What's wrong? I feel all right, I just hurt a bit.' But Carla and I made the best of it and even began to laugh a little. But when I laughed, I was in terrible pain. All the muscles in my face would go up, and it was agony because my scalp had tightened and scabs had formed which made me feel like a puppet with all its strings attached to my scalp. I had to hold my hands over my face to keep the muscles from moving because I hurt so much with the bruising and swelling. Funny things kept happening, things that we could smile about, but smiling was agony."

Dorothy and Carla stayed in the hospital for another few days before they were released to go to the hotel. They had no clothes to leave in, so Fran Wood and a Pan Am mechanic set off to buy some. When they returned, the mechanic told them that the hardest part was shopping in Spanish for underwear for two ladies he hardly knew. Fran had found a big, fluffy cotton outfit for Dorothy, a garment with huge gathered sleeves and an elastic waist, so that she could pull it on over her broken arm with ease. "She was so thoughtful to think of something like that," adds Dorothy.

When they finally arrived at the hotel, the reporters began circling around Dorothy like hungry sharks. They recognized her immediately because of her broken arm and bruised face and they wanted to devour her, the heroic victim. But Pan Am employees also met her, surrounded her before the reporters could reach her, snatched her away, and whisked her in the service elevator up to her room. "That room was like a funeral parlor, it was so full of flowers. Bouquet after bouquet kept arriving, and at one point I had to fill the bidet with water for them.

"It was non-stop from then on. Telephone ringing. Reporters lurking in the hallways. Cameras everywhere. People with microphones popping up everywhere. At one point we were able to escape with Fran, just for a walk in the park, just to take some air, away from all this. I remember that very, very vividly—walking with Fran in the park."

Before they could go home, the crew members had to give their statements to the National Transportation Safety Board, the Federal Aviation Agency, and to Pan Am. With their testimonies behind them, the atmosphere for the crew began to lighten a little and became more social. "We were protected by various people, engulfed, and in that way we could go down to the bar, have some drinks, and eat in the restaurant. It was a release of tension to socialize, not that we were being insensitive, but you had to let go of the tension from the previous week and try to maintain some sense of normality, or to get back into it. But I still tired very easily and did a lot of napping, although I couldn't sleep more than 30 minutes at a time, and suffered headaches and general discomfort.

"Pan Am would approve whom I could talk with. That's when I became closely involved with Jeff Kriendler. He acted as my front man and he would brief me, although he never said 'Don't say this, don't say that.' He never spoke for me. After the first or second interview, he said 'You're doing fine.' I knew what I was not supposed to say—you just didn't divulge everything. There was too much liability involved. I did a lot of interviews for the Americans and for the Europeans. I knew that people were interested and I would rather they heard facts than fiction or speculation. I wouldn't be terribly dramatic and didn't divulge all the gory details because I was well aware of the fact that those who were left behind needed to be protected. They already had enough to deal with."

The next hurdle for Dorothy was the memorial service in the cathedral in Tenerife. That was when the sheer enormity of the death toll hit her, packaged as it was in the formality of funeral dogma and tradition. People from all over the world flew in, the King of Spain's representative arrived, and as always, the media were circling round, menacing. Pan Am was concerned about Dorothy's safety. "There were various Pan American employees, as well as military, F.A.A., N.T.S.B., and embassy people, and a combination of these people escorted us whenever we went anywhere. Several of them were very tall, especially one Pan Am executive who devised a plan to protect me as I entered the cathedral. He and several others encircled me and we went in via a side entrance. But, of course, the reporters were there too. I found it so thought-provoking that people should have to provide me with a physical guard.

"Once we were inside the cathedral, the men sat on both sides and behind me in the pews. There at last, we were immune from the mob. We were left alone, physically and emotionally. Perhaps it was the solemnity of the occasion and the pervasive spiritual aura that daunted even the most unscrupulous journalist. The service was very moving because finally the magnitude of the disaster became a vivid reality. One could only turn inward to ponder and question how to accept it all. There in that soaring, candlelit vastness, filled with the traditional sounds of medieval music and chant, reeking with the scent of flowers and incense, I watched as the richly vested elite of the Church delivered the prescribed liturgical ritual, praising God, thanking Him, begging forgiveness and mercy for the departed and consolation for the living. All this ancient drama and spectacle unfolding around me did not comfort me

but only served to confuse and confound me. The forever unanswerable
dilemma of a just God became a ponderous and stinging reality for me."

✈ ✈ ✈ ✈ ✈

It was nearly time to go home. Pan Am had arranged for a 707 to pick
up all the Pan Am people and some of the media from New York. "I was
suffering some really throbbing headaches at that time, which was under-
standable, considering my head injury. I remember waiting in the terminal
and then sneaking away to a quiet place just to meditate. Having people
around me all the time, having to be protected all the time, and having to be
pleasant too, was a trying experience."

When the flight was called and Dorothy started the walk out across
tarmac, a military guard lined up at the foot of the stairs to the aircraft. They
all raised their arms in salute. As the small, damaged figure walked past them,
their leader stepped forward and said in words that conveyed more admiration, respect, and love than any medal or decoration ever could:

"Dorothy, we salute you."

✈ ✈ ✈ ✈ ✈

Pan American World Airways
June 9, 1977

Mr. John J. Carroll
Executive Vice President and Managing Director
Flight Safety Foundation
1800 N. Kent St.
Arlington, VA 22209

Dear John:
Pursuant to our recent discussion, Pam Am wishes to submit the
names of its employees on board charter flight B150 of March 27,
1977, as deserving of special recognition of their exemplary actions at the Tenerife tragedy.

Nine New York based cabin crewmembers died in the performance of their duties: purser Francoise Colbert de Beaulieu and
flight attendants Mari Asai, Christine Ekelund, Luisa Flood, Sa-
chiko Hirano, Marilyn Luker, Aysel Sarp, Carol Thomas, and
Miguel Torrech. Although we may never know the full extent of

their heroism, we firmly believe that many people owe their lives to the dedication of these crewmembers.

In spite of injuries to her head and arm sustained at the time of impact, first class purser Dorothy Kelly coolly and professionally directed passengers out of and away from the burning aircraft, then repeatedly reapproached the wreckage to assist the injured, including Captain Victor Grubbs, to safe areas beyond the range of explosions and flying debris. After she was relieved at the scene, Ms. Kelly arrived at the hospital where she continued for some time to work with the doctors in tending to passenger injuries and compiling information on other survivors. Captain Grubbs has recalled how Ms. Kelly assisted him in the attached statement.

Ignoring a broken ankle suffered in jumping down from the shattered cockpit, first officer Robert Bragg immediately took charge of the situation on the ground. He guided ambulances as close to the burning aircraft as possible, and assisted litter carriers in getting to the most critically injured passengers first. As able bodied survivors and local people became available, he organized their efforts in assisting passengers into the arriving cars, buses and jeeps. He then proceeded to the terminal operations office to establish communications with Pan American. When he finally arrived at a hospital, he learned that the majority of survivors were at a second hospital, and he continued there to complete the information he knew would be most helpful to the Company and investigating authorities at home. It was only when satisfied that all this had been accomplished that he had his own injury attended.

Flight engineer George Warns, operations representative Juan Murillo and mechanic John Cooper all escaped from the cockpit with difficulty. John Cooper assisted passengers away from the vicinity of the left wing, where they were hesitating while the engines continued to run and the fuselage took fire. Even after fuel tanks in the right wing had exploded, Mr. Murillo remained at the aircraft to pull out several passengers and remove them to a safe distance. Cooper and Murillo joined first officer Bragg in completely searching the area, and after local authorities had taken charge, began coordinating preliminary information back to Pan Am headquarters.

After impact, stewardess Carla Johnson oriented herself to her bewildering surroundings, and aware of the increasing intensity of the fire in the wreckage behind her, encouraged and command-ed stunned passengers to quickly get off the aircraft. Momentarily trapped when flooring gave away beneath them, stewardesses Su-zanne Donovan and Joan Jackson crawled upwards to exit with passengers by working their way forward and down along the ex-terior of the twisted and constantly shifting fuselage. These three eventually joined survivors on the ground and provided comfort and assistance to the injured awaiting transportation.

On June 7, the nine survivors were presented the President's Award at the monthly meeting of the Pan American Board of Directors. Chairman Seawell, who presented each with a gold medallion and a certificate, told the nine "We're proud of you." The certificate cit-ed the ... professional, courageous and compassionate conduct and action at the time of the tragic accident at Tenerife Island... present-ed with highest honor and respect on this day, June 7, 1977.

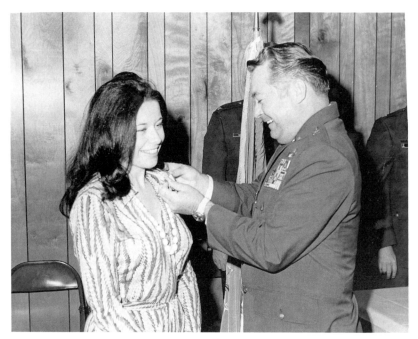

Brigadier General Carl Miller, U.S. Air Force, pins on the Silver Medal of Valor.

The nine crewmembers who died in the crash will be presented the President's Award posthumously.

The attached "Awareness Newsletter" attests to the admiration and respect these brave people have earned from their fellow Pan Am employees. Your recognition of their extraordinary efforts is very much appreciated.

Very truly yours,

Francis L. Wallace
Director-Flight Safety Analysis and Information

✈ ✈ ✈ ✈ ✈

Statement By Captain V.F. Grubbs

After exiting the airplane, I found myself alongside it in a stunned condition, unable to move. I could feel the intense heat of the fire, and was aware of burning metal and debris being scattered all around me.

I noticed Ms. Kelly running toward me. (She had already reached safety and was coming back to get me.) Ms. Kelly urged me to get away from the aircraft. I tried to move, but my body seemed to be glued to the ground. I told her I could not walk. I could hear her say "Crawl, Captain, crawl." I began to crawl, but recall wanting to stop several times—the grass felt so cool under me. She insisted that I keep crawling, and then grabbed hold of me from under my arms and I could feel her pulling me. Although I wanted to stop, she continued to pull me and insisted we must reach the concrete first. Ms. Kelly had been injured herself. There was blood coming from a wound in her forehead, and it was trickling down her face. I learned later that she also had a broken arm.

After we reached the concrete about 200 feet away, I was able to stand. I found myself aiding passengers into an ambulance. I don't remember seeing Dorothy after that; I believe she was assisting injured passengers on the grass.

Fiftieth Anniversary Celebration

O for a pleasure trip up to the Pole!
Rossiter Johnson, "Ninety-Nine in the Shade"

I n 1977, because of the pall that the Tenerife disaster cast and because the company began to suffer acute financial strain, there was a desperate need for an eye-catching stunt to improve Pan American's image in the public's eye. What could be better than celebrating the golden anniversary of Pan American's first flight?

The previous year, to commemorate the U.S. bicentennial, Pan American had flown a Boeing 747SP, dubbing it *Clipper 200—Liberty Bell Express*, on a record-breaking (in terms of commercial aircraft) round-the-world-at-the-Equator flight. The Clipper carried 98 fare-paying passengers at a cost of $2,912 for a first-class seat and $1,838 for economy, and the flight paid for itself. What a grand scheme it would be to fly the same Clipper in a record-breaking round-the-world-over-the-Poles flight! Pan Am's Public Relations department went into a frenzy of activity.

Flight 50, using the same 747SP, renamed *Clipper New Horizons*, would originate in San Francisco, then head north to reach London in one leap over the North Pole. After a fuelling break in London, it would head south for a non-stop flight to Cape Town. From Cape Town, the Clipper would fly due south again to cross the South Pole en route to Auckland, and finally from Auckland back to San Francisco. The flight would try to break a 1965 Flying Tiger 707 record of 62 hours and 27 minutes. Miss U.S.A. and Miss Universe would accompany the passengers all the way around the world. Miss England, Miss South Africa, and Miss New Zealand would join the flight en route.

The 165 first-class passengers would be showered with souvenirs: certificates, itineraries, menus, make-up kits, shaving kits, slippers, and glasses engraved with '50' and the Pan Am logo; and postcards with stamps already on them so that they could be mailed on arrival at each stop. Old time movies, such as *Casablanca, The Road to Morocco*, and *It Happened One Night* were selected to entertain the passengers on the long legs. Fourteen carefully planned meals would be served along the way by handpicked cabin crews, each crew flying just one leg. (Although the cockpit crew also changed along the way, those who flew the first leg remained on board so as to be on hand to make the landing in San Francisco on returning there.)

Pan Am first offered to sell 172 first-class seats on the 50th anniversary flight to those passengers who had been aboard the bicentennial flight and also advertised it in *The Wall Street Journal.* Within three days, all the seats were sold. Who, you might ask, would be crazy enough to want to go on a two-and-a-half day flight around the world? Isn't it tough enough to spend seven hours crossing the Atlantic? There are people for whom record-breaking events are of paramount interest. They will do anything to be part of history. They will even pay $2,200 to fly around the world in a weekend.

In the weeks before the flight took off, the company sent out question-naires to the passengers, inquiring why they wanted to participate in such a flight and offering a prize for the best response. The winner was a man who said that he was sick and tired of his wife's saying that he never took her anywhere; he hoped that by taking her around the world for a weekend he could shut her up for the rest of her life.

Frank Papouschek was the senior purser chosen to work on board the first leg of the 50th Anniversary flight. Frank was born in New Jersey, and raised in Cleveland and Philadelphia. Looking for adventure, he had moved to San Francisco in 1950 and joined Southwest Airlines (S.W.A., later renamed

*Frank
Papouschek
and jans.*

Pamela Taylor (far right) and co-workers on the 50th anniversary flight encourage Mike Jarnigan.

Pacific Airlines), a DC-3 local service or feeder line which flew between San Francisco and Los Angeles, a five-hour, ten-stop flight. (Feeder is hardly appropriate in this context; there was not even time for a coffee service between stops.) But, like other local service airlines, S.W.A. was often the flight attendant's stepping stone to larger airlines, and many of their employees went on to fly with Pan American. Frank was one of these, and soon his energy and enthusiasm for Pan Am was (and still is) boundless. He loved the airline with a passion, he adored working on public relations jaunts, and was often chosen for special charters. It came as no surprise that he was selected for the honor of heading up the cabin crew, which included Pamela Taylor (see page 188), on the first leg of Flight 50. Frank already had several special flights under his belt, having flown on the last Stratocruiser flight and the first 707 Round-the-World flight, but this particular event had a double meaning for Frank; it also happened to be the 20th anniversary of the day on which he started to work for Pan American.

At noon on 28 October 1977, Pan Am threw a bon voyage party, complete with a giant 50th anniversary cake, at San Francisco Airport for the passengers of Flight 50, just before they took off. After the party, Frank and his crew, along with Miss Universe, Janelle Commissiong, and Miss U.S.A., Kimberly Tomes, welcomed the passengers aboard, and shortly after they were aloft, served the first of the many elegant meals. After dinner, the passengers were entertained with a Gucci fashion show.

Pamela adds: "The company hired professional models for the women's fashions, one of whom was a Pan Am flight attendant, who also worked for an agency in New York. They were all incredibly glamorous and sophisticated. There was a hairdressing salon in the 747's upstairs lounge, where their hair and make-up were attended to. When they were ready, they would whirl down the curved staircase, fly down the aisle, and loop back up through the cabin. Mike Jarnigan, one of our flight service supervisors, modeled the men's fashions. He was the only non-professional, but he looked terrific in a wonderful fur hat and coat."

"One of our pilots had wanted to be a passenger on the trip," says Frank, "but no Pan Am people were allowed as paying passengers. Instead, he talked one of his neighbors into going, and he introduced her to me at the reception. Now, Gucci had donated a beautiful ladies' two-piece suit, and after the fashion show, the captain drew a name out of a hat. The pilot's friend had won the suit. She came to me later and said 'Frank, you didn't have to do that!' She couldn't believe her luck; she simply assumed that I had fixed it for her.

"The passengers were wonderful. One man found pennies from 50 years ago which he presented to all the passengers and crew, another celebrated his 50th birthday, and still another man dressed as Santa Claus because he wanted to go up and down the aisle when we went over the North Pole to welcome people to his part of the world."

Janelle Commissiong, Miss Universe, models a sporty outfit. Mike Jarnigan waits his turn.

Pamela remembers a slight diversion from the flight plan: "It was night when we went over the North Pole, so we couldn't see anything, but the captain made the airplane bump up and then down, as though we were jumping a fence. It made a thump as though we were actually hitting the Pole. A guitarist played and sang, and we handed out glasses of champagne to everyone. Frank made a toast." In his words: "I toasted all the people below us. The whole world was below us at that moment! But Santa had sampled the brandy a bit too much, and by the time we went over the Pole he was truly red-nosed. He kept saying, 'Wait till you see the penguin outfit I have for the South Pole!' I think he must have slept over the South Pole because nobody ever saw the penguin outfit."

After the Clipper circled the Pole, it continued on its long flight to London, but what with meals, movies, the fashion show, the ceremony over the Pole, and a little sleep, the time passed very quickly for the passengers. "When we landed at London's Heathrow Airport," Frank says, "the door opened and the Lord Mayor of Hillingdon, in which Greater London borough Heathrow is located, came in, wearing his full regalia. He pounded on the floor of the cabin with his big cane, saying, 'Hear ye! Hear ye! Welcome to England!'"

After a two-hour refuelling stop, *Clipper New Horizons* took off again, flying south. As the 747 crossed the Equator, the captain welcomed the passengers to the southern half of the world. On arrival in Cape Town, local time 11 p.m., there was a large reception for the passengers at the airport, and the mayor of Cape Town welcomed them to the "finest cape in the world."

After another two-hour refuelling stop, the Clipper took off again for the most thrilling part of the journey in terms of the breathtaking views from the aircraft. Flying out of the darkness into the dawn, the passengers were treated to a crystal-clear sunrise over territory that few have ever had the opportunity to see. Antarctica revealed itself: an endless succession of mountains, glaciers, snowfields, unimaginably huge and pristine. The Clipper flew over the South Pole in brilliant sunlight, in vivid contrast to the dark North Pole, but by the time it reached Auckland, it was night again, and the aircraft landed in a terrific rainstorm. Even though it was 3 a.m. local time, the passengers were welcomed by Maori dancers, who invited them and the captain to join them in some unusual dance routines around the airport.

On the last leg of the flight, across the Pacific from Auckland back to San Francisco, the passengers watched as the sun rose once again. After more food, more movies, and crossing the international dateline soon after leaving New Zealand, *Clipper New Horizons* made it back home. The total flying time was 54 hours, 7 minutes, and 12 seconds.

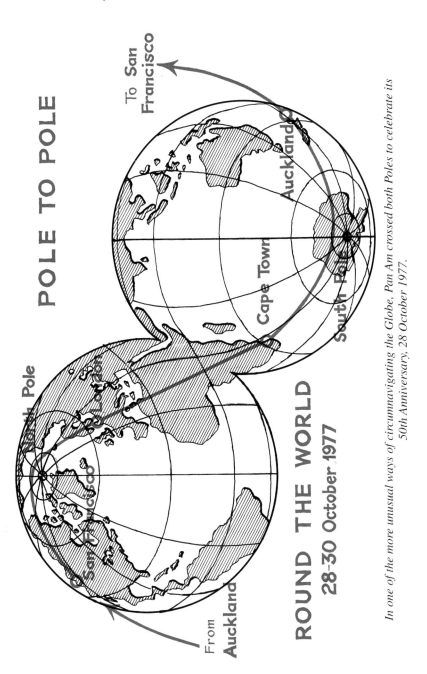

In one of the more unusual ways of circumnavigating the Globe, Pan Am crossed both Poles to celebrate its 50th Anniversary, 28 October 1977.

Frank and his crew had dearly wished to continue onward from London with Flight 50, but that was not to be. Instead, they did the next best thing. They overnighted in London, and then immediately returned home, just in time to greet the exhausted 50th anniversary passengers when they arrived in San Francisco. Frank says that, in spite of the ordeal of going round the world in a weekend, "They came off that 'plane just as bubbly and wild as they were at the beginning. They will never stop talking about going round the world in a weekend. If Pan American could have something like that again, they would sell out in no time flat."

Clipper New Horizons is the only aircraft ever to have circled the globe at the Equator and over the Poles. A plaque was placed on board, describing this distinction, and whenever Frank worked on that airplane thereafter, he would make an announcement about its achievement, adding, "If anyone is interested in hearing stories about the 50th anniversary flight, one of our cabin crew is in a strong position to tell them to you."

Who else but Frank Papouschek himself?

The Cross,
The Cushion

He is brought as a lamb to the slaughter.

Isaiah, LIII, 7

During the seven years between 1966 and 1974, a time of huge expansion in international air travel with a concomitant need for cabin crew with Asian languages, Pan American hired a number of Japanese nationals to fly in the Pacific Division. Young women who wanted to apply were invited to telephone to schedule an interview. That 'phone call was, in effect, the initial interview, and it was conducted solely in English because Pan Am recognized that someone who could speak fluently on the telephone, with no complementary facial expressions and hand gestures, would certainly be able to converse fluently under less challenging conditions.

Yoshiko Oana (Maeda) was born in Nagano, in the Japanese Alps, but has spent most of her life in Tokyo. With an older brother and a younger brother, she refers to herself as the best part of a sandwich. As she grew up, she found herself torn between two driving interests, the adventure of travelling as a flight attendant for Pan Am and the pursuit of an intellectual and spiritual education. As things have turned out, she has been able to fulfil both her desires.

Although she felt that her life experience made her more suited for work for a Japanese airline because, apart from one vacation in Europe, she had not been exposed to other cultures, she wanted desperately to work for an international carrier, and accordingly, she picked up a Pan Am brochure, and dialled their number as instructed. Yoshiko passed that first hurdle and was invited to an all-day interview at the Palace Hotel in Tokyo. At 9 a.m., she was invited to step on a scale and given the sombre news that she was "a little bit overweight and oversized of the hips" and that she might not make it. She was then interviewed, again in English, by four people, two from the New York office, one from Honolulu, and one from Japan. She passed that hurdle too. In the afternoon, she underwent the language listening and comprehension tests. She left the Palace Hotel at 6 p.m., utterly exhausted but triumphant.

Yoshiko Maeda

As Yoshiko Maeda had hoped, her life as a flight attendant has not only given her the opportunity to travel and to be of service to the public but also the time and opportunity to fulfil her quest for intellectual and spiritual satisfaction. She is now not only a flight attendant (she continued to fly after United purchased Pan Am's Pacific routes) but an accomplished singer, artist, and poet.

On 12 August 1982, Yoshiko Maeda was working on the Boeing 747 flight PA830 from Tokyo to Honolulu. Until about half an hour before landing in Honolulu, the flight had been routine. There was a large party of Japanese businessmen in the rear of the aircraft, but the rest of the cabin was not overcrowded. Suddenly, there was the sound of a large explosion. The flight attendants immediately thought that it was a rapid decompression and expected the oxygen masks to drop down. That did not happen, but the captain's terse voice over the public address system instructed the cabin crew to take their seats immediately. Yoshiko, who was working in business-class, turned around to take her seat, but somebody was already sitting in it.

"I had to go some place else, and I started running towards the back of the airplane. Then I encountered a small, elderly Japanese man coming towards me in the aisle, begging, 'Help me. Oh, my son is killed. Killed.' I was so shocked by that word that I forgot the situation we were in and whether or not we were decompressing. If we had been, I would not have my life. I ran to the back with him, and there I saw the disastrous scene.

"Normally, if I look at a film and see blood, I scream. I can never look at those bloody things. But this time, my professional mind took over. I looked at the boy's body so clearly. His internal organs were partially coming out and one side of his leg had been blown off. But from his waist to the top of his head, there was nothing wrong with him. He was moving his head, saying '*Itai. Itai*,' which means 'painful.' I wrapped him in a blanket. I made myself do it. I couldn't believe that I could deal with it.

"Other flight attendants were working in that part of the cabin and trying to assist me, but somehow I was the one to end up with that boy until he died. I stayed with him until he died.

"The bomb had been placed between the seat cushion and the seat. The boy had been blown upwards and then dropped in the aisle. We started calling for a doctor over the P.A. Four of them were on board, and one by one they looked at the boy and turned away, saying there was nothing they could do. They also feared a second explosion. The fourth doctor was Japanese, and I grabbed his arm and begged 'Please, please stay with me even though I know we can't do anything.' He was shaking but I was somehow so calm. I went back to the galley to get some ice. When I asked the girls for it, they were also lost, trying to give me different things. I was so calm. Usually I am such a clumsy person, but I found myself a different personality.

"I was so sad because I couldn't do anything; nobody could do anything. I wanted to at least reduce his pain. I asked the doctor if aspirin would help because we had no morphine. I tried oxygen, but that didn't help. Finally, I didn't know where I could put my feeling of sorrow, of uselessness, of helplessness, so I just told the boy 'If you are in such pain, why don't you bite my hand?' He understood me. He bit me right away. He bit my right hand so hard. Then I came back to reality and thought 'Maybe I'll lose skin and muscle.' I had to take my hand back, and the mark remained for a long, long time. But the boy had understood me.

"The only word he could express was '*Itai*.' I stroked him, I calmed him. I said 'It's all right. Be alive. Be alive.' I stroked him all the time. I was so calm when I was taking care of him. Until three minutes before we landed, when I covered him completely, I hadn't recognized the damage to the airplane. Only then did I look up and recognize the reality of what had happened. The fuselage, the panels were all peeled off and all the machinery was exposed. I couldn't believe it; I never knew there was such precise machinery in the fuselage. And the ceiling had dropped down and you could see all the machinery in the ceiling too. The skin of the airplane was exposed.

"If the bomb had exploded while the boy was in the bathroom, it would have penetrated the skin of the fuselage, and we would all have died. The boy made the difference. He was the Cross, he was cushion. I was shocked and impressed. He took the bomb, all by himself, for everybody else.

"His relatives, his brothers were sitting near or next to him or behind him. Some of them got a little fire and were burned. Hair was burned, stockings were burned, but there was no other major physical injury.

"After the airplane arrived, and we had been interviewed by the F.B.I. and had written reports for Pan Am, all my tension released. I cried and cried and cried. I did not sleep at all for three days. I could not eat. Pan Am said, 'Yoshiko, why don't you rest for a while? You probably need a rest.' The president of the company invited all the crew members of that flight to a luncheon in Los Angeles, but somehow it was cancelled.

"When the time came for me to go back on the aircraft, it was not hard for me. Even though flying is not the same nowadays as it used to be, I try to make myself enjoy it, especially when I am talking to passengers. I tell myself that there is a reason why I see these particular passengers today in this world. Maybe it's just once in my life that I see them, but it is a very precious once.

十字架のクッション

"Seven years after the death of the boy, when I was in Seattle on a layover, I turned on the T.V. in my hotel room to watch the news. I learned that they had finally arrested the man who bombed PA830. He was a Palestinian terrorist with a bomb prepared in Hong Kong. His act was one of unlimited murder, aimed at the United States. That meant that anyone could be the target, but preferably the whole aircraft, full of people. It happened that the body of one 16-year-old Japanese boy saved all our lives."

The Cross, the Cushion.

Baby on Board!

...the place of our birth...sung always will be
as the shell ever sings of its home in the sea!
                                Frances Dana Cage, "Home"

W hile some people die on board of natural causes, others insist on being born. All flight service personnel are given training in how to deliver babies, which nowadays usually takes the form of a lecture and a movie of an actual delivery. However, Helena Cioffi Stoffel remembers that in 1946 flight service trainers in New York were at a loss as to how to handle the birth problem. The solution: they sent the trainees over to the Planned Parenthood offices in Manhattan where they spent a couple of days learning how to assist at a delivery.

Here are accounts of three births on board Pan Am Clippers as told by the midwife-stewardesses themselves. Of interest is how the instructions for delivering a baby have changed over the years, especially with regard to cutting the umbilical cord.

JACK
by *Olga Iturrino*

[Olga Iturrino, who assisted at Jack's birth, was hired in Puerto Rico in 1950 during Pan Am's first hiring of Hispanic women. Five hundred young women applied for the job, and seven were chosen. Olga's engaging personality and quick wit served her well at her interview, so well, in fact, that the interviewers failed to notice that at 4' 11", she was well short of the regulatory minimum height (at that time 5' 2"; later on 5' 4").]

I was the purser on the flight from Puerto Rico to New York. The woman was quite big.

"Don't you feel good?" I asked her when I saw her rubbing her stomach as she came on board.

"I feel fine," she said.

"When are you going to have that baby?" I asked again.

"Not for a while, maybe another month."

Olga Iturrino.

"If you think you are going to have that baby, I must tell you that this 'plane is not equipped to handle births. We don't have anything to take care of you," I warned her.

"Don't worry about it. I'm not going to have that baby," she said.

It was an eight-hour night flight, and we left around 11 p.m. After the passengers were all settled, I told the stewardess that I was going to take a rest for an hour, and then she could have her turn. While I was resting, she rushed to me saying:

"Hey, hey, hey. You better go back to the men's room. I think I hear a baby crying."

At that time, the bathrooms were divided into men's and women's, just little cubby holes, not much room. I opened the door, and there was the woman in a squat position, and the baby was on the floor, still attached. I rushed to the cockpit and told Captain Harvey. He came back with me and looked at her and said to me:

"Do you have a pair of scissors?"

"No, you know we don't carry scissors," I replied.

"Give me your scout knife, then," he said.

I quickly boiled water and disinfected the knife, and then he tried to cut the cord.

"This doesn't cut at all," he said.

"The only thing I can give you is the sandwich knife," I suggested.

So I disinfected that and gave it to him, and he cut the cord and handed me the baby.

"What am I going to do with it?" I asked.

"Just take care of it."

That poor baby; he was so slippery, and I was juggling him, trying to hold on to him. Finally the stewardess came with a blanket and we wrapped him up. I asked the mother if she had any clothes for him, and she said:

"Not a thing. I didn't expect to have this baby here."

Then came the problem of tying the umbilical cord. I asked for a doctor over the P.A. There was no doctor but a pharmacist offered his help. He came over and tied it, just made a knot in it. He turned out to be a cousin of mine that I had never met before.

We cleaned the baby as much as we could, and we fixed three seats as a bed for the mother. Then all of a sudden we ran into this bad weather, a bad August storm, up and down, up and down. It was terrible, and I was so worried for the mother, but she was fine. This was her fourth baby, and her husband was supposed to be waiting for her at the airport, to fly home to Chicago with her, but he never showed up. An ambulance took her to the hospital. We made a collection for her expenses, and Pan Am contributed to her ticket from New York to Chicago.

The baby was named Jack after the captain, Jack Harvey, and he was the first child born on board a Pan American Clipper.

ANNA VICTORIA
by Anne Wasse-Lyon

[Anne Wasse-Lyon was a midwife in London before joining Pan Am in 1967. Her job was to ride around North London on her bicycle, its basket holding a

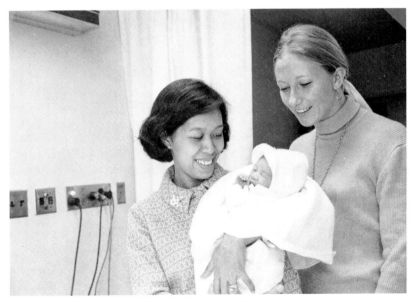

Dr. Roberta Romero, Anna Victoria, and Anne Wasse-Lyon.

small bag of equipment, and to deliver babies, usually in the middle of the night. While on vacation at her parents' home in Bermuda, she met their neighbor, a Pan Am captain, who arranged for a recruiter to fly from New York to interview her. The recruiter's flight was late, the turn-around swift, and Anne was hired in the space of ten minutes. She has been flying ever since, but has only once had to call upon her earlier skills as a midwife.]

I was on a Rest & Rehabilitation trip between Saigon and Hong Kong, and we had a five-day layover in Hong Kong. As soon as we arrived, I went on a shopping spree; I ordered shoes and dresses, everything custom made, and then returned to the hotel and went to bed feeling secure that I would be able to attend fittings during the next couple of days. It seemed as though I had been asleep for a mere two minutes when Scheduling telephoned and told me to be ready for pick-up in one hour. I made every excuse I could think of: I had been drinking, my hair was wet, and so on. I made so many excuses that finally they had to send a taxi for me because I missed the pick-up. We flew to Tokyo, and the next day I found myself on *Clipper Victor*, Flight 864 from Tokyo to San Francisco. The delivery happened on a flight I wasn't meant to be on at all.

Four hours after our departure, just as we were ready to start the dinner service, we hit some bumpy weather, so we decided to hand out the landing forms instead of serving the meal just then. I picked up a bunch of forms and went through the first-class curtain. Dr. Roberta Romero, her three children, and her niece, whom she was using as a nanny, were sitting in the first two rows.

"Do you need a landing card?" I asked.

"I think I'm in labor," she replied.

"You can't possibly be," I said, in deep denial. "Take a deep breath, relax, and forget about it."

I gave her a glass of champagne, and she seemed to follow my instructions, while insisting that she was not full term. Dr. Romero was travelling to Canada to join her husband, also a doctor, who was on the staff of McGill University Hospital.

Mind over matter is not usually effective when a baby wants to be born, and it was not long before Dr. Romero was back in labor. One of the other flight attendants and I went into action. We moved two men from the last row of first-class seats to the lounge of the 707, and made a bed for her on the seats, with blankets hung around it to give her some privacy. We used vodka to sterilize ourselves, and we put out a call over the P.A. system for a doctor. Not until after I had delivered a little girl (who I am sure was full term), and after I had cut the cord, had bathed her, and wrapped her in a blanket did a very drunken doctor appear. He was worse than useless. He had nothing to do with the delivery itself; he turned up afterwards and pulled her placenta out. You just don't do that. So she bled, and for the next hour or two I had to massage her stomach. This keeps the uterus tight, otherwise it goes flaccid and bleeds. If you massage it, it contracts and stops bleeding. There are drugs that help too, but obviously I didn't have those on board. The other thing that helps is breast feeding. Hormones at work.

There was some consternation when we arrived in San Francisco with 121 passengers instead of 120. This perplexed Immigration. An ambulance took Dr. Romero away, but left the three children and the young niece on the aeroplane. We kept asking, "What is going to happen to these people?" Pan Am dropped the ball, and said they didn't care. So I took them all home with me for three days until their mother was able to travel again. My poor roommates! Can you imagine their faces when I came home with four children and said, "Hey, look what I've got!"

[Dr. Romero decided to name her new daughter Anna Victoria, in honor of the stewardess who had delivered her and the Clipper on which she was born.]

PAM ANN
by *Katherine Beard*

[Kathy Beard is a fifth generation Floridian from Jacksonville. After spending her junior year in France, she wanted to continue travelling. She joined Pan Am in 1970, the year after she graduated from college. During her flying career, she acquired a degree at the New York School of Interior Design. She was particularly happy she had made the effort to carve out a second career when she learned early on the morning of 4 December 1991, just as she was ironing a couple of shirts for a flight to Mexico that day, that Pan Am had ceased operations.]

We joined the flight in Beirut, headed for London. I was in the C-zone, the front part of the economy-class section in the Boeing 747. (I mention that because later on there was nowhere to hide anything that was going on.) I saw a large Indian family—a father, a mother, and seven children—return from the transit lounge and take up two rows, which was not unusual.

The previous crew had told me that this lady was not feeling well, and apparently they had already investigated her doctor's certificate about how far along her pregnancy was, and the note said six months. She had boarded Pan

Kathy Beard

Am in Delhi, but had started her journey in Bombay, and her destination was London. After take-off, she told me she did not feel well. I noticed she didn't eat anything, didn't even nibble, and I asked her if she felt she was in labor. She shook her head.

When we arrived in Istanbul, our first stop, she was still feeling discomfort, and I again questioned her about what was going on, and she said she just didn't feel well, she just didn't want to eat. However, it seemed as though she was asking me for help because she kept saying she didn't feel well and wanted to be alone. I did not want her on the aircraft because I knew in my bones she was going to have that baby, and as she was in my section I would be the one to deal with it. We took off for the two-and-a-half hour flight from Istanbul to Frankfurt, and once again she didn't eat a thing. Moreover, she was feeling worse and worse. I was convinced that she was in labor because, although I hadn't had a baby myself, my Labrador retriever had recently delivered pups and I recognized the signs. She refused to admit it because she was determined to get to London. By this time, all the crew knew that something was going on and I jokingly told the In-Flight Director, "You have got to get this woman off the 'plane in Frankfurt because I don't intend to deliver a baby today." Then I went forward to my mother who was travelling in the B-zone and jokingly told her that I expected her help in delivering the baby because she'd had the experience of having me. She said, "No way!" and stayed firmly in the B-zone. I never once thought I would actually have to deliver a child.

When we arrived in Frankfurt, the authorities came on board and looked at the woman's passport and realized how many children were on it already. If they took her off, they would have to take the whole family too. They fussed. So the captain, who wanted to keep to his schedule, said, "Well, let's get out of here." We took off, and he poured it on all the way to London.

As soon as we we were airborne, the woman told me that she was bleeding. I said, "You mean your water's broken?" She said, "No. I'm bleeding." So I stuck my hand under her to check, and sure enough, I was right: her water had broken. That was when I called for help, and we took the blankets down from the overhead compartments and made a screen around her.

The In-Flight Director found the first aid kit, got the manual out, and started reading the instructions aloud. We had a bain-marie of hot water, we had ice, we had linens, blankets underneath her and around her. Someone immediately paged for a doctor (of course, you had to say medical doctor so that a doctor of history wouldn't volunteer). There wasn't a single M.D. on board. The closest we could get was a medic, who at least could help this woman with her breathing.

That baby came out like greased lightning, absolutely no problems. A little girl. As per instruction, nothing was cut—we just tied the cord in two places. We didn't wash her, just wiped around her eyes. We put her on the woman's stomach, to keep her close and warm.

It was a healthy baby and the mother was fine. The other seven kids were in the row behind their mother, all bouncing up and down. The husband wrung his hands a bit, but he wasn't too concerned because he was getting free medical attention. He thought we were all doctors or nurses and that we did this sort of thing every day of the week.

The captain was thrilled to have made that 70-minute flight in 62, but was disappointed to find out it wasn't quite fast enough. The baby was born just as we were touching down. A day or two later, we learned from the London *Daily Mail* that the baby had been named Pam Ann.

Thank goodness I only had to do it once.

Siege at Karachi

*For you, O dearest among women, you only
had the hard courage to give your life...*

Euripides, Alcestis

In 1985, Pan American began what it referred to as a 'regional hiring' program, and what the I.U.F.A. referred to as the 'hiring of foreign nationals.' The program was controversial. The company claimed that its intention was to acquire cabin crew who spoke the languages of the countries to which its aircraft flew and that it had every right to set up bases in Poland, Turkey, India, Kenya, Israel, and Thailand and to hire flight attendants in those countries. The union rejected this argument, claiming that the company's intention was to acquire cabin crew to whom it could pay lower wages. A shaky compromise was reached: hiring of foreign flight attendants would be limited, and they would do no trans-Oceanic flying.

Neerja Bhanot was one of several Indian flight attendants hired in 1985. From Bombay, she was a true beauty, and had worked as a model before joining Pan American. As competent as she was beautiful, she checked out as purser as soon as she had completed her probation, and by September 1986 had been flying for ten months. On the fifth of that month, Pan American's Flight 73, a Boeing 747, from Bombay to Frankfurt and New York, with Neerja working as senior purser, made its usual stop in Karachi. It was 5 a.m. and still dark, but the night had made little difference to the brooding summer heat.

At the aircraft doors, the cabin crew welcomed the Karachi passengers as they boarded the flight; with the new arrivals, there would be a total of 382 passengers that day. Suddenly, the orderly boarding process was shattered. A van carrying four men, two of them dressed in airport security clothes, roared across the tarmac towards the airplane. Reaching the foot of the steps, they sprang out of the van, brandishing automatic rifles and grenades. After spraying the tarmac with bullets and wounding two baggage handlers and a passenger, they ran up the steps and into the 'plane, shoving the boarding

Neerja Bhanot.

passengers out of their way. At the top of the steps, one of the men grabbed a stewardess (affectionately known as Sunshine) by the hair and held a gun to her head as the other terrorists entered the aircraft, firing off rounds and ordering the passengers to raise their hands. "What are you doing?" the terrified stewardess screamed. "This is a hijacking," the terrorist responded.

Neerja Bhanot was in charge of the first-class cabin and was standing by the L1 entry door when the hijackers burst into the cabin. As soon as they made a sudden left turn and ran for where they thought they would find the cockpit, she fled up the spiral stairs of the 747. She had been told repeatedly during training that the most important step to take in a hijacking on the ground was to disable the aircraft by removing the flight crew. With a grounded aircraft, the terrorists might be persuaded to give up their quest. She quickly alerted the pilots to the crisis so they could make their escape through the cockpit hatch. The captain, the co-pilot, and the engineer immediately locked the cockpit door and set about their escape, clambering through the hatch and winching themselves to the ground.

Neerja then ran back down the stairs and picked up the intercom to make an 'All Call,' a two-beep signal which alerted all the flight attendants on board to pick up their receivers. The message from Neerja was that they should put all their doors on automatic so that the moment they were opened, the chutes would be deployed.

This was the start of a protracted ordeal of intimidation and negotiation that lasted 17 hours. The sun rose and began beating down on the aircraft.

Because there was no cockpit crew, it was almost impossible for the Pakistani officials to establish contact with the aircraft. They tried first, and unsuccessfully, with a bull horn, but the terrorists refused to communicate in any language other than Arabic. Finally, after more than two hours, radio contact was made with the aircraft. With the aid of a Saudia official to translate, the authorities learned the hijackers' demands. They wanted a new, Arabic-speaking crew to fly the aircraft to Cyprus, where they intended to liberate some 'friends' from jail. They gave the officials until 7 p.m. to provide the crew. If they did not comply, they would start shooting the passengers one by one.

As senior purser, 23 year-old Neerja Bhanot was now in command of the aircraft, and she knew it was her responsibility to do everything in her power to calm and reassure the cabin occupants. She remained unflustered and unflinching, made encouraging announcements to the passengers, and never once demonstrated anything other than absolute confidence in a happy outcome. She talked to her crew about the importance of loyalty to their passengers; she insisted that they, like herself, should radiate confidence that the horror would pass.

The horror did not pass. The day wore on, and the heat intensified as the aircraft's power generator struggled to keep the cabin cool. The terrorists refused to allow commissary to replenish supplies, and soon the food on board was exhausted, and as the thirsty passengers consumed their drinks, the flight attendants realized that all their supplies of liquids would soon run out. With nearly 400 passengers and crew members on board, conditions in the lavatories soon became unsanitary.

Morning wore on into afternoon.

During the day, the terrorists remained relatively relaxed, as long as they felt that their demands would be met. They bantered with the passengers, who said that they were 'very polite,' and they played with the children. After more negotiations, they agreed to release the women and children and possibly the elderly when the new crew arrived.

As the afternoon wore on, babies and little children screamed with hunger while their emotionally exhausted parents were at a loss as to how to help them. The flight attendants did all they could to comfort and assist the families. In the middle of the afternoon, the negotiators informed the hijackers that the new flight crew would not arrive until the middle of the night, which put the terrorists in the awkward position of having to extend their deadline. They began showing signs of edginess. They collected everyone's passport, and called for Mike Chexton, a Briton, to come forward. At first, Chexton decided not to respond, but realizing that he might anger the hijackers by not identifying himself, he bravely approached them. They passed him over.

Rajesh Kumar was not so lucky. Suddenly, they decided to demonstrate their deadly intent. They called Kumar, a U.S. citizen, forward to the first-class cabin, shot him, and threw his body out of the 'plane onto the tarmac below. After murdering Kumar, the terrorists politely apologized to the passengers for their act, stating, "Our argument is not with you."

Afternoon became early evening, and darkness began to fall again.

Under cover of darkness, anti-terrorist commandos crept towards the airliner and took up position. Meanwhile, at 8:30 p.m. the oil for the 'plane's generator ran out, and the aircraft automatically switched over to its auxiliary batteries, which would keep the cabin illuminated for about 90 minutes, but which could not operate the air-conditioning. The temperature in the cabin began to rise and the air became stale.

As the darkness deepened, the ordeal seemed to go on forever. The hijackers started talking desperately to each other, arguing, waving their hands; the lights became dimmer and dimmer; and the passengers were panic-stricken by the loss of light and fresh air inside the aircraft. The flight attendants tried to reassure them that power would soon be restored.

Angered by the loss of electricity, which they considered to be a ruse on the part of the negotiators, the hijackers sprang into action shortly before 10 p.m. They herded the passengers into the center of the aircraft, seating some of them in the aisles. Some of the crew members and passengers, realizing that this might be their last bid for safety, struggled open the emergency doors and began to slide down the chutes, which had immediately deployed when the doors were opened. Neerja's 'All Call' in the opening minutes of the siege, requesting that the doors be put on automatic, was responsible for saving many lives.

Seeing their hostages escaping was the final straw; the terrorists suddenly began throwing hand grenades and shooting wildly into the crowd. In the mayhem of gunfire and screams, Neerja Bhanot stepped in front of her passengers, saving the lives of three children while sacrificing her own.

During the wild burst of shooting, the terrorists expended most of their ammunition, but they still had enough to keep the commandos at bay for nearly 15 minutes. When the commandos finally took control of the aircraft, wounding two of the terrorists and arresting all four, 21 people aboard Flight 73 had been murdered and more than 50 had been injured. Neerja Bhanot died on her 23rd birthday.

✈ ✈ ✈ ✈ ✈

Neerja Bhanot was posthumously awarded the Ashok Chakra Award, India's highest award for bravery, and is the only woman ever to have received that honor. She was also posthumously awarded the Flight Safety Foundation Heroism Award on 28 October 1987, (an honor received by Dorothy Kelly ten years earlier). This award is sponsored annually by Kidde Graviner and is represented by the Graviner sword.

The Neerja Bhanot-Pan Am Trust Award has been established in her memory. This recognition is granted to the Indian flight attendant who best exemplifies its objectives as displayed in Neerja's character: devotion to duty, concern for justice, self-respect, and courage in adversity.

Lockerbie

Suddenly, there was a whistling noise in the air: in the blink of an eye something else appeared on the hillside within yards of the gravestones: the cockpit and forward first-class cabin of Clipper Maid of the Seas *smashed on to the grass. The portion fell on its port side and there she lay like a huge smashed egg.*
    Kate Anderson stepped inside that wreckage. She came upon the body of a stewardess, her flesh still seemed warm. Possibly, she was still alive for just a few moments, but died as Kate touched her.
From Allan Edwards *Flights into Oblivion*

IN MEMORIAM

Babette Avoyne

Noelle Berti

Siv Engstrom

Stacie Franklin

Paul Garrett

Elke Kuhne

Nieves Larracoechea

Lilibeth Macalolooy

Gerry Murphy

Joycelyn Reina

Myra Royal

Irja Skabo

Milutin Velimirovich

Desert Storm

August 1990
2-3; Iraqi troops, armor and helicopters swarm into Kuwait,
pushing quickly to the Saudi frontier. President Bush orders a
U.S. economic embargo of Iraq.
4-6; European Community and U.N. announce similar embar-
goes. Saudi Arabia requests U.S. military assistance. Operation
Desert Shield *begins.*
7-8; Bush orders combat forces to the Arabian Gulf.
Thomas Taylor, *Lightning in the Storm*

ania Anderson was on a trip to Frankfurt on 2 August, the day of
Iraq's invasion of Kuwait. When she arrived home, she found a
cryptic message on her answering machine: "If Tania is interested,
we have an S.P.A. [special assignment] available this week. This is her supervisor speaking. Please have her return my call if she wants to sign up for it."
Tania was immediately interested. She returned the call and was faced with a
barrage of questions: "Is there anybody Jewish in your family? Is your middle
name Jewish? Do you have visa stamps from Israel on your passport? Have
you visited Israel in the past year?"

"It felt like going on a secret mission, but I had expected the call. I had
intended to volunteer anyway because I love special assignments. I had
figured that Pan Am would be flying troops in to Saudi Arabia because of our
Civil Reserve Air Fleet program (C.R.A.F.). We had convertible 'planes—
aircraft that could be changed in about 30 hours from commercial wide-
bodied jets into troop and matériel carriers. The military would yank out all
the seats, rearrange the galleys, and put tracks on the floor so that they could
load on different types of equipment. Pan Am had been part of the C.R.A.F.
program for decades. It was a good deal for Pan Am because the military did
major overhauls on the aircraft in return for our making them available in
national emergencies. Pan Am was always first in and last out when things
were really bizarre, and other airlines would not touch certain types of volatile
situations that Pan Am would."

Tania Anderson is from McLean, Virginia, but spent her high school
years at Millfield, a progressive boarding school in England. She flew back to

the United States on Pan American three times a year for her school vacations, loved flying, and made careful notes on the flight attendants' diplomatic style. After receiving degrees in political science and international studies at Washington, D.C.'s American University, Tania worked for the Marriott and Sheraton hotels, but in 1985, her desire for adventure came to the forefront, and she applied to Pan American for a job. Even though Tania joined the company at a time when its fortune was hardly at its zenith and flight attendants were already having to pepper their service with excuses for lacks of this and that, she says, "I felt that old company loyalty even then. You could write a whole book about Pan Am company loyalty, which is still very much in evidence today."

Tania proved to be extraordinarily game and extraordinarily competent. She checked out as purser after three years and made sure that she saw as much of the world as possible, always taking side trips at her destinations, always on the alert for a new diversion. When she learned that the White House press charters were a closed shop, she became determined to have that experience too. "I couldn't even get on the list for a year and a half. I would overhear people whispering in the galley, and I'd ask, 'Are you guys talking about the press charters?' I'd get zip for an answer. It was like the National Security Agency. But I kept bugging my supervisor about it because I felt I had something to contribute, being well apprised of current events and belonging to several clubs that meet regularly on the Hill, including the California State Society, the Virginia State Society, and the English Speaking Union. I also had lots of letters of recommendation. Finally Scheduling called and asked for my permission to give my date of birth and social security number to the Secret Service so they could do a background check. My chance came up shortly after that."

Desert Storm was another challenge, and when her family and friends learned that Tania would be flying troops into Saudi Arabia, they were not surprised. When they learned that she was accompanying them home again, they were still not surprised. They almost expected it.

"I flew into Dhahran for the first time a couple of weeks after the invasion. Bangor, Maine, was our launching point. The Pan Am Boeing 747 crew deadheaded from Kennedy to Bangor, picked the troops up there, and flew with them to Fiumicino [Rome]. During the briefings before the flights, I would say to the flight attendants, 'As far as I am concerned, we have 425 V.I.P.s on board,' with which they would heartily agree. The interaction between the crew and the passengers was wonderful and the atmosphere in the cabin very cohesive. However, it's strange to get on an airliner that's loaded with guns. The ammunition clips are in the belly, but you have 425 troops, each with a sidearm and an M-16 automatic assault rifle. Some of them had M-60s, which weigh about 26 pounds. When you get on board and see these grenade launchers, you know they mean business.

"We didn't use a full 747 crew, because it was a simple service. The soldiers could not drink and everybody ate the same thing, so ten of us could do a converging service, meeting in the middle. Our crew would disembark and have 24 hours off in Rome, and a fresh crew would take the troops on to Dhahran. Then we would do the rotation the next day. It was a five-and-a-half-hour flight to Dhahran—almost like doing a New York to Los Angeles. We were vectored in over secure territory, past Riyadh, past Bahrain, out over the water and back in. Once we arrived and the troops had disembarked, it would take a couple of hours to unload all the tons of equipment from the belly, all sorts of support equipment. We were really setting up camp in Saudi Arabia. I never saw a Saudi the whole time we were there; it was just like going to a base in Oklahoma, and the crew enjoyed loading up with T-shirts that said 'I'll fly 10,000 miles to smoke a camel.'

"We were on the ground there for about two and a half hours—no layover because of security—and then we'd ferry back to Rome. As the 16 January date approached, troops were flown in to Riyadh and Al Jubail, close to the Kuwaiti border, but I never went to those places."

As the deadline for an Iraqi withdrawal drew closer and the threat of war became more and more a reality, the flight attendants were given instructions in the use of gas masks. The commanding officer and his assistant would gather the cabin crew in the back galley and demonstrate how to don the masks and how to interpret visual signals because once the cumbersome mask was in place, it was impossible to hear instructions during a SCUD alert. Tania continues, "Yellow signs being held aloft would mean there was an incoming alert, red would mean run for it with your gas mask on, and white would mean all clear. We were told that in case of an emergency, it would be each person for himself. The mask became one of the things we were required to take with us—like our manual, our cockpit key, and our flashlight."

On the long flights from Bangor to Rome and from Rome to Dhahran, Tania found herself becoming endeared to the troops she was accompanying. As senior purser on board, she made sure that her announcements were as reassuring and as caring as possible, and she and her crew became the recipients of many stories and much admiration. Tania could not help grinning when the staff sergeant addressed the troops: "Now, listen up, men. Take a good, long, last look at these ladies because they're going to be the last women you're going to see for some time. I'm going to be your Momma from now on." On the final approach into Dhahran, Tania never failed to send the troops off without her promise: "I look forward to the day I get the call from Crew Scheduling to bring you guys home, and I promise you I'll be right there. It's been a wonderful, valuable, and memorable experience meeting all of you, one I'll never forget. God bless you all. You are in our thoughts and our prayers. Vaya con Dios."

On 16 January 1991, *Desert Shield* became *Desert Storm*, and the war was quick, lethal, and spectacular. Two days after it started, Tania had a nightmare. "I must have had it because I had spent so much time with the soldiers, listening to their stories, getting a good feeling about who they were. A lot of them were from middle America and had never been in a big city, and all of a sudden they were 10,000 miles from home. They were such young boys; just kids really. Anyway, I dreamt that I was in the military and the sergeant said, 'The fighting has started. Who is going to watch this town?' You could hear bombs constantly going off in the distance. One of the other troops and I put our hands up and said, 'We will.' I immediately felt terribly embarrassed because it showed what a chicken heart I was, and everybody knew that I had chosen to do the safe thing rather than going into the heat of the action. I kept hearing the bombs going off in the distance. Then all of a sudden, I sat up ramrod straight on my bed, and I felt as though someone had poured iced water all through my veins and into my lungs. I could feel it running down through my arms.

"I attributed the dream to the fact that I had bonded with the troops so readily, and had empathized with all their fears. I believe I was taking on some of what they were feeling. Maybe I wanted to be with them at that point; but who knows what good I could have done? You bond with them because they're your passengers, because they're fellow human beings, because they are sensitive people who tell you their stories, and you feel protective of them."

On 1 April 1991, Tania kept her promise. She flew to Dhahran to bring out the paratroopers, the members of the 82nd Airborne Division, the 'All Americans.' Tania and her crew decorated the cabin with welcome home signs and yellow ribbons from nose to tail, dressed up in patriotic shirts, carried bouquets of yellow flowers and ribbons, encouraged pillow fights, and wished their passengers "Happy Easter" and "Welcome home." Most of the troops of the 82nd were jubilant about returning because they had been the first to go in to Saudi Arabia and had spent many months there, but a few of them were anxious about their re-entry into American society and what they would find back home as several of them had received 'Dear John' letters. One paratrooper asked Tania, "Has there really been a lot of support at home?" She recognized from the tone of his question that he had served in Vietnam, and reassured him, "Yes. There are yellow ribbons everywhere. Bumper stickers everywhere. People have signs up in their windows. The

Homeward Bound! (Photograph by Tania Anderson.)

flags are flying all over the country." He remarked, his eyes filling with tears, "It was terrible when we came home from Vietnam."

Tania continues, "When we came in to land, the air was electric because everyone was so excited. I had my camera with me and I got a picture of the whole E-zone, with the troops all waving their arms and going crazy. I said to them, 'Thanks, fellas; that was a real Kodak moment.'

"As we were coming up to the blocks, the big thing was to have a soldier flying the American flag out of the cockpit hatch. That could almost empty a terminal. Passengers from other flights would rush to the windows to watch us arrive, and would flock to Gate 3 at Kennedy Airport, which was reserved for the 'planes coming in from Saudi to witness this exuberant and historic moment. The 'plane would refuel at Kennedy before taking the troops back to their home base.

"When they got off the aircraft, the guys would walk down the air bridge, and each would have a different reaction. One guy got down and kissed the ground, another just touched the walls, not saying a word, and another just yelled 'ALL RIGHT!' It was the only time in my airline career that passengers made me cry. It was a deeply personal and touching moment for each soldier that I witnessed as they disembarked."

Tania with the 82nd Airborne Division on arrival at Fort Bragg. (Photograph courtesy Tania Anderson.)

Tania was invited to the tickertape parade in New York by an Air Force staff sergeant, Shelley Ousak, with whom she had become friends in Dhahran during her two-and-a-half-hour turn-arounds, and with whom she has remained in contact ever since. Colonel Dan Fake from the Big Red One (the 16th Infantry Regiment) in Fort Riley, Kansas, invited Tania to the 8 June victory parade in Washington, D.C. She adds: "I sat with his family catty-corner from the Presidential box, and I saw Colin Powell, Dick Cheney, and Norman Schwartzkopf walking ahead of his troops. There was also a fly-by of all the aircraft flown in the Gulf War, from helicopters right up to the Stealth fighter. It was incredible. But best of all I saw the guys I had flown with, and here they were home again, celebrating. The 101st Airborne from Fort Campbell and the 82nd Airborne from Fort Bragg."

✈ ✈ ✈ ✈ ✈

3 December 1991. Tania continues: "I was working on a White House press charter. I had met the crew at Andrews Air Force Base, and we flew to Sarasota on the Boeing 727 alongside the presidential aircraft, Air Force One, tail no. 28000. When we arrived, President Bush went to the Tropicana plant,

and I went to talk to his chief pilot, Colonel Danny Barr, and to see the 'plane (I had already been on board the alternative Air Force One, tail no. 29000). The flight attendants kidded me, saying, 'Tania, they're identical. You've been on the other one.' But I said to them, 'I want to go on board this one because you never know when the party will be over.' However, I was really confident that we would fly with the President to Hawaii on 7 December when he was visiting Pearl Harbor for the 50th anniversary of the bombing.

"In flight from Sarasota to Meridian, Mississippi, John Sununu submitted his letter of resignation to the President, and the Press was really excited. They went downtown to do the satellite feed, hoping it would be the lead story on the national news that evening. While they were downtown, all a-flutter, and we were killing time at the airport, the pilot of our 727 emerged from the cockpit. His face was ashen, and he said, 'I've been listening to the radio, and it's really bad news for us. Delta's pulled out of the deal to finance Pan Am Two out of Miami.' It was 1400 hours."

Pan Am did not officially cease operations until the following morning, but one by one the Clippers began their final journeys.

Water Cannons
At Dinner Key

The party's over, it's time to call it a day.
They've burst your pretty balloon and taken the moon away.
Betty Comden and Adolph Green, "The Party's Over"

an Am ceased operations officially at 9 a.m. on 4 December 1991. Ask any flight attendant and she or he will line up a roster of reasons for the demise: the purchase of far too many expensive 747s; the oil crisis in the 1970s; ill-judged desire for domestic routes and greed for more aircraft; the costly and untimely acquisition of National Airlines in 1980, a marriage which was not exactly designed in heaven; deregulation shortly after the acquisition, which meant that Pan American could have had for nothing what it had spent millions to acquire; a bloated management; poor decision-making; golden parachutes; overstaffing and overspending; the hasty sale of precious assets at bargain prices; and the terrible tragedy of Lockerbie.

The clarity with which those who worked out on the line perceived what management apparently could not is impressive. The flight attendants knew that an airline whose employees had taken pay cut after pay cut to keep it flying could not remain in the air with an ill-advised and edacious manage-ment. They were well aware that a corporation which dropped money-making flights (San Juan, for instance) because at 100% capacity there was no room for improvement, was not looking for bread and butter. They were quick to notice when the Bermuda schedule suddenly acquired an early Saturday morning flight so that the Chief Executive Officer could go to his house for weekends; they noted the escalation of almost empty flights to the Turks and Caicos Islands to serve the C.E.O.'s wife's diving school. Not much missed their scrutiny.

They recognized that they were always apologizing for their airline. There were never enough blankets or pillows. The cabins looked scruffy. They were chronically short of meals, and regularly went without their own (which was against the regulations) so that their passengers could eat. There was never enough of anything. They made excuse after excuse.

263

Cyndee Davis, Exie Soper, Mark Pyle, Chuck Freeman, Jeanne Cleary, Bob Knox, and Jeanne Katrek in Barbados on 4 December 1991, just before they boarded Pan Am's final flight.

One by one, Pan Am sold its treasures, its money-makers: the Pacific routes (lock, stock, barrel, aircraft, infrastructure, for a knock-down price), Intercontinental Hotels, the Pan Am Building, and the New York–London route. Finally, there would be little left but the still profitable Latin American Division, and Delta Air Lines was interested in striking a deal, forming a Pan Am/Delta cooperative, Pan Am Two, which would keep Pan American aircraft and employees flying south. But at the eleventh hour, Delta backed out.

Exie Soper, Jeanne Katrek, Jeanne Cleary, and **Cyndee Davis** were the flight attendants on Pan Am's final flight. I interviewed Exie and Jeanne Katrek at the Doubletree Hotel (the old Coconut Grove Hotel) in Coconut Grove, a suburb of Miami, Florida. It overlooks the old Pan Am building, the hangars, and Dinner Key Marina. It seemed such a fitting place, right there at Pan American's first base, right there where the whole beautiful, big, blue dream took off.

Jeanne Cleary decided not to join us because she was still suffering from depression caused by the loss of Pan Am, and did not wish to stir up painful memories. At that time, I was unable to find Cyndee Davis, but subsequently interviewed her in Southern Pines, North Carolina. Exie, Jeanne Katrek, and Jeanne Cleary had all flown for National before the Pan Am acquisition, but Cyndee Davis was Pan Am throughout her career. Before the last flight, the four women had spent a whole month working together, and Cyndee describes the cameraderie: "We had worked through all the interpersonal conflicts that arise with four people on an airplane, and we operated really well together. Right at the end of the month we had two days in Bermuda, and decided to spend them sight-seeing. We walked all over town and had a lovely time, telling stories, and enjoying the magnificent weather."

The crew flew from Bermuda to New York on 3 December, and spent the night at the airport hotel. They were called early the next morning for the 7 a.m. flight to Barbados. It was a bright, cold day in New York, with the temperature hovering around freezing. "We knew that while we were in the air, our fate would be in the balance," Cyndee says. "Doomsday was coming, but we still thought that Delta was going to bale us out. There was a code of honor, and they would do what they said."

Clipper Goodwill, a Boeing 727-200, made a calm and uneventful flight to Barbados during which the flight attendants served a hot breakfast. The weather was clear and the temperature was 80° F. when they landed. Exie, the purser, was the first crew member off the aircraft. As she crossed the tarmac, the station manager came rushing up to her, waving a telegram and yelling "We ceased operations at 9 o'clock this morning." Exie felt the news like a blow to her stomach. She took the cable and ran back to the cockpit. Aghast, Mark Pyle gathered the crew together and read the telegram:

SUSPENSION OF SERVICES - STATUS NBR 1

SUBJECT/ANNOUNCEMENT

PAN AM PRESIDENT & CEO REGRETS TO ANNOUNCE THAT PAN AM CORP HAS WITHDRAWN ITS MOTION FOR CONFIRMATION OF THE CHAPTER 11 PLAN OF REORGANIZATION FOR PAN AM AND ITS AFFILIATED COMPANIES AND THAT AS A RESULT IT IS CEASING FLIGHT OPERATIONS EFFECTIVE IMMEDIATELY. FURTHER INFORMATION REGARDING THE SPECIFICS RELATED TO THIS WITHDRAWAL WILL BE PROVIDED THROUGH A COMPANY PRESS RELEASE.

PAN AM MANAGEMENT HAS BEEN DIRECTED TO IMPLEMENT A SHUT DOWN PLAN GUIDED BY THE FOLLOWING PRINCIPLES:

*IMPLEMENT SUSPENSION OF SERVICES IN A SAFE AND PROFESSIONAL MANNER

*ENSURE CUSTOMER-DRIVEN ACTIONS THAT MINIMIZE INCONVENIENCE TO TRAVELING PUBLIC, SHIPPERS, AND OTHER CUSTOMERS

*PRESERVE AND PROTECT THE ASSETS OF THE COMPANY

SPECIFIC SUSPENSION OF SERVICE STATUS BULLETINS WILL BE ISSUED BY THE CENTRAL COMMAND POST

WANGERIEN

"At that point, I was in shock," says Cyndee, "Exie broke down, Jeanne Katrek broke down, and the other Jeanne just walked it off." Then came the questions—Could the Clipper make the return journey to Miami? Could it even find fuel?

The news spread like wildfire around the terminal that this would be the last time Pan Am would fly into Barbados. Local reporters arrived on the scene to photograph the aircraft and interview the crew. One by one the airport personnel approached the flight attendants bearing huge bouquets and paying tribute. "There was this lovely little farewell ceremony. It was so touching—they were terribly sad, too, that they would never see the blue ball again. It was heart-wrenching. Pan Am had been flying into Barbados for 60 years! Exie broke down several times, but I remained fairly stoic because I didn't believe it was actually happening," says Cyndee.

Somehow fuel became available, and it was agreed that the return flight would operate as scheduled. The station manager asked the crew if they would mind delaying the flight somewhat to accommodate some more passengers. Exie was under the impression that they were being asked to wait for Pan Am employees who would otherwise be stranded in Barbados with no way to return to Miami. Mark Pyle agreed to wait for a while, but the wait

Cyndee Davis.

dragged on and on, and the cabin crew started boarding passengers. Still there was no order to leave, and people continued to dribble onto the aircraft. Eventually, Exie realized that the tickets she was taking were marked Barbados/New York instead of Barbados/Miami and she was boarding people whose flight was not due to take off until 4.45 p.m. "There we were," she says, "All crying our hearts out, ready to leave forever, and still the passengers kept coming." Jeanne Katrek adds, "We were walking around like zombies at that time." Cyndee says, "We were the morning flight and we were waiting for the afternoon flight, but I've always been easy-going in that respect—hey, I'll wait. I don't care. I may grumble here and there, but it doesn't bother me. I realized we were pulling people from everywhere, but I thought whoever we could take home might as well join us."

But Exie felt a strong responsibility to her Miami passengers. "I went up to the captain and said, 'This isn't fair. All these other people are trying to get to Miami just so they can get a flight from there to New York. This could take forever. Our Miami passengers have waited long enough. There's a point where you've gone far beyond the call of duty. We're there. We're there.'" She continues, "I could tell Mark was desperate, too. He was trying to console everyone else, trying to be helpful, but he was crying inside."

Captain Pyle gave the order to close the doors, and Pan Am's final journey began. The Clipper carried 111 passengers from Barbados to Miami, most of whom had no idea of part they were playing in the last chapter in the history of the world's most extraordinary airline.

"There was food," Jeanne Katrek says, "and surprisingly there was even a choice of meal. We had a major decision to make: since we had officially ceased operations, we could sit down and do nothing—or we could go to work. For a brief moment we entertained the idea of saying, 'Here's the galley. The meals are hot. Have at it.' Instead, we decided we would give away as much liquor as people wanted and would do the service with all the dignity that we had been trained to observe and maintain. The ship was going down and Fate had decreed that we were the crew to go down with the ship. We would do it with class."

Cyndee says, "We all pulled together. We did an excellent job. We worked hard and if somebody wanted a drink, we offered them the cart. 'Take whatever you want,' we said. 'You want a pillow, take a pillow. Keep it. You want a blanket, take a blanket.' They were such nice people for the most part. A few were getting on our nerves because they were greedy, taking everything, yet they were the same people who started a collection for us. We had no idea that was going on. Just before we touched down, they handed Exie an envelope and said 'This is so that you people can have a Christmas dinner. We know you aren't going to get paid, and this is for doing such a good job.'"

"It was the passengers helping out the flight attendants. It was so kind, so sweet," says Exie.

As the Clipper began its descent into Miami International Airport, Chuck Freeman, the engineer, received word from the tower that *Clipper Goodwill* was the very last Clipper to return home. The tower then requested a low pass over the field.

"When the Clipper approached Miami," says Jeanne Katrek, "dammit if the tower didn't make us go straight over Biscayne Bay, right over the old Pan Am building at Dinner Key, and Mark tipped the wing, just a little tip, and he said 'Isn't that fitting?' The cockpit crew had difficulty in keeping their own composure under the circumstances."

"Then he let us know he was going to do the flyover," says Exie.

"You know, where he actually does drop the gear so that he can go down enough but doesn't actually do a touch and instead keeps going," adds Jeanne.

"We were LOW," says Cyndee. "About 150 feet off the runway."

"I did the whole thing standing up in the aisle. With my knees bent. I let us come down, down, down, and then back again. I did it with my hand over my heart, " says Jeanne Katrek.

"I stayed by the window and watched the Miami International Airport flash by," says Cyndee. "Then we came round again, and it was an unremarkable landing. Mark put it down very smoothly. As we turned onto the taxiway, just before approaching the gate, the water cannons started pouring water over us in the traditional gesture of recognition of an historic moment. At that moment I realized it was the end. We were crying and crying, and a woman turned to us before she got off and said, 'I have never flown with you before. I don't know you girls from anybody, but I'm so sorry that this is happening to you.' She came up to us and hugged us all. At that point we were heaving and sobbing."

"Even more impressive than the water cannons," adds Jeanne Katrek, "was that all the Pan Am personnel remaining at Miami International Airport lined up in a row, a nice straight line, I'd say 20 to 30 of them. As soon as the water cannon business was finished, they all saluted the Clipper."

"Once we had parked, we looked down," says Cyndee, "and who was unloading the aircraft? None other than the upper management. People who had never lifted a passenger's bag in their life. Everybody from the office came out to touch the last Clipper in some way or another. All the other Pan Am aircraft had vanished."

Jeanne Katrek adds, "It was as though the airline had never existed."

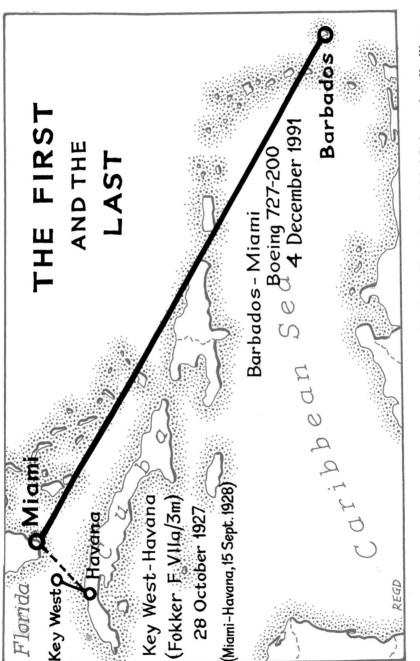

THE FIRST
AND THE
LAST

Miami

Key West

Havana

Florida

Key West - Havana
(Fokker F.VIIa/3m)
28 October 1927

(Miami–Havana,15 Sept. 1928)

Barbados - Miami
Boeing 727-200
4 December 1991

Caribbean Sea

Barbados

REGD

Almost as if pre-ordained, Pan American returned to its place of birth, Florida. Its first scheduled flight was from Key West to Havana, on 28 October 1927, its last was from Barbados to Miami on 4 December 1991.

Epilogue

S o that's it. Or is it? You could say that the aircraft are not flying any more, but some of them are. You could say that the flight attendants are not flying any more, but many are. You could say that the Pan Am spirit is dead, but you would be dead wrong.

Signs of life are everywhere. Let me give you an example. Last year, Tania Anderson, who is now a flight attendant with American Airlines, took a leave of absence so that she could 'fly the Haj' with Kabo Air. This meant being based in northern Nigeria and flying Muslim pilgrims to Jeddah to visit the holy site of Mecca. When Tania arrived in Sokoto she was astonished and delighted to find that the cockpit crew, mechanics, and cabin crew were almost entirely made up of Pan Am people. What was even more astonishing was that the Clipper they worked on was the Boeing 747 whose registration was N747PA. It was the *Juan T. Trippe,* the first 747 built for commercial use. (N747PA was the second 747 off the assembly line. Boeing held on to the first for its own purposes.)

During the two months that Tania spent in Nigeria, she trained Nigerian flight attendants in addition to taking her flights to Jeddah. She became deeply attached to the people she met in Sokoto and, as the result of a chance trip to a little grocery store, found herself moved by the plight of some lepers she encountered sitting outside the store in the blazing heat. "I started thinking about it," Tania says, "and the more I thought, the more I realized how desperate their need was for a shelter. It gets to be 112 degrees there in the summer. I am going to provide that shelter for them. I am going to raise the money." Even as I write this, Tania is in Nigeria, bearing with her the blueprints for the shelter, talking to the Sultan, picking a site.

On another leave, Tania went to Tajikistan to help that country set up international operations for its airline and to train its flight attendants. She worked on their inaugural 747SP flight from London to Dushanbe, and remarks, "It was all Pan Am alumni again, even the pilots. There we were, standing on the tarmac in Dushanbe, and I turned to a colleague, Linda Oja, and said, 'Do you realize, it's exactly two years to the day that Pan Am died, and here we are, half-way round the world, still showing them how to fly?'"

Yes, signs of life are everywhere. If you take a look at the *New York Times* best seller list, you'll find that a Pan Am flight attendant's name appears on a regular basis: **Mary Higgins Clark**. Mary, who started writing as a child, kept a journal during her Pan Am years. When she left the company to get married, she determined to become a professional writer and started taking courses at New York University. "The professor was terrific," she says. "He advised me to write about what I knew, and suggested that I should start by using my airline background, taking the most dramatic incidents and asking myself two questions: 'Suppose?' and 'What if?'"

In 1949, Mary was a stewardess on the last flight to Prague before the airport was closed to western aircraft. "We didn't bring anyone in. We were picking up seven Americans and going back to Frankfurt. The Soviets were having an air show, and there were thousands of people at the airport watching those military formations. When our lone little Constellation broke through the clouds, the crowd turned as one and began to cheer and clap and wave to us. On disembarking, we found our passengers, all men, huddled together in the terminal, watched over by Soviet guards with their hands on their guns. Our captain said to me, 'I don't like it here. We're going to fuel up and depart. Don't wander away.' The crowd watched us leave in perfect silence. They didn't wave; they didn't cheer. One of our passengers was weeping, and he said, 'There is no one in that crowd who would not give half of the rest of his life to be on this 'plane.'"

Mary took this incident and said to herself, "Suppose the stewardess went back on board the 'plane first. Suppose there was an 18-year-old member of the underground trying to hide on her 'plane. Suppose the searchers were heading towards the aircraft. Suppose, suppose, suppose. Then I remembered that on one of my previous flights the purser had been sick, and had remained in the bunk behind the flight deck, but his jacket was left out. I asked myself, 'What if the stewardess threw the kid the jacket and told him to put it on? What if she gave him the manifest...?'

"That became my first short story, 'Stowaway.' The professor said, 'This is a professional story and it will sell.' It did—six years and 14 rejection slips later." Mary went on to write several more stories using her Pan Am experiences as inspiration before turning her hand to the suspense novels for which she is so justly famous.

What else? Patricia Ireland is president of the National Organization for Women; Marcia Young is an undercover detective on the Portland, Oregon, vice squad; Lou Rena Hammond is president of her own New York public relations company, Lou Hammond & Associates (founded in 1984); Nonna Cheatham has been Field Director for the Girl Scouts, a Line Officer in the U.S. Navy, and a prime mover for archaelogy and ornithology projects for Earthwatch in California; Kristina Testor is a financial advisor with Smith

Barney Shearson, Inc. in Washington, D.C., where Ada Pena owns and operates Uniglobe, a large travel agency; Monique Quesada is a Foreign Service
Officer; Gunilla Crawford teaches jet emergency to flight attendants from all
over the world at the Pan Am Flight Academy in Miami; Joan Williams
Ashton, a tri-athlete, has a Spanish language school in Guatemala; Cathy
Centorbe-Moon owns and operates the Balboa Café in San Francisco and a
winery in Napa; Jeanne Clover is the Mother Theresa of animals and provides
for them through the Clover Animal Fund in Salinas, California; Norma Jean
Travis Gaskell has taught business education in Arlington County, Virginia,
schools as part of the Job Training Partnership Act; Roberta Brown, presently
on special assignment in Saudia Arabia, plans to build an orphanage for the
victims of civil strife in her native Liberia; Annie Ogle is an artist, living in a
small village in Bali. But I merely scratch the surface.

Others are still flying. Some who no longer work in the airline industry
have had to face a tough re-entry into a world that often operates on a narrow
and predictable nine-to-five schedule, anathema to flight attendants. Many
now work in other transport-related professions.

Strongest of all is the reunion spirit. Each year, Pan American people,
wherever they may be, join together during the first week of December to
celebrate having been part of an extraordinary international aviation team and
to mark the anniversary of the death of the airline they loved so much.
Members of the Pan Am community stay in touch through the *Pan Amigo
News,* published and edited six times a year by Patricia Jackson in Miami, and
circulated to former Pan Am employees and friends all over the world.

World Wings International, Inc., the association of ex-Pan Am flight
attendants, enjoys a larger membership than it ever did when Pan Am was
flying and is now nearly 2,000 members strong. Members have donated more
than $2 million to worthy charities. Since 1982, World Wings has given
support to Gallaudet University in Washington, D.C. (Gallaudet was signed
into law by President Lincoln in 1864, authorized to confer liberal arts
degrees upon deaf students from all over the world or those wishing to work
with the hearing impaired.) The association has contributed $130,550 to the
university and established the World Wings Endowed Research Fund, which,
through matching grants, reached a total of $240,900.

In 1993, the World Wings membership voted that CARE, Inc. become
its new international charity. Members are already hard at work raising funds
through book sales, fashion shows, luncheons, and raffles to support CARE
in that league's work to feed and teach the impoverished in 40 countries
around the world. In addition, each of World Wings' 34 chapters supports a
local charity such as a children's home in Brussels, a hospice in Hawaii, a

foundation for autistic children in Paris, an educational foundation for orphans in Tokyo, and a family guidance center in New Jersey.

What about the beloved blue ball? Do not imagine that you have seen the last of it. The word is that it will rise, phoenix-like, in the Pan Am Alliance logo. Cobb Partners of Miami has purchased the Pan Am name, the logo, and the frequent flyer plan. Participating international airlines with complementary routes will benefit from collective marketing, reservations systems, central ticketing offices, and airport V.I.P. lounges. Passengers, too, benefit because they will accumulate mileage on a single frequent flyer program, World Pass. The great Pan Am name may yet have a future as well as a past.

And, wonder of wonders, that past has been retrieved, thanks to the tireless efforts of the Pan Am Historical Foundation and the University of Miami. Together they have snatched the company archives and much memorabilia from the jaws of hungry profiteers, and this material is now safely housed at the University's Richter Library. It is a treasure trove of aviation history. The Foundation is also at work on the creation of a documentary film and the establishment of an aviation museum.

Again the nightmare occurs. This book is hot off the press, and the 'phone starts ringing. "Why did you leave out this incident?" "Why did you leave out that story?" "How come you didn't include so-and-so?" "Surely you must have heard about old what's-his-name?"

There is so much more to tell. Help me out. Write up the missing stories. Get them in the record. Let me have a good night's sleep. The good news is that several others are already hard at work: Harry La Porte, Opal Hess, Eugene Dunning, John Ferrugio, Jay Koren, Sharon Flescher, and Sebastine Amédume-Beaumier, to cite just those I know about.

We must never forget the glory that was Pan Am and the part that flight attendants played in its history.

They reckon ill who leave me out.
When me they fly, I am the wings.

Ralph Waldo Emerson, "May-Day"

Where Are They Now?

Tania Anderson lives in Virginia, and is now a flight attendant with American Airlines. She has committed herself to the establishment of a leper shelter in northern Nigeria, and remains open to adventure wherever she finds it.

Katherine Araki became an elementary school teacher after she left Pan American. She is now a real estate agent in Oahu, doing general brokerage sales for Newtown Realty.

Nelida Perez Beckhans was based in New York until 1981, when she moved to Miami with her new husband, a Pan Am maintenance supervisor. They both worked for Pan Am until the end. Nelida is now a flight attendant for another major U.S. carrier.

Robert Betancourt returned to Miami from New York in 1955, and continued to fly for Pan Am until his retirement in 1982. Since then he and Martha have been living quietly, next door to one of their sons. They enjoy travelling in the U.S.A. and to Europe; their two grandchildren often join them on their vacations.

Neerja Bhanot lives on in the awards to her memory.

Lois Thompson Blanchard left Pan American in 1947. After 40 years of marriage, she has been a widow for seven years, living in Seattle, blessed with three children and four grandchildren "who inspire me to keep up with our fast-moving world." Lois stays involved in volunteer work, education, and recreation, and with her Pan Am birds of a feather, relives the exciting and history-making experiences of working for the flagship of the world.

Dottie Bohanna is a third order Carmelite. As a eucharist minister, she dispenses daily communion, makes home visits to shut-ins, and during the course of two years, makes contact with every house in the parish of St. Bernard in Levittown, N.Y.

Jerry Cameron worked for Pan American for almost 39 years, most of the time as a purser, but also providing flight service training and supervision.

With co-author Phil Parrott, he wrote the first Atlantic Division flight service training manual. He lives in Solvang, California, with Mary, his wife of 56 years. Always interested in food service, Jerry purchased a pick-up which he uses for his volunteer work, delivering food to and from food banks.

Phil Casprini went from flight service in the 'forties to reservations until the mid-'sixties, then on to customer relations as a supervisor until retirement in 1980. He is enjoying his retirement in Bayside, New York, with his wife, Margaret, and keeps in touch with his sons in Manhattan and France, as well as with other relatives and friends, some of whom were Pan Am employees.

Mary Higgins Clark, who has earned the title 'America's Queen of Suspense' for her 12 best-selling novels and two collections of short stories, never fails to give Pan American credit for her early inspiration. She lives in Saddle River, New Jersey.

Beverly Mogensen Cowden. After her marriage to Bill Cowden, Bev moved with him to such places as Shanghai and Canton Island before he became airport manager in Hong Kong, where they lived for 28 years and raised their three sons. They spent the following ten years in Boston before retiring to Santa Rosa, California.

Madeline Cuniff has worked tirelessly for the University of Alabama's scholarship program, and the award in her name provides support for young women entering the world of aviation. In 1993, the university celebrated 31 outstanding women, and planted trees in their names; Madeline was included because of her role in the history of women in aviation. She belongs to the Ninety Niners and the Women's International Air Space Group, and is a member of the New York and Fort Lauderdale chapters of World Wings International.

Cyndee Davis lives in North Carolina and spends much of her time riding horses. She found work with charter airlines after Pan Am's demise, and she says, "I went through the last airline in record time. They were a disaster waiting to happen, and I was let go for refusing to work a 24-hour day. I saw more F.A.A. violations and emergency situations in five months than I did in 15 years with Pan Am. So now I am doing what I planned for my retirement, which just came early and unplanned."

Mickey de Angelis. On 27 October 1958, Mickey had the honor to be the chief purser on Pan Am's first commercial jet flight. He retired after 33 years with Pan American, and now enjoys living in Hiawassee, in the beautiful Georgia mountains.

Verne Edwards is deceased.

Alice Flynn retired from Pan Am in 1987, started her own desktop publishing business, continued to oil paint and, with her husband, opened Impulse Travel Agency in Burlingame, California. She has worked on the committee that fought for medical benefits for Pan Am retirees during the bankruptcy case, and has made a video about women and negotiations (available through Harvard University).

Jerry Galindo closed Jerry Galindo's Airport Men's Shop at Miami in 1992. He is father to Geraldine and Raymond, grandfather to Sean and Kimberly, and great-grandfather to Shane. Jerry, who used to be able to see a cockroach at three miles, now has trouble with his eyes. At 82, he is otherwise in excellent health and is an endless fund of stories from his flying days.

Lari Hamel. Since leaving Pan Am, Lari has become the mother of two, a cub scout den mother, a wildlife rehabilitator, and is active in the parent/teacher's organization and other community affairs.

Virginia Smith Hart lives in Claremont, California. Her daughters in San Diego and Santa Barbara provide her with year-round enjoyment. She is also active in the Sierra Club, Pomona Valley Community Services Respite Care, American Red Cross Blood Donor Services, Joslyn Center Senior Volunteers, and West Coast Dixieland Jazz Festival participation!

Artha Gruhl Hornbostel found the right man in Hawaii, married, left Pan Am, and moved to Germany for two years. When she and Milton returned, they settled in the Denver area where Artha started writing for Golden Books. They adopted an Hawaiian child, and once he had started elementary school, Artha joined a structural design engineering company, eventually becoming a partner. Now retired, she adds, "We've recently landed in Parachute, Colorado, where we continue to operate as Scanmasters, a computer typesetting business for publishers in New Jersey and Arizona."

Olga Iturrino flew for almost four years until company regulations forced her to resign because of marriage. After her divorce, she moved to Annapolis, where she has lived for nearly 40 years. She and her long-time friend and roommate, Helen Marino, worked for the AFL-CIO in Washington, D.C. for many years. After her retirement, Olga was for six years the sole care-giver for Helen, who had suffered a paralyzing stroke.

Ted Johnson retired from Pan Am in 1984, since when he has spent considerable time travelling domestically and to Asia. He is now treasurer of the San Francisco Chapter of World Wings International, and is preparing for its convention to be held in that city in October 1995. He revels in the continuing Pan Am camaraderie.

Lois Smith Kelley left Pan Am to get married and raise a family. She has worked as a volunteer for over 40 years, first as director of the Foster City (California) Museum Gallery, and for 21 years as the director of the San Mateo County Fair Annual Art Exhibition. She is also director of art galleries in Burlingame, San Mateo, and Hillsborough. Lois will make an appearance in the 1995 edition of *Who's Who of American Women*.

Dorothy Dawson Kelly spent 18 months recovering from her injuries at Tenerife before going back to flying out of New York. In 1986, she transferred to the London base. After the Lockerbie disaster, she took time off to help members of the flying community deal with the terrible loss of life as well as their loss of confidence. She continued to fly for Pan American until early 1991 when she lost her job at the time of the United Airlines takeover of London operations. Since then she has been involved in a class action lawsuit to regain her job, has trained for career transition, and has pieced together various part-time jobs, the most consistent of which has been with Sothebys, where she has the opportunity to pursue her enduring interest in the arts.

Alice Lemieux Jacobsen was one of four sisters who were flight attendants for Pan Am. "I married a Pan Am pilot, now deceased, with whom I had 44 beautiful years, but I am fortunate to have three great children, and I have recently become grandmother to a second grandchild." Alice lives in Scottsdale, Arizona, and always looks forward to the World Wings Arizona chapter meetings.

Jeanne Katrek spends her time in Deland and Miami, and enjoys early retirement, reunions with friends from her flying days, and making occasional use of the real estate license she acquired after Pan Am's last flight.

Jay Koren. After Jay first retired, Pan Am hired him back as a consultant to build flight attendants' scheduling bidlines. He says, "I proved that by hand-building, I could create better bidlines than the computer. There was a way of pleasing almost everyone, but it was rather like doing ten *New York Times* crossword puzzles in a couple of days." When he finally retired, he and Joe Kapel moved to Rio de Janeiro but now spend their time in Connecticut and San Miguel de Allende in Mexico, where they have built their dream house.

Kathy Beard Long. Before Pan Am folded, Kathy was able to attend school during the week and fly at weekends for five years so as to become an interior designer. She now has her own interior design company, Katherine Beard Interiors, with clients from Florida to Maine as well as in Europe. She also enjoys being a mom and having traded in her galley shoes for golf shoes.

Ingrid Gabrielli Lubienicki retired from Pan American in 1988, and since then has divided her time between Skaneateles, New York, where she enjoys watersports, and Innsbruck, Austria, where she enjoys skiing.

Sharon Madigan lives in Arlington, Virginia, and has just started her second term of office as Secretary-Treasurer of the Association of Flight Attendants.

Yoshiko Maeda is now a flight attendant with United Airlines, flying between Asia and the United States. She is a specialist in the ancient art of dyeing images onto silk for kimonos and is an accomplished singer. In 1994 she sang with a group from Tokyo in a concert at Carnegie Hall.

Marleane Thompson Mitchell lives with her husband in Arlington, Virginia. They have a daughter, Rana, and a son, Jai. In 1984, Marleane went back to work for Pan Am, in administration, first in the downtown D.C. office and later at the airport. When Delta Air Lines purchased the Pan Am Shuttle in September 1991, Marleane was one of the assets included in the transfer. After three and a half years of work in an office capacity, Marleane learned that Delta was making flight service positions available through its employee transfer program, and she jumped at the opportunity. After five weeks of intensive training, Marleane will once again take to the skies.

Sheila Nutt left Pan American in 1989. She is now Director of Multicultural Programs and AHANA student advisor at Emmanuel College in Boston. She has remarried, produced a third daughter, and continues to write about flight attendants. (AHANA is the acronym for African-American, Hispanic, Asian, and Native American.)

Frank Papouschek. Since his retirement, Frank has remained extremely active in the Pan Am community. He is the first male to serve on the World Wings International board, is a past co-president of the San Francisco chapter, and is chairman of the upcoming international convention. He is also on the board of directors of CARE of Northern California.

Gwen Persson. While on a layover in Buenos Aires in 1974, Gwen was badly injured in a limousine accident. After a month in hospital, she returned to the U.S., where she remained on medical leave for five years. It was the end of her flying career. However, her languages once again proved useful when she applied to S. Christian of Copenhagen's store in San Francisco; she was hired immediately and worked there for many years. She is not working at the moment, and is considering retirement. Gwen will be 70 in January 1996.

Charles (Bebe) Rebozo, who is best remembered for his loyal friendship to Richard Nixon, remains active in real estate and community affairs in the Miami area. He is president of Key Land Company, Inc.

Amaury Sanchez. [I have not been able to locate him.]

Barney Sawicki is deceased.

Doris Bulls Scher co-chaired the San Francisco Chapter of I.U.F.A. until her death on 31 October 1989. She made her last flight on 12 July 1989. Doris and her husband, Arnie, travelled via Pan American to faraway places on vacation at least twice a year, something that Arnie has yet to find interest in doing again since she died.

Exie Soper cried for three days after Pan Am's demise, and then applied for unemployment and enrolled in retraining programs. She was subsequently employed by Norwegian Cruise Lines as a ground agent and is now part of their pier management team. She adds, "My husband, Don, is also working at Norwegian, and now we take cruises instead of flying; the same passengers are out there!"

Fred Stecher lives in Longboat Key, Florida. He retired in 1980 after 40 years of service with American Overseas Airlines and Pan American. He is a volunteer worker at Sarasota-Bradenton Airport, Ringling Museum of Art, and Selby Botanical Gardens. He still enjoys travelling, but most of it is done by cruise ship these days.

Mary Lyman Talbot married George Talbot of Pan Am's Traffic Department in 1947. They live in Moraga, California, where they spend time with their three sons and seven grandchildren. They are enjoying retirement and stay in touch with Bev and Bill Cowden.

Kelly Tangen accepted Pan Am's 'early out' offer on 1 January 1990, after having flown for 28 years. She now operates the 1890 Colonial Bed and Breakfast in a large, comfortable, and elegant house in Sharon, Connecticut.

Sam Taormina retired from Pan American in 1980, after a 38-year career. He still enjoys travelling and playing golf, and is grandfather to seven and great-grandfather to one (so far). He has not forgotten Pan American: he is active in the Pan Am Association, a member of the Historical Foundation, and Corresponding Secretary of the San Francisco Chapter of World Wings.

Pamela Borgfeldt Taylor continued to fly for Pan American until it sold its Pacific routes to United Airlines, at which time she made the difficult decision to leave Pan Am for United. After eight more years of flying, she retired in Washington, D.C. to study art and interior design. Pam and her husband, author Thomas Taylor, plan eventually to return to Northern California.

Tony Volpe's travelling has been restricted because of a neurological problem which affects his right leg and requires him to use a cane or a walker. He lives in Bethpage, New York, where he keeps an eye on the incoming flights from Europe descending towards Kennedy Airport. He remarks, "I am constantly reminded that the famous Pan Am logo, recognized throughout the world, is no longer visible in the sky." He has enjoyed talking to other Pan Am people as a result of participating in this book.

Grace Burtt Walker left Pan Am to get married after five years of flying. Once her three children were raised, she returned to Pan Am, first in its Washington, D.C. federal affairs office and then in sales and marketing where she remained until the bitter end. Since December 1991, she has done volunteer work at Children's Hospital and for the Clinton campaign and transition. She is now a volunteer at the White House. She also writes newletters for World Wings and for various hotel chains.

Jane Bray Wessman does volunteer teaching in Archer, Florida, attends senior citizen luncheons, and helps out at Presbyterian Hospital and Oak View Retirement Community.

Bibliography

Baker, Trudy and Rachel Jones. *Coffee, Tea or Me?* New York: Bantam, 1967.

Bamford, Jack. *Croissants at Croydon.* Sutton, Surrey: Sutton Libraries and Arts Services, 1986.

Beaty, David. *The Water Jump: The Story of Transatlantic Flight.* New York: Harper & Row, 1976.

Binding, Tim. *In the Kingdom of Air.* New York: Norton, 1994.

Brock, Horace. *Flying the Oceans: A Pilot's Story of Pan Am.* Lunenburg, Vermont: Stinehour Press: 1978.

Brock, Horace. *More About Pan Am.* Lunenburg, Vermont: Stinehour Press, 1980.

Bender, Marylin and Selig Altschul, *The Chosen Instrument: The Rise and Fall of an American Entrepreneur.* New York: Simon & Schuster, 1982.

Cohen, Stan. *Wings to the Orient: Pan American Clipper Planes 1935 to 1945.* Missoula, Montana: 1985.

Daley, Robert. *An American Saga: Juan Trippe and his Pan Am Empire.* New York: Random House, 1980.

Davies, R.E.G. *Pan Am: An Airline and its Aircraft.* New York: Orion Books, & McLean, Virginia: Paladwr Press, 1987.

Davies, R.E.G. *A History of the World's Airlines.* London & New York: Oxford University Press, 1964.

Davies, R.E.G. *Airlines of the United States since 1914.* London & New York: Putnam, 1972.

Edwards, Allan. *Flights to Oblivion.* McLean, Virginia: Paladwr Press, 1993.

Gandt, Robert L. *China Clipper: The Age of the Great Flying Boats.* Annapolis, Maryland: United States Naval Institute, 1991.

Glines, Carroll V. *Round-the-World Flights.* New York: Van Nostrand Reinhold, 1982.

Hager, Alice Rogers. *Wings over the Americas.* New York: Macmillan, 1940.

Harwell, Elizabeth. *Cabin Pressure.* New York: St. Martin's, 1989.

Hochschild, Arlie Russell. *The Managed Heart*. Berkeley: University of California Press, 1983.

Jablonski, Edward. *Sea Wings: The Romance of the Flying Boats*. Garden City, New York: Doubleday, 1972.

Josephson, Matthew. *Empire of the Air*. New York: Harcourt, Brace: 1944.

Kane, Paula. *Sex Objects in the Sky*. Chicago: Follett, 1974.

Lindbergh, Anne Morrow. *Listen! the Wind*. New York: Harcourt, Brace, 1938.

Lindbergh, Anne Morrow. *North to the Orient*. New York: Harcourt, Brace, 1935.

Masland, William M. *Through the Back Doors of the World in a Ship That Had Wings*. New York: Vantage, 1984.

McLaughlin, Helen. *Walking on Air*. Denver: State of the Art, 1986.

McLaughlin, Helen. *Footsteps in the Sky*. Denver: State of the Art, 1994.

Nielsen, Georgia Panter. *From Sky Girl to Flight Attendant: Women and the Making of a Union*. ILR Press, Cornell University: 1982.

Parrott, Philip J. *The History of In-Flight Service*. Miami Springs: International Publishing Company of America, 1986.

Purl, Sandy *Am I Alive?* San Francisco: Harper & Row, 1986.

Turner, P. St. John. *A Pictorial History of Pan American Airways*. London: Ian Allan, 1973.

Waterman, Sherry, *From Another Island: Adventures and Misadventures of an Airline Stewardesss*. Philadelphia: Chilton Company, 1962.

Wilson, Ned. *For Pilots' Eyes Only*. McLean, Virginia: Paladwr Press, 1993.